The Experiences of a Hunter and Naturalist in the Malay Peninsula and Borneo

William T. Hornaday (front right), with the other members of a Central American expedition, on Porous Red Lava, at the Papago Tanks, 1876. Reproduced by permission of the British Library.

The Experiences of a Hunter and Naturalist in the Malay Peninsula and Borneo

WILLIAM T. HORNADAY

With an Introduction by
J. M. GULLICK

KUALA LUMPUR
OXFORD UNIVERSITY PRESS
OXFORD SINGAPORE NEW YORK
1993

Oxford University Press

*Oxford New York Toronto
Delhi Bombay Calcutta Madras Karachi
Kuala Lumpur Singapore Hong Kong Tokyo
Nairobi Dar es Salaam Cape Town
Melbourne Auckland Madrid*

*and associated companies in
Berlin Ibadan*

Oxford is a trade mark of Oxford University Press

Introduction © Oxford University Press 1993

First published as Two Years in the Jungle:
The Experiences of a Hunter and Naturalist
in India, Ceylon, the Malay Peninsula and Borneo
*by Charles Scribner's Sons, New York, 1885
Reissued as an Oxford University Press paperback 1993*

ISBN 967 65 3034 4

*Printed by Kim Hup Lee Printing Co. Pte. Ltd., Singapore
Published by Oxford University Press,
19–25, Jalan Kuchai Lama, 58200 Kuala Lumpur, Malaysia*

PUBLISHERS' NOTE

With the addition of an Introduction by J. M. Gullick, this volume is a reprint of the second half of William T. Hornaday's *Two Years in the Jungle*, of which Part III covers the Malay Peninsula and Part IV, Borneo. (The two preceding Parts describe India and Ceylon.)

To avoid confusion, the present volume has been retitled. The text has also been repaginated and the pagination of the Contents and List of Illustrations amended accordingly. The Appendices and the Index included in the original volume have been omitted.

INTRODUCTION*

The Author

IN the course of two years spent in the jungle, Hornaday travelled southwards through India, then on to Ceylon, Malaya, and finally Sarawak. His purpose was to obtain specimens, in particular of large animals such as crocodiles, tigers, elephants, and orangutans, for display in American museums. It was a task which sent him for weeks or months to live in villages, rest-houses, and jungle camps, so that he saw a great deal of local communities and tropical landscape which he found as fascinating as the fauna which were his primary interest. This is a book about countries and people, as well as wild animals.

When, in July 1878, he reached Kuala Lumpur, which was at that time a mining village in the remote interior of Selangor, he went to replenish his stock of provisions at the only Chinese shop which supplied such things. Here he says, 'We struck a bonanza. We found Mumm's champagne for sale at sixty cents a quart.' After trying in vain to persuade the bewildered *towkay* that 'he must have made a mistake in marking his goods ... engaging the strongest coolie we could find we loaded him with champagne ... my only regret is that I did not fill a tub and take a bath in it, for champagne is the only artificial drink I really like' (p. 26). The sheer exuberance of this young naturalist of twenty-three adds a great deal of colour and human interest to his narrative. He enjoyed life and he applied himself to the task in hand with energy and much practical skill. Not the least of the impressive features of

---

*Grateful acknowledgement is made (for help received) to the British Library, the General Library of the British Museum (Natural History), and the Library of the New York Zoological Society.

the book is the author's account of how he prepared for and surmounted the problems of each stage of his safari through southern Asia.

Hornaday came from the tide of European migrants who had spread across the Middle West of the United States in the nineteenth century. His grandfather, Ezekiel Hornaday, was one of four brothers who emigrated from England soon after the end of the American War of Independence in 1783. His father, William Hornaday, married Martha Varner, daughter of a Dutch father and a Scots mother. From North Carolina, where William senior was born, he moved to take up new land at Plainfield, Hendricks County, Indiana. Here the author of this book, William Temple Hornaday, was born on 1 December 1854, the youngest of his parents' four sons; in addition, he had two half-brothers, born to his mother in a previous marriage. When young William was four, the family moved to a larger homestead in Wapella County, Iowa, at the edge of the virgin prairie at that time. Under the vast open sky, the boy saw 'the great flocks of migrating pigeons, the soaring turkey vultures, the huge gatherings of prairie chickens'. During a visit to one of his half-brothers who had remained in Indiana, he saw a showcase of mounted birds. In an autobiographical fragment, he remembered that as a student 'it was Audubon's *Birds of North America*, Samuel's *Birds of New Zealand* and Tenney's excellent *Manual of Zoology* that revealed to me the existence of the great world of wild creatures, and fired my farm-bred soul with a desire and purpose to see a whole lot of it'. One can understand his enthusiasm. Audubon's book, in particular, is still a classic; it contains more than a thousand coloured prints of birds and cost the astronomical sum (in 1827) of £20,000 to produce.

But the frontier life in which Hornaday grew up was hard. By the time he was fifteen both his parents were dead, and for the next few years he lived in the homes of various relatives. It was not easy to get an education but, with characteristic pertinacity, he struggled on to become (in 1872) a student at the Iowa State Agricultural College, where he spent two years but had not graduated when he left—all the academic training he ever had. This was a period when colleges and museums throughout the United States were becoming alive to the need to present 'natural history' to students and to the general public through collections of preserved, and later, of living animals. The Iowa College must have recognized his enthusiasm and aptitude, for he was given the job of preparing specimens of animals and birds for its museum. In this work, he had to teach himself the craft of taxidermy, at which he became very proficient.

In the United States at this time, the pioneer and leading practitioner in the field was Henry Augustus Ward (1834–1906), Professor of Natural Sciences at the University of Rochester since 1861. On Ward's initiative, the University set up a 'Natural Science Establishment' on the campus. It was a wide-ranging collection. Ward's own speciality was geology, in particular fossils and meteorites. But to help him build up collections in other fields, he recruited assistants. In November 1873 Hornaday, not yet nineteen, obtained a post under Ward as the assistant in charge of the zoological part of the collection.

Ward soon sent him off to collect specimens in other countries. Hornaday's first expedition (in 1874) was to Florida, Cuba, and the Bahamas, and two years later he visited South America. When, late in 1876, he set off in the company of Ward, for an expedition to southern Asia, he had a great deal of practical experience. This was what he needed. In his Preface to this book, he describes it as 'a record ... of action rather than observation, and opportunities for study were few and far between'. But the chapters herein on the orang-utan and on the Dyak show that Hornaday was perhaps being rather modest in his claims. He had remarkable powers of observation and description, both of people and animals.

No museum or wealthy philanthropist funded the enterprise. Hornaday says that Ward provided 'ample funds for expenses ... and a good salary besides'. But Ward's resources were fully stretched, and Hornaday was expected, in the early part of his expedition, to send back specimens which Ward could sell to museums and others to generate cash for carrying on the programme upon which Hornaday had embarked. His task was not only to track and shoot wild animals, which were often elusive and fast-moving, but to retrieve their carcasses, reduce them to skin and skeleton, preserve the skins against decay by generous use of salt, pack them up, and dispatch them to Ward from the nearest port of shipment.

In one passage, he describes skinning and 'skeletonizing' an Indian elephant which had stood 9 feet tall when alive and had a dead weight of 4 tons. In tracking and in preparing his specimens, Hornaday had to direct local tribesmen in tasks which they sometimes found unpleasant as well as unfamiliar. He had to cajole or sometimes to outwit, while keeping within the law, local authorities from field staff to fairly senior officials, if they were obstructive, as some of them were. In these encounters, as he describes them, one sees the combativeness of the man. But overall it was a productive and successful expedition, marred only by the fact that he could not, as he had hoped, go on to Australia (p. 198).

Hornaday and Ward set off for Europe at the end of 1876 and they travelled together to the Red Sea, where Ward turned off to pursue his own, briefer, programme. Hornaday took a dislike to Victorian London, 'a vast inhospitable wilderness of brick', only partly redeemed by 'its wonderful museums and galleries of art'. He found the British Museum a 'wonderful storehouse' and its scholarly, but expensive, catalogues 'truly astonishing'. It made him a little jealous that the United States as yet had no comparable resources. He passed through Paris to Rome, which he found 'a desert for natural history'. Rome had abundant marble statues 'but she cannot stuff an animal so that it is fit to be seen'. They began their stay in Cairo at the Grand New Hotel, but the other guests looked supercilious and disapproving as Ward and Hornaday carried through the foyer to their rooms the 'queer animals' which they had bought. This experience convinced Hornaday that in his peculiar trade small and unfashionable hotels would suit him better—and they were of course cheaper.

As a tourist himself, albeit a zoologist, Hornaday had a hilarious encounter with an Egyptian camel which objected noisily to being mounted by 'a Christian infidel dog'. He was learning fast; later on he has much to say about Hindu religious objections to his killing animals, and how he got round them. At Jeddah, Ward and Hornaday parted, and the arduous two-year stint in the Asian jungles began, with only brief respite in the major cities through which he passed. In the chapters reprinted herein, the author has clearly gained confidence by experience—as will be described later. In February 1879 he 'reached Rochester safe and well' after an absence of two and three-quarter years. Then he married Josephine Chamberlain, who had waited so patiently for his return; when the book was published, he dedicated it to her as 'the sunshine of my life'.

Looking back over his productive career as a writer, he reckoned that 'my "fortune" in books, figuratively speaking, was made by *Two Years in the Jungle*'. It also established his reputation as 'an expert taxidermist and field naturalist'. From 1882 to 1890 he was chief taxidermist at the United States National Museum in Washington. It was much more than just preparing animal specimens as exhibits. He was a pioneer in the presentation of animals in a background which showed their natural habitat, and his 'famous bison group' became a model for many other museum curators.

From taxidermy he moved on into the mainstream of his career, the conservation of living animals in zoos or in the wild, taking his opportunities as they came. He argued that the effective display of animal specimens in museums came from knowing how the living animals behaved—their posture and appearance, as much as their environment. He may not have been the originator but he certainly developed the Museum collection of living animals, kept in improvised surroundings for observation by taxidermists in his department. He made a 'much publicized tour' of the United States to collect animals, and by 1889 he had a collection of 225 living animals. Under the encouragement of Langley, Secretary of the Smithsonian Institution, which administered the Museum, he became Curator of the Department of Living Animals. This led to the project for founding a zoological park in Washington.

Hornaday was able to secure a spacious site for the zoo on the outskirts of Washington. From the outset he believed that wild animals in captivity should be allowed to roam in enclosures and not be confined to cages, as was the normal practice in many European zoos of that time. But there were problems in building up a collection of wild animals in the national capital. If a foreign ruler gave an animal to the President—the gift of a lion from the Ethiopian Emperor Menelik was such a case—it was passed on to the zoo. At a humbler level, a circus which had surplus animals, such as the cubs born to a lioness, offered them to the Washington zoo. On one memorable occasion, a circus elephant marched through the capital, attended by numerous small boys, on its way to the zoological park. Few of these fortuitous and uncoordinated additions to the collection were refused. But their arrival made it impossible to develop a balanced collection, housed in proper buildings. Hornaday was once obliged to decline the offer of eighteen bison, made by the celebrated W. T. Cody (Buffalo Bill) because he could not accommodate them. These and other difficulties tried Hornaday's patience—not his most abundant quality—beyond endurance. In 1890 he resigned and withdrew altogether from the animal world to make a living in real-estate dealing in Buffalo, New York.

But the onward march of animal conservation was unstoppable

and after six years recalled Hornaday to his chosen metier. As we shall see, Hornaday felt justified in killing animals to obtain specimens for exhibition in museums, and he accepted the practice of selective hunting of big game for sport, though he denounced the type he called 'a game butcher or a market hunter' who slaughtered on a large scale for personal display or for profit. In this attitude, he was typical of his time. Men of greater influence than he in America—such as Theodore Roosevelt, the future President—were big-game hunters who deplored the threat of *wholesale* shooting of species in their own or other countries. In 1887 Roosevelt and other wealthy enthusiasts had formed the exclusive Boone and Crockett Club (the names are those of legendary American frontiersmen and hunters), which was opposed to 'uncontrolled and unprincipled methods'. In 1893 Madison Grant joined the club; he was an advocate of a scheme for forming a zoo in New York, so that it would no longer lag behind other great cities of the world in that respect.

This group had the political clout and the money needed to get the project started. The New York City administration offered to provide a site if the sponsors would raise $250,000 for the buildings and other development. In their plutocratic world, that was no problem. In April 1896 Hornaday was engaged as Director of the projected New York Zoological Park, a post which he held for the ensuing thirty years. He selected a 260-acre site in what was then the open countryside of South Bronx. Hence, it became the 'Bronx Zoo' to New Yorkers until, to suit changing perceptions, it became the International Wildlife Conservation Park in 1993. Hornaday's site still had abundant tree cover and included rocky outcrops and other existing features which could be adapted to reproduce the natural habitat of various species. He went off on a tour of European zoos to acquaint himself with their practice and ideas, but came back more than ever convinced that open enclosures were the best layout. It took fifteen years to complete the building programme, and the quality of these structures was such that in the 1960s there were doubts about replacing them with buildings of more modern design.

The Bronx Zoo, described in Hornaday's obituary as 'the greatest monument to his memory', was soon much more than a centre for showing living animals to the public. It undertook a programme of breeding endangered American species, such as the buffalo, to provide stock which could be dispersed across the country. Already in his brief time at Washington, Hornaday had been associated with the Yellowstone National Park. In 1905 the Wildlife Survival

Centre at the New York Zoo founded the American Bison Society to provide 'a reserve where they could live and breed in peace'. In 1913–14 Hornaday took the lead in raising $100,000 to endow a Permanent Wild Life Fund. In later years he received formal awards from the Montana Bison Range and the Elk River Game Reserve for his part in their progress. He and Madison Grant, who was President of the New York Zoological Society in Hornaday's time, donated their numerous trophies to form a Heads and Horns Museum within the Zoo.

There was still time and inclination for the occasional expedition into the wilds. In 1907, after a trip to the Canadian Rockies (described in his *Camp Fires in the Rockies*), Hornaday joined a party which made a journey by mule from Tucson, Arizona, southwards across the Sonora desert in northern Mexico and climbed to the summit of the volcano, Pinacate. It was a strenuous and quite eventful trip through unknown country which Hornaday described, in rather gung-ho fashion, in his *Camp Fires on Desert and Lava*. This book was more than just an entertaining account of a journey through the back of beyond. Three of the eight members of the expedition were scientists, who did some fieldwork, and three were proficient photographers. There was some selective shooting of game, but at the end of the book Hornaday sets out guidelines, entitled 'A Sportsman's Platform', advocating that trophies should be limited to 'very few' for each hunter, and arguing that 'a fine photograph of a large animal in its haunts is entitled to more credit than the dead trophy of a similar animal'. A few years later he published in book form (*Wild Life Conservation*, 1914) a series of lectures delivered at Yale, illustrated by horrifying photographs of large numbers of birds and animals slaughtered and then displayed *en masse* to gratify the vanity of the 'sportsmen' who had shot them.

His obituary notes that

with voice and pen he waged a militant battle in defense of the nation's wildlife. He had an uncommon faculty of making enemies, men who were opposed to his ideas and methods, but the opposition only increased the vigor of his campaigns. Fearless and courageous beyond ordinary reckoning, he never minced words but spoke and wrote as his judgment dictated.

The preservation of American migratory wildfowl led to a vigorous campaign against the shooting lobby and their allies, the manufacturers of sporting guns. He was one of the group who promoted the federal Bayne Law to restrict the sale of native game; another law prohibited the import of the plumage of wild birds for millinery purposes.

Although not a teetotaller, he was a vehement critic of the evils which could follow the unrestricted import of alcohol into traditional societies. His *Free Rum on the Congo* (1887) was a diatribe against the commercial interests which had prevented the Berlin Conference of 1884 from banning the import of alcohol into the Congo basin. His novel, *The Man Who Became a Savage*, based on his experiences in his trips abroad, he called 'a story which leans towards the side of temperance'. This came oddly from the man who wished he could have bought enough champagne in Kuala Lumpur to bathe in it. During the period of American neutrality in the 1914–18 war, he wrote a pamphlet, 'Awake! America', and in 1917 came *A Searchlight on Germany—Blunders, Crimes and Punishment*, which advocates continuing the war until Germany should surrender unconditionally.

His *Two Years in the Jungle* went through many editions—the twelfth was published in 1929. But in his own opinion his *magnum opus* was his *American Natural History* (1904), a solid and well-illustrated tome of 449 pages, written for the practical purpose of filling the gap between the zoology textbooks written for college students and the 'nature study' booklets used in primary schools. But this is more than a sound secondary school textbook; in systematic and orderly fashion, Hornaday works into it an immense amount of knowledge, gained by firsthand observation, of American fauna and some other animals found in zoos. Ever the evangelist, Hornaday sought to dispel prevalent 'false notions', such as the idea that all species of crocodile are likely to attack man and a tendency to impute to animals 'a full measure of human intelligence'. In that connection, he has some fascinating material on training orang-utans in the Bronx Zoo to perform in human fashion—like a chimpanzees' tea-party—for an audience. At a more technical level, he had produced a handbook, in 1891, on *Taxidermy and Zoological Collecting*.

Animal intelligence and behaviour was an absorbing interest which prompted him to write *The Minds and Manners of Wild Animals—A Book of Personal Observations* (1922), which he rated 'my most scholarly and well written book'. It is a study of animals presented thematically rather than by species, to consider facets of temperament such as fear, aggression, intelligence, language, and other forms of communication. It is the summation of a lifetime's close observation of animals, both in the wild and in captivity. There are many shrewd and humorous touches. He remembered, for example, how in India the langur monkeys 'used to glare down at us and curse us horribly whenever we met'. He points out that some birds build elaborate nests which provide much better shelter than the overnight shanties of branches with which the Jakun of Malaya and the Punan of Borneo are sometimes content.

Like many a writer who had a facile pen and an urge to communicate, Hornaday wrote too much. There is a considerable difference in quality between his best books and his lesser effusions. He himself was much attached to 'the imp of the brood', *Wild Animal Interviews and Wild Opinions of Us*. Another in the same vein is *Tales from Nature's Wonderlands*, a book for children, based—he said—on stories told to his grandchildren, on the evolution and extinction of living and some vanished species, such as the dinosaur and the American elephant.

Much of this writing was in his later years—he retired from his post at the Zoo in 1926 but kept in touch. He lived on to die on 7 March 1937, honoured by many universities for his talents and achievements as 'a man of firm convictions and indomitable will'.

Two Years in the Jungle: The Expedition and the Book

Before reaching South-East Asia in May 1878, Hornaday spent a year and a half collecting specimens in north and south India (where he spent a long spell in the Animallai Hills) and then in Ceylon. The most important part of his varied bag were Indian crocodiles (gavials) and elephants.

In this early part of his long expedition, he was 'on a learning curve', acquiring skills in stalking and shooting big game in Asian conditions, in recruiting and using the services of local huntsmen, and—not least—in coping with officialdom, such as obstructive customs departments. He wrote of his parting from Ward at Jeddah: 'I was left to go on alone to the East Indies, and work out my own salvation with fear and trembling.' But when he enters the pages of this reprint with his arrival at Singapore, he had become very proficient and confident in the manifold requirements of his mission.

His established routine was to select a suitable area, recruit local people to work for him—with a merger of their technique and his own to achieve maximum results—and then to go into action. The description of catching a crocodile at Jeram (p. 25 ff) illustrates how he did it.

It is worth noting that throughout his book he writes as a naturalist, as well as a collector of specimens. Chapter X, 'Facts about the Orang-Utan', demonstrates that aspect of his work, and is the record of it. He was also, because he was interested in people, something of an ethnographer, as appears in his description of Dyaks in Sarawak.

Like Isabella Bird,[1] he sought an 'escape from civilisation' and so found Singapore fully as uncongenial as she did a few months after him. But he has some vivid comments, such as the narrow passage into the New Harbour being 'like getting into a house through the scullery window' (p. 2). He also notes that there was already a brisk trade in captured wild animals for zoos and circuses, such as Charles Mayer describes (in *Trapping Wild Animals in Malay Jungles*) early in this century. Hornaday was offered a tiger for $150 and a rhinoceros for $250 and a variety of monkeys and other fauna (p. 8). But he preferred to obtain his own specimens in the field and his agents, Katz Brothers, advised him that Selangor would be 'a good collecting ground' (p. 11). He set off with a letter of introduction to Tunku Kudin, who—as it happened—was about to relinquish his office of 'viceroy' of Selangor. He travelled up the coast on the steamer *Telegraph*, which had carried Kudin to Selangor ten years before, and much appreciated the 'thoughtful kindness' of Hood, the chief engineer, whom Emily Innes so cordially disliked.[2] It is a pity that during his brief visit to Selangor Hornaday did not encounter the waspish Emily.

Hood introduced Hornaday to Harry Syers, the Superintendent of Police in Selangor. In 1878 Syers was only at the beginning of a career which took him from service as a private soldier in a regiment stationed in Singapore (he left in 1875) to Commissioner of Police, Federated Malay States, in 1896, and then a tragic death while hunting *seladang* (*bos gaurus*) in 1897. Hornaday, something

---

1. Isabella Bird, *The Golden Chersonese and the Way Thither*, London, John Murray, 1883; reprinted as *The Golden Chersonese: The Malayan Travels of a Victorian Lady*, Kuala Lumpur, Oxford University Press, 1967; and Singapore, 1980, p. 109.

2. Emily Innes, *The Chersonese with the Gilding Off*, London, Richard Bentley and Son, 1885; reprinted Kuala Lumpur, Oxford University Press, 1974 and 1993, Vol. 1, p. 129.

INTRODUCTION [xvii]

of a romantic himself, warmed to Syers who was 'fit to do duty as the hero of a vigorous romance' (p. 13). Here for the only time in his expedition, Hornaday found a European companion of his own age and temperament. After trapping a crocodile at Jeram on the Selangor coast, using native methods illustrated in one of his drawings, Hornaday set off with Syers, who was also a fine shot and a naturalist who gave specimens to local museums, for the interior of Selangor. This is one of the most attractive and interesting passages in the book, and it conveys the exhilaration of two young men exploring as well as hunting. They came to Kuala Lumpur, where champagne was on offer at a ridiculous price, and Hornaday provides one of the earliest extant descriptions of the place as it was in 1878. He and Syers explored the Batu Caves, possibly the first Europeans to do so. He describes the Jakun aborigines and compares them with the Punan whom he met later in Borneo.

He went to Sarawak mainly to obtain specimens of the orangutan, whose habits—like those of the Dyaks—he describes in detail. This species seems to have become a favourite with Hornaday; he wrote about them in his books and trained four to perform at the New York Zoo. Of the Dyaks and other traditional peoples of Sarawak, he wrote:

Savage tribes deteriorate morally, physically, and numerically, according to the degree in which they are influenced by civilization. Those which yield most readily to the mild blandishments of the missionary, the schoolteacher, and the merchant are the first to disappear from the face of the earth ... modern vices and diseases [are] more deadly than the spears and poisoned arrows of the savage (p. 153).

This opinion brought down upon his head the wrath of some reviewers, whose reception of his book was otherwise generally favourable. But, quite unrepentant, in 1887 he denounced the 'devil's work' of the dealers in drink in tropical countries (*Free Rum on the Congo*, p. 39).

The modern reader perhaps finds more fault with Hornaday's conviction that he was justified in using his rifle to kill an animal 'in a moment's time and preserve it to be admired by thousands of other men, rather than leave it to be pulled down and torn to bits' by a predator in the wild. He based his case on 'my fixed principle ... never to kill a harmless animal which I do not need as a specimen or else to eat'. In confirmation of that principle, the story is told that when Hornaday as a youth went hunting on the Iowa prairie for the family larder, he decided to give up shooting squirrels for fun. The story sounds like one of those improving nineteenth-century myths told for the edification of Little Arthur, but it may be true.

However, the scale of killing to obtain museum specimens is disturbing. To give two examples, he shot forty-three orang-utans (p. 150) and twenty-six Indian crocodiles. But his catch by itself would not have endangered the species, which were comparatively abundant at the time, and he argued that 'the demands of various scientific museums ... for East Indian forms' were finite. His 'novel' expedition was the first of its kind, and he probably obtained the required specimens with less mortality among animals than if he had resorted to the more expensive method of buying his specimens. He is honest enough to admit that hunting wild animals in this way was more than a job to be done. It was exciting. The elephant in particular is not easy to hit in a vital spot even at close range; that is why the hunting in the Animallai Hills was so prolonged and frustrating. When he came close to a wild elephant, 'it is a fair and square encounter every time, and the hunter backs his skill and nerve with his life against the great mountain of physical strength and impregnability'. This, of course, is the argument of the big-game hunter out for sport rather than for museum specimens. Hornaday acknowledges the 'moment of triumph' in first handling the carcass of what had been a dangerous foe.

In later years he might have been less disposed to write 'what a romantic life it was to hunt'. But in the 1870s he was a young man experiencing 'the mystic spell of life in "a vast wilderness"', exhilarated by 'the pursuit *for a good purpose* of the living creatures' in it (p. v—emphasis supplied). 'I learn as I grow older,' said Socrates.

Hornaday's book is both a mine of information, about animals, hunting, places, and people, and a record of a personal experience of a gifted man. He evidently took much trouble in converting his notes and diaries into the published text. He says that he sat up late at night to work on it after a long day's toil at other things. That may explain why six years elapsed between his return to the United States in 1879 and the publication of the first edition in 1885.

Woodford Green,   J. M. GULLICK
Essex
February 1993

Further Reading

There is an excellent short study of Hornaday in *The Dictionary of American Biography*, 22, 2, London, Oxford University Press, 1942. His successor as Director of the New York Zoo, W. Reid Blair, wrote his obituary in the *Bulletin of the New York Zoological Society*, 40, 2 (1937), illustrated by a striking portrait photograph of Hornaday in his later years. His papers are held at the Manuscript Division of the Library of Congress. These include an incomplete autobiography, entitled 'Eighty Fascinating Years', but his expedition to Asia is apparently among the unwritten chapters. An autobiographical note, mainly on his books, is printed in S. J. Kunitz and H. Haycraft (eds.), *Twentieth Century Authors*, New York, H. W. Wilson, 1942. Lord Zuckerman (ed.), *Great Zoos of the World*, London, Weidenfeld & Nicolson, 1980, has informative essays on the early years of the zoos at Washington and New York by J. Toovey and M. Edwards respectively. Hornaday's books are full of personal reminiscence; the later ones (but not *Two Years in the Jungle*) are generously illustrated with photographs of animals and scenery (but not of the author).

TWO YEARS IN THE JUNGLE

THE EXPERIENCES OF A HUNTER
AND NATURALIST

IN INDIA, CEYLON, THE MALAY PENINSULA AND BORNEO

BY

WILLIAM T. HORNADAY

DIRECTOR OF THE NEW YORK ZOOLOGICAL PARK
LATE CHIEF TAXIDERMIST, U. S. NATIONAL MUSEUM

WITH MAPS AND ILLUSTRATIONS

"There is a pleasure in the pathless woods,
There is a rapture in the lonely shore."—*Byron*

NEW YORK
CHARLES SCRIBNER'S SONS
1885

To

MY GOOD WIFE

JOSEPHINE

WHOSE PRESENCE BOTH WHEN SEEN AND UNSEEN

HAS EVER BEEN THE SUNSHINE OF MY LIFE

THIS BOOK

IS AFFECTIONATELY DEDICATED

PREFACE.

As a matter of simple justice to myself, I must inform the reader that the journey of which this book is a record was one of action rather than observation, and opportunities for study were few and far between. Owing to the circumstances under which the trip was carried out, all my waking hours were occupied in a ceaseless warfare for specimens, and my only regret comes when I think what "it might have been," for me at least, had I not been obliged to shoot, preserve, care for and pack up nearly every specimen with my own hands. From first to last I had no other assistance than such as could be rendered by ignorant and maladroit native servants. Even in the preparation of these pages the demon of Work has still pursued me, and the task has been accomplished only by the aid of "midnight oil," when wearied by the labors of the day.

What follows is offered merely as a faithful pen-picture of what may be seen and done by almost any healthy young man in two years of ups and downs in the East Indies.

He, at least, who loves the green woods and rippling waters, and has felt the mystic spell of life in "a vast wilderness," will appreciate the record of my experiences. I love nature and all her works, but one day in an East Indian jungle, among strange men and beasts, is worth more to me than a year among dry and musty "study specimens." The green forest, the airy mountain, the plain, the river, and the sea-shore are to me a perpetual delight, and the pursuit, for a good purpose, of the living creatures that inhabit them adds an element of buoyant excitement to the enjoyment of natural scenery, which at best can be but feebly portrayed in words.

In the belief that the average reader is more interested in facts of a general nature than in minutiæ, I have avoided going into natural history details, but have endeavored instead to indicate the most striking features of the countries visited, and the more noteworthy animals and men encountered in their homes.

As the pages which follow will presently reveal, this is in every sense a personal—I might even say a first-personal—narrative, in which the reader is taken as a friend into the author's confidence while they make the trip together. The writer addresses, not the public, in general, but The Reader, individually. To him I would say, confidentially of course, that as a duty to him, in the preparation of these pages I have labored earnestly to avoid all forms of exaggeration, and to represent everything with photographic accuracy as to facts and figures. It is easy to overestimate and color too highly, and I have fought hard to keep out of my story every elephant and monkey who had no right to a place in it.

I consider it the highest duty of a traveller to avoid carelessness in the statement of facts. A narrative of a journey is not a novel, in which the writer may put down as seen any thing that "might have been seen."

To a great many kind friends in the East Indies my thanks are due for aid, comfort, and advice; but I will not consign their names and the acknowledgment of my gratitude to the obscurity of a preface, and each will be found in its own place in the story. But for the friends I made as I went along, and the kindly interest they manifested in my welfare and happiness, I would have felt like a rogue elephant—solitary, uncared for, and even spurned by the other members of the social herd.

Curiously enough, nearly all my East Indian friends were English, and to my American reader I would say, when you meet an English traveller treat him kindly for my sake.

W. T. H.

WASHINGTON, D. C.

CONTENTS.

PART I.

THE MALAY PENINSULA.

CHAPTER I.

SINGAPORE.

New Harbor.—A Back-door Entrance.—Mangrove Swamps and Malay Houses.—Street Scenes.—The Sailors' Quarter.—Well-planned City.—Chinese Shops and Houses.—Populace.—Social Life.—The Curse of the East Indies.—The American Consul.—Two American Travellers.—A Model Millionaire.—The Climate of Singapore.—Market for Live Animals.—A Visit to Mr. Whampoa's Villa.—Curios.—A Tigerish Orang-Utan.—Curiosities in Gardening 1–10

CHAPTER II.

ON THE SELANGORE SEA-COAST.

Malacca.—Selangore.—Klang River and Town.—A Kindred Spirit.—Visit to Jerom on the Sea coast to Collect.—Bamboo Creek.—A Filthy Chinese Village.—A Foul Stream.—Crocodiles.—Catching a Twelve-foot Crocodile with Hook and Line.—The "Alir."—A Harvest of Saurians again.—Crocodiles in the Sea.—Birds.—Shrimp-eating Monkeys.—An Iguana.—The Slowest Race on Record.—Remarkable Fishes.—Catching *Periophthalmi.*—An Adventure in Mud.—Various Vertebrates.—Centipedes and their Doings.—Doctoring a Ray-stung Fisherman.—Malay Character.—Return to Klang.. 11–23

viii CONTENTS.

CHAPTER III.

HUNTING IN THE INTERIOR OF SELANGORE.

PAGE

A Trip to the Interior.—Road to Kwala Lumpor—The Town.—"The Captain Cheena."—A Bonanza in Champagne.—Sungei Batu.—A Foolish Feat.—Our House.—Feasting on Durians.—A Jacoon House and Family.—Resemblance to the Dyaks.—An Impromptu Elephant Hunt.—Attack in a Swamp.—Death of a Young Tusker.—Plague of Flies.—Another Elephant Hunt.—A Close Shave and a Ludicrous Performance.—Discovery and Exploration of Three Fine Caves.—Cathedral Cave.—Mammals.—Visit to a Tin Mine.—Chinese *versus* Malays.—Political Condition of Selangore.—Statistics.—Snakes.—Good-by to Klang.—Mr. Robert Campbell, my Good Genius............................ 24–42

PART II.

BORNEO.

CHAPTER IV.

SARAWAK, PAST AND PRESENT.

Geographical Position and Area of Borneo.—Explorations.—From Singapore to Sarawak.—The Finest City in Borneo.—Historical Sketch of Sarawak Territory.—Sir James Brooke.—Anarchy and Oppression.—Cession of the Territory.—Order out of Chaos.—Evolution of a Model Government.—A Wise and Good Rajah.—Justice in Sarawak and the United States.—Present Prosperity.—A Lesson for Political Economists............................ 43–56

CHAPTER V.

FROM SARAWAK TO THE SADONG.

Hunting near Kuching.—Crocodiles in the Sarawak.—A Dangerous Pest.—War of Extermination.—From Sarawak to the Sadong.—The Simujan Village.—A Hunt for an Orang-utan.—In the Swamp.—On the Mountain.—Valuable Information at Last..... 57–63

CHAPTER VI.

AMONG THE ORANG-UTANS.

Start up the Simujan.—Boat-roofs.—Among the Head-hunters.—A Dyak Long-house.—Monkeys.—Fire-flies.—A Night on a Tropical River.—Mias' Nests.—" Mias, Tuan."—Death of the First Mias.—Another Killed.—Screw Pines.—" Three Mias in one Day ! "—Laborious Work.—Swamp Wading.—Padang Lake.—Cordial Reception at a Dyak House.................................... 64–75

CHAPTER VII.

DOINGS IN THE ORANG-UTAN COUNTRY.

Preparation of Orang Skins and Skeletons.—Return down the Simujan.—Three Orangs Killed.—A Troublesome Infant.—Accessions from Native Hunters.—Seven Orangs in One Day.—Miscellaneous Gatherings.—A Battle-scarred Hero.—The Bore in the Sadong.—Another Trip up the Simujan.—Doctoring an Injured Hunter.—The Dyak at his Worst.—Death of a Huge Orang, "the Rajah."—Dimensions.—A Rival Specimen.—Two Captives 76–87

CHAPTER VIII.

COLLECTING AROUND SIMUJAN.

Native Hunters.—Two Orangs Killed at Simujan.—Nest-making by an Orang.—A Harvest of Mammals.—A Deputation of Dyaks from the Sibuyau.—An Inviting Invitation.—The Rise and Progress of the Baby Orang.—An Interesting Pet.—Humanlike Habits and Emotions.—A Tuba-fishing Picnic.—Third Journey up the Simujan.—Snake Curry.—A Voyage in the Dark....... 88–99

CHAPTER IX.

COLLECTING AT PADANG LAKE.

A Hunt on Gunong Popook.—A Lost Hunter.—A Handsome Dyak.—A Reception by Torchlight.—More Orang-utans.—How an Orang Sleeps.—Proboscis Monkeys.—Living *versus* Stuffed Specimens.—A Remarkable Nose.—Luckless Gibbon-hunting.—Luckless Wild-hog Hunting.—Mud and Thorns.—Picturesque Vegetation.—Fresh-water Turtles and Fishes.—Return to the Sadong........ 100–107

CHAPTER X.

FACTS ABOUT THE ORANG-UTAN.

Distribution of the Orang-utan.—Its Affinities.—External Appearance.—Remarkable Facial Ornament (?).—Color of Skin.—Hair.—Eyes.—Mode of Fighting.—Pugnacity.—Food.—Unsocial Habits.—Young at Birth.—Nesting Habits.—Locomotive Powers.—Inability to Walk or Stand Erect.—Height of Adults.—General Measurements.—Two Species Recognized.—Characters of *Simia*, *Wurmbii* and *Satyrus*.—Individual Peculiarities.............. 108–118

CHAPTER XI.

A MONTH WITH THE DYAKS.

Journey to the Sibuyau.—The River.—A Malodorous Village.—Barriers.—Proboscis Monkeys and Flying Lemurs.—Head of Canoe Navigation.—Swamp-wading.—Our Journey's End.—A Lodge in a Vast Wilderness.—Fine Hunting-grounds.—Source of the River.—Hunting Gibbons.—Lively Sport.—Gibbons' Remarkable Mode of Progress.—A Mias.—A Successful Hunt.—Affection and Courage of a Male Gibbon.—Helplessness of the Baby Orang in Water.—A Live Tarsier.—More Gibbons Shot.—Argus Pheasants.—Dyak Mode of Snaring.—A Deadly Pig-trap.—A Shiftless Village.—A Magnificent Bird.—Curious Rodent.—Visit to Lanchang.—A Village of Head-hunters.—Trophies of the Chase.—A Fine Dyak Specimen 119–135

CHAPTER XII.

A MONTH WITH THE DYAKS—*Concluded.*

Leeches.—Model Making.—Poor Shooting-Boots.—Bad Ammunition.—A Big Buttress.—Wild Honey.—Human-like Emotions of the Baby Orang.—My Guides go on a Strike.—Flying Gibbons.—Boils and Butterflies.—Bear and Muntjac.—Delicious Venison.—Lee Tiac's Omen Bird.—Dyak Shiftlessness in Trade.—Gathering Gutta.—Lee Tiac Climbs a Tapong Tree.—A Perilous Feat.—Ah Kee gets Lost.—A Torch-light Search in the Swamp.—Another Bear.—Return to the Sadong.—The Last Orang.—The Nipa Palm.—A dangerous Squall.—Nesting Habits of the Crocodile.—Farewell to the Sadong...................................... 136–152

CHAPTER XIII.

THE ABORIGINES OF BORNEO.

Civilization an Exterminator of Savage Races.—Stability of the Dyaks.
—The Survival of the Fittest.—The Typical Dyak.—Four Great
Tribes.—*The Kyans.*—Their Strength and Distribution.—Tribe
Misnamed Milanau.—General Characteristics.—Mechanical Skill.
—Modes of Warfare.—Aggressiveness.—Cannibalism of certain
Sub-tribes. — Tattooing. — Ideas of a Future State. — Human
Sacrifices.—Houses.—*The Hill Dyaks.*—Distribution.—Takers of
Head Trophies. — Fighting Qualities. — Physique. — Dress and
Ornaments.—A Curious Corset.—Weapons.—Houses.—The Pangah.—Social Life.—Strict Morality without Religion.—Prohibition of Consanguineous Marriages.—Marriage Ceremony.—Honesty.—Disposal of the Dead.—A Relic of Hindooism.—Ideas of a
Supreme Being and Future State.—*The Mongol Dyaks.*—Remains
of Former Chinese Influence.—An Advanced Tribe.—Position.—
Physique.—Dress.—Houses.—Skill in Agriculture.—Implements
of Husbandry.—Independent but Peaceful.—The Muruts.—Dress
and Ornaments.—Houses.—The Kadyans.—Comparative Estimate
of the Four Great Dyak Tribes.............................. 153–168

CHAPTER XIV.

THE SEA DYAKS.

Habitat. — Number. — Sub-tribes. — Their Physique. — Sea Dyak
Women.— Their Dress and Ornaments. — The Men. — Their
Weapons.—War Boats.—Fighting Qualities.—Head-taking and
Head-hunting.—A Mania for Murder.—Houses and House-life
of the Sea Dyaks.—Communal Harmony.—Daily Occupations.—
Amusements.—Music-making.—Feasts.—Gentlemanly Drunkenness.—High Social Position of Women.—The Doctrine of Fair
Play.—Strict Observance of the Rights of Property.—A Race of
Debt-Payers.—Morality without Religion.—Infrequency of Crime.
—Dyak Diseases.—Mode of Burial.—The Future of the Race.—
Can Christianity Benefit the Dyaks?....................... 169–185

CHAPTER XV.

A PLEASURE TRIP UP THE SARAWAK.

The *Firefly.*—Mr. A. H. Everett.—The Chinese Gold-washings at
Bau.—Caves and Crevices near Paku.—Walk to Tegora.—The
Cinnabar Mines of the Borneo Company.—Romantic Boat Ride

CONTENTS.

down the Staat.—Trip to Serambo Mountain.—Dyak Bridges.—Village of Peninjau.—The Rajah's Cottage.—Magnificent View.—Return to Kuching.—Farewell to Borneo.—Singapore once more.—End of the Expedition.—Retrospect.—Conclusion 186–199

LIST OF ILLUSTRATION

CATCHING A CROCODILE WITH HOOK AND LINE,	*To face page*	16
THE JUMPING FISH.—(*Periophthalmus Schlosserii*),	"	19
A JACOON HOUSE,	"	29
VERTICAL SECTION OF A CAVE IN SELANGORE,	"	37
MALAY HOUSES ON THE SARAWAK RIVER,	"	48
PLAN OF A DYAK LONG-HOUSE,	"	66
EXTERIOR OF A SEA DYAK LONG-HOUSE,	"	66
INTERIOR OF A SEA DYAK LONG-HOUSE,	"	67
WADING AFTER A WOUNDED ORANG-UTAN,	"	71
FEMALE ORANG-UTAN, INFANT AND NEST,	"	78
A FIGHT IN THE TREE-TOPS,	"	85
HEAD OF *Cynogale Bennettii*,	"	90
EMBRYO OF *Crocodilus porosus*,	"	90
THE "OLD MAN,"	"	91
THE THREAD FISH,	"	96
Stegostoma tigrinum,	"	97
Luciocephalus pulcher,	"	97
THE GOURAMI,	"	99
PORTRAIT OF A PROBOSCIS MONKEY,	"	105
THE GIBBON'S MODES OF PROGRESSION,	"	125
THE TARSIER.—(*Tarsius spectrum*),	"	130
BUTTRESSES OF A TAPANG TREE,	"	138
DYAK WEAPONS, UTENSILS, ETC.,	"	153
KYAN WARRIOR,	"	157
GROUP OF SEA DYAKS,	"	169
A SEA DYAK. (SERIBAS CLAN),	"	170
A SEA DYAK BELLE,	"	171
DYAK HARP,	"	179
DYAKS USING THE BILIONG, OR AXE-ADZ,	"	194

MAP

BORNEO, ETHNOGRAPHIC AND GENERAL, . . . *Opposite page* 43

PART I. — THE MALAY PENINSULA.

CHAPTER I.

SINGAPORE.

New Harbor.—A Back-door Entrance.—Mangrove Swamps and Malay Houses.—Street Scenes.—The Sailors' Quarter.—Well-planned City.—Chinese Shops and Houses.—Populace.—Social Life.—The Curse of the East Indies.—The American Consul.—Two American Travellers.—A Model Millionaire.—The Climate of Singapore.—Market for Live Animals.—A Visit to Mr. Whampoa's Villa.—Curios.—A Tigerish Orang-Utan.—Curiosities in Gardening.

THE twentieth of May found us steaming down the Strait of Malacca, close along the shore of the Malay Peninsula. The strait was almost as smooth as a river, and all day long we sat comfortably under the double awning, enjoying the slowly moving panorama of forest-clad hills and mountains, stretches of level jungle, a river mouth and a Malay village here and there, and pretty green islets rising jauntily out of the water along the shore. The next sunrise saw us threading our way through a bewildering maze of islands, large and small, a perfect archipelago in fact, with only a narrow passage for us at best. Presently we passed a flag-staff upon a hill, and a little later three buoys described a semi-circle to the left around a group of islets, and then we saw far across the water many ships at anchor, and back of them a long line of white buildings two stories high, with a monotonous row of upper windows staring across the water at us. Beyond that lay a background of low, green hills.

This is Singapore, the great central ganglion of the Malay Archipelago and Southeastern Asia, the hub of the Far East. The spokes are steamship lines running in almost every direction, to Bangkok, Saigon, China and Japan, Manilla, Sarawak, Pontianak, Batavia, Sumatra, Ceylon, Calcutta, Rangoon, and Malacca.

We had scarcely exclaimed, "Yonder is Singapore!" when it

began to pour in literal earnest, and kept it up during the greater part of that day.

Our steamer, instead of making straight for the town, describes a perfect fish-hook on the chart, leaving Singapore away off to our right and behind us. We enter a little strait which at first we take to be a river, it is so narrow and so completely shut in by green hills and banks of reddish brown shale. But there are large ocean steamers and ships, wharves, dry docks, and coal sheds all along the northern side ; so this must be New Harbor.

Having reached the barb of our fish-hook, we tie up at the Borneo Company's wharf, and pull our relaxed energies together for another collecting campaign in a strange locality. I was very loth to quit such a delightful ship as the *Yengtse*, and actually envied the passengers who were going on to Japan in her. Usually, however, one does not feel so.

This is indeed the end of our voyage, but we are still three miles from the European quarter of the city, so off we go in a rickety bandy with a cart-load of trunks and boxes following slowly after.

Entering Singapore by way of New Harbor is like getting into a house through the scullery window. One's first impressions of the town are associated with coal-dust, mud, stagnant water, and mean buildings, and I found it required quite an effort to shake them off. This back-door entrance is by no means fair to Singapore, for under its baleful influence the traveller is apt to go away (by the next steamer usually) with a low estimate of the city, every way considered.

For the first stage out from New Harbor, the road is built through a muddy and dismal mangrove swamp. Here and there we pass a group of dingy and weather-beaten Malay houses standing on posts over the soft and slimy mud, or perhaps over a thin sheet of murky water. Delightful situation, truly, for the habitations of civilized human beings. Monkeys would choose much better. A Malay prefers to build over water; and, failing that, he builds over the softest mud he can find, usually on the bank of a river or lagoon. His house is quite in keeping with its location. The roof is made of palm leaves, and very often the walls also. The windows are mere slits across the wall near the floor, with clumsy wooden bars across; there is not a speck of paint or whitewash or colored paper visible anywhere, and the whole structure reminds one of an old crow's nest.

Farther on, we emerge from the swamp and pass a Chinese Joss house and cemetery on a hill-side, beyond which we have for a mile, on our right hand, a solid row of Chinese shops and dwellings, and on the other side of the road, a creek flowing mud and slime instead of water. Talk of malaria! It could be cut in that creek, in blocks a foot square, like ice in the Hudson. And the worst of it is that creek stinks—pardon, I mean sticks—by us until we are well into the city itself.

How odd the Chinese shops look with their huge red lanterns, wonderful signs, and flaming inscriptions in black on red paper pasted on the door-posts, lintels, and window-casings. How fat and sleek and hearty-looking are all the Chinese men and women, and how plump and saucy-looking are all their children. I am sure the Chinese are more fleshy, man for man, than any other people in the world.

Rattling on we go. Here are Chinamen smoking big stems of bamboo, large enough for hitching-posts; here is one having his pig-tail combed and his head shaved as he sits smoking unconcernedly on a bench. We pass four Chinamen with a huge and clumsy coffin upon a cart in which there will soon be a fifth, please heaven. Here is a Malay woman combing her hair in a doorway, and here, ah! old enemies! Here are three shops kept by Tamils, or Klings, as they call them here.

How odd everything looks. The houses are all two stories high, with part of the lower story cut out to give a dry passage way, and the overhanging upper portion supported by huge square pillars of masonry.

Aha! The sailors' quarter, it would seem, if we may judge by the tavern signs. One announces, quite regardless of space,

THEMANONTHELOOKOUT,

and displays the portly figure of a Jack tar holding a small Krupp cannon up to his eye, while he squints horribly into the muzzle. Another sign in base imitation of the former proclaims,

THEMANATTHEWHEEL;

and another, the best painted of them all, sets forth, in beautiful letters but homicidal orthography,

THE SILVER ANKER.

Still another proclaims

THE ORIGINAL MADRAS BOB,

which is equivalent to the assertion that there are spurious Madras Bobs about, and "all others are base imitations, unless stamped by our trade mark, and liable to be prosecuted according to law." Verily human nature seems to be very much the same in Singapore as in Rochester.

The streets are wide, the shops are trim and orderly, and apparently filled to overflowing with their respective wares. What fine times we shall have loafing about these queer streets, and poking our nose into everything that is new!

Just now, however, it is pouring rain, so we rattle on through the Chinese bazaars, across an iron bridge, spanning a sort of inner harbor for lighters and small boats (Singapore River), and, without having passed a single European house or shop, we alight at a hotel just at the foot of Fort-Canning-on-the-hill.

Singapore is certainly the handiest city I ever saw, as well planned and carefully executed as though built entirely by one man. It is like a big desk, full of drawers and pigeon-holes, where everything has its place, and can always be found in it. For instance, around the esplanade you find the European hotels—and bad enough they are, too; around Commercial Square, packed closely together, are all the shipping offices, warehouses, and shops of the European merchants; and along Boat Quay are all the ship chandlers. Near by, you will find a dozen large Chinese medicine shops, a dozen cloth shops, a dozen tin shops, and similar clusters of shops kept by blacksmiths, tailors, and carpenters, others for the sale of fruit, vegetables, grain, "notions," and so on to the end of the chapter. All the washerwomen congregate on a five-acre lawn called Dhobi Green, at one side of which runs a stream of water, and there you will see the white shirts, trowsers, and pajamas of His Excellency, perhaps, hanging in ignominious proximity to and on a level with yours. By some means or other, even the Joss houses, like birds of a feather, have flocked together at one side of the town. Owing to this peculiar grouping of the different trades, one can do more business in less time in Singapore than in any other town in the world.

Architecturally considered, Singapore has little to boast of except solidity and uniformity. With but few exceptions the buildings are all Chinese, and perfectly innocent of style. It is a two-story town throughout, solidly built of brick, plastered over, and painted a very pale blue or light yellow. There is a remarkable scarcity of the tumble-down, drunk, and disreputable old buildings so essential to the integrity of all other large cities. Some of the Chinese shops and dwellings of the rich merchants are quite elaborately ornamented on the front with fancy tile and brick work, figures of apocryphal dragons and Chinese lions in high relief, and surrounded by beautifully kept gardens of tropical plants and shrubs. All of these impart a tasty and luxuriant air to the streets. The wealthy Chinamen take very kindly to European luxuries of all kinds except in matters of dress. They are lavish in the use of fine furniture, wines, and food, and their turnouts are really dazzling with their fine open carriages, matched horses, elegant harnesses, and liveried servants, though in dress they draw the line at the white stiff hat of English make. Their dress is cool and roomy, made of white silk or linen, and they wear no jewelry whatever.

The population of Singapore (about one hundred thousand) is a sort of *omnium gatherum* from the various over-crowded countries of Southern Asia generally. The Chinese are by far the most numerous, the most thrifty and enterprising, and the most satisfactory to deal with. The Malays come next, and after them the Tamils from Southern India and Ceylon. The population includes a goodly sprinkling of Portuguese half-castes, a few Javanese, a few Siamese, and of Europeans, a mixture of English, Dutch, Germans, French, Swiss, and last but not least, three Americans, our consul and his daughters.

Of the social life of Singapore I know nothing ; but from what I was told, I judge it is not at all different from other British colonies. There are the usual balls and dinner parties, and the usual number of grades in society, each of which knows its station to a line and never ventures beyond it. To an American it seems extremely silly for wholesale merchants and their clerks to hold themselves, socially, above the retail merchants and their clerks, regardless of the amount of business they do, and their moral and intellectual standing. For my part, I have no patience with society's nonsensical standards, in accordance with which a man's business or profession is everything, and he himself is nothing. Thank God for America, where every man stands on his merits, if he has any.

The hotels of Singapore are all bad, and life in them is exceedingly dull. The liquor consumed in them, and the drunken men one sees almost daily, keep the abstemious traveller in a state of perpetual disgust. The extent to which intoxicating liquors of all kinds are drunk in the East Indies is simply appalling. The drinking habit is so universal, that, as a general thing, when you go to call on an acquaintance at his house, or to visit a stranger in company with other friends, the greeting is, "What will you have to drink?" If you say you do not drink, or do not wish anything, you are urged most urgently to "take *something*," until it becomes positively disagreeable; and really the easiest way is to compromise by taking a glass of their beastly lemonade or abominable soda. Furthermore, when your new acquaintances, or old ones either, for that matter, call upon you at your hotel for half an hour's chat, you are expected to order drinks for the crowd, until the crowd is full of whatever it likes best. To omit this feature is to give positive offence in some cases, and even at the best to send your visitors away saying that you are uncivil and not worthy the acquaintance of gentlemen.

Again and again, I have seen men sit down in a hotel and deliberately drink themselves drunk and helpless. At the old Sea-view Hotel in Colombo, there is a room down-stairs kept for the exclusive use of gentlemen who get too intoxicated to leave the premises. Some get foolishly drunk at the dinner-table with their wine; some drunk and quarrelsome; some destructively drunk; others disgracefully, and many helplessly. It was painful to see polished and intelligent young men make free exhibitions of themselves in the public rooms, and become objects of contempt even to the hotel servants. The curse of the East Indies is brandyism. Wrecked livers and stomachs are always charged to the "beastly climate," but in many, many cases the beastly bottle is to blame. Of course no one will be so unthinking as to suppose there are not hosts of good and true men in the East who draw the line at Bass' pale ale or claret, and who never think of touching more fiery intoxicants; there are plenty such, but I fear they are in the minority.

In due time, I called upon our consul, Major Studer, to pay my respects, little thinking that in him I would meet a "fellow-citizen" from my own proud State, Iowa, and be received almost with open arms. Yes, that was my good fortune, and more than that, I had the pleasure of an early introduction to the Major's charming daughter, then Miss Studer, but now a lass no more, a genuine American girl—which is the highest praise I can bestow upon a young lady. It was a great treat to me all around, and their kind hospitality made my stay in Singapore, at the three different times I was there, far more endurable and free from social dulness than would otherwise have been the case.

I think Major Studer is one of the most efficient consuls with whom

I have yet become acquainted. First, last, and all the time, he is uncompromisingly American, loyal to the backbone, and devoted heart and soul to the interests of the government he represents. In addition to this he has the stamina which such a position requires, and does his duty without the slightest fear of what those around him may say or do. I was not surprised to learn that his official acts have not always met the approbation of those most affected by them, for to my mind no consul can do his duty unflinchingly without making some enemies. From him I learned more of the political history of the Straits Settlements, and the Malay Archipelago, both inside and out, than I could ever have obtained elsewhere.

It was at the Major's, one evening after my return from Borneo, that I met two Americans of the kind one is proud to meet abroad, and pleased to meet at home. Mr. Andrew Carnegie and Mr. Vandevorst ("Vandy") had just then reached the "half-way house" on their pleasure trip around the world, where they stopped for a few days to see the sights. In spite of his Scotch blood, Mr. Carnegie is quite an ideal American, with nothing but praise for his adopted country and all her institutions. More than this, he is what I should call a model millionaire, whom great gain has not rendered insatiably greedy for more, and who industriously coins his money into human happiness instead of reversing the operation, as most of our wealthy men do.

It increases one's estimate of human nature to meet such a man, who, in manner, is as cordial and unassuming as one's best friend, whose human sympathy is his most conspicuous trait, and whose greatest happiness is found in making others happy. While these tardy pages have been in course of preparation, Mr. Carnegie has finished that journey, and made another; and now the public knows him well through the charming pages of "Around the World," and "An American Four-in-Hand in Britain," both of them books of the kind which it warms one's blood to read.

The city of Singapore is situated on an island of the same name, twenty-five miles long by fourteen broad, which is separated from the mainland of the Peninsula by a strait from one-half to three-fourths of a mile wide. The island is covered with low hills, the highest of which has an elevation of about five hundred feet. Although Singapore is only seventy miles north of the equator, the temperature is by no means so hot as might at first be supposed. The thermometer seldom rises above eighty-seven degrees in the

shade, and usually stands at about ten degrees lower than that
There are absolutely no seasons, and nothing to mark the climatic
changes which occur elsewhere. It rains nearly every day, copious
showers of short duration, quite unlike the all-day down-pour of
the monsoons in India. The air is very humid, so that the heat is
far less noticeable than would otherwise be the case. One does
not swelter as in Calcutta or Madras, although a daily bath is as
necessary to comfort as daily bread. Taken altogether, Singapore
is really a delightful resting-place for a traveller, full of interesting
sights, and pleasant walks and drives. The Raffles Library and
Museum, the well-kept Botanic Gardens, the Fort, the markets, the
Joss houses, and various bazaars, are all well worth visiting and
enjoying. The harbor in front of the town often contains some
queer craft, including lumbering Chinese junks and Malay trading
proas of thoroughly antique design.

With the exception of shells, star-fishes, and corals, I found
nothing on the island that I cared either to collect or buy, and
even these were not nearly so abundant as I expected to find them.
The Malays assured me it was not the right time of the year for
them; but I believed this was only an excuse with them, until I
returned from Borneo in December, when they brought me shells
and coral, star-fishes, and huge Neptune's cups, literally by the boat
load.

Had I been a showman or collector of live animals, I could have
gathered quite a harvest of wild beasts in Singapore, at very small
cost. I was offered a fine tiger at $150; baby orangs at $20 to $30,
a fine pair of proboscis monkeys at $100; a pair of full-grown
tapirs at the same price; manis and slow lemurs at $2; and a rhi-
noceros at $250. These were the asking prices, and it is quite
certain that much smaller sums than those named would have purchased the animals in question. The greatest bargain I heard of,
was the sale of a full-grown orang-utan (*Simia satyrus*), four feet
two inches in height, to the Hon. H. A. K. Whampoa, for the ridiculous sum of $65, or $35 less than the price first asked. My desire
to see this animal led me to pay a visit to the country seat of his
owner, a very wealthy Chinese merchant, quite advanced in years
and honors. I went by invitation, and the call was one to be remembered.

On one side of a quiet street in the suburbs, there is a wall en-
closing a spacious garden. Passing through an open gate, the
posts of which are very high and ornamented with carved figures

of Chinese dragons, we drove through a well-kept garden, sighted a spacious but unpretentious white house, and drew up before the massive and finely carved front doors. A gardener, who was trimming a shrub close by, took my card and thrust it through the open carving. Presently the doors opened wide, and I saw Mr. Whampoa coming slowly from the farther end of the wide hall to meet me. He was an old man with a low stoop in his shoulders, a large head, a very thin queue of white hair, small twinkling eyes with a very pleasant expression, perfect manners, and a very kind, unassuming smile. He speaks English as well as I, and has the honor to be Chinese Consul, Turkish Vice-consul, member of the Legislative Council, and the happy possessor of many, many dollars as the result of his labors.

My errand was to see the big orang-utan, but the contents of that lofty hall quite drove the charming creature out of my mind. The first thing that caught my eye was a rounded gray stone about the size of a small coal-scuttle, lying upon the floor as if it were of small account. I scanned it idly, until my glance rested on a spot that had been polished, and I saw that it was jade! Value about three thousand dollars, a present from the owner of a mine for whom Mr. Whampoa had once done some business. We passed through three large, square apartments, which formed a grand saloon, in which were tables for the reception of rare objects of virtu, and the walls and niches were quite filled with "curios." On a table stood a bronze elephant with a pagoda on his back, three feet high, Japanese work evidently, and exquisitely done. Near it hung a huge Chinese gong, four feet in diameter, on which were two dragons inlaid in gold. Above that, hung a huge—almost colossal—pair of stag-horns, on the massive branches of which were perched stuffed birds of paradise. Bronze storks stood upon the floor, and elsewhere were numerous dragons in bronze, elephant tusks, spears, etc. The furniture was all of ebony, exquisitely carved and lavishly inlaid with mother-of-pearl and ivory. On the walls and cornices were divers and sundry inscriptions in Chinese characters, painted very large and very red. I had hard work to repress the curiosity I felt, and the questions that rose to my lips at every step; but I did not wish to tire the feeble old gentleman, or make him regret my visit, so I held my peace.

Then we went out into the back yard to see the orang. He was a perfect monster in size, compared with all other orangs I had seen in captivity, and as savage as a tiger. My presence seemed particularly obnoxious to him, for he scowled and growled at me, made faces, and sprang at me against the wooden bars of his cage in great rage. When I approached him for a nearer view, he thrust his big, hairy arm out from between the bars for about four feet, it seemed to me, and made a grab in my direction, with his huge, black hand. His canine teeth were very large, almost like those of a bear of medium size, and I was very glad he had not an opportunity to try them on my flesh. The brute really acted as if he recognized in me an enemy to his race, and foresaw the slaughter to his kind my visit to Borneo afterward caused. Mr. Whampoa had had him about six months. He was fed with leaves, plantains, and pineapples, and seemed in very good condition, but a few months later he died ; his skin was stuffed, and is now on exhibition in the Museum.

Besides the orang, I was shown quite a collection of live animals, including tortoises of three species, argus pheasants, golden and silver pheasants, a gazelle, porcupine, kangaroo, and some beautiful mandarin ducks. I regretted to see that the latter so completely surpass our pretty summer duck (*Aix sponsa*).

Having viewed the animals, we walked through the gardens, which have been gotten up regardless of expense, and are kept in fine order. One of their most notable features is the abundance of a little shrub, a species of box (*Buxus*) which has been trained and trimmed into various animal forms. The leaves are small, stiff, and very thickly set, and the branches seem willing and able to assume any form which is desired. It was fashioned into Chinese dragons, elephants, tigers, pigs, rhinoceroses, and even deer with antlers. Every animal was perfectly recognizable at a glance, and the effect was heightened by the addition of large wooden eyes painted somewhat like life. Some of the animals were four or five feet high, while a representation of a Chinese junk, of which there were several, was quite eight feet in length, and very carefully reproduced.

There were flowers after flowers, and shrubs by the score, but what pleased me most was a tank containing an old Demerara friend, the Victoria regia, queen of lilies. Yet a bed of touch-me-nots took me back like a flash to the terrace flower-beds at college, and further still, to my mother's mounds at our old home, so very, very long ago. Ah, me! The Victoria regia was eclipsed.

CHAPTER II.

ON THE SELANGORE SEA-COAST.

Malacca.—Selangore.—Klang River and Town.—A Kindred Spirit.—Visit to Jerom on the Sea-coast to Collect.—Bamboo Creek.—A Filthy Chinese Village.—A Foul Stream.—Crocodiles.—Catching a Twelve-foot Crocodile with Hook and Line.—The "Alir."—A Harvest of Saurians again.—Crocodiles in the Sea.—Birds.—Shrimp-eating Monkeys.—An Iguana.—The Slowest Race on Record.—Remarkable Fishes.—Catching *Periopthalmi.*—An Adventure in Mud.—Various Vertebrates.—Centipedes and their Doings.—Doctoring a Ray-stung Fisherman.—Malay Character.—Return to Klang.

A WEEK after landing in Singapore, I set off up the coast toward Malacca, in search of good collecting ground. I took with me an intelligent young Portuguese half-caste as assistant and interpreter, my regular jungle outfit, and all the information I could procure regarding that region. Messrs. Katz Brothers, merchants in Singapore, had advised me to visit the newly opened Territory of Selangore, above Malacca, and supplied me with a letter of introduction to Tunku Dia Udin, a Malay noble, living at Klang, the capital, in case I should decide to go there.

Malacca is about ninety miles up the coast from Singapore. It takes four dollars and fourteen hours by steamer to get you there, and after you have reached it you find only a dull and uninteresting, but prettily shaded town. A few hours spent in industrious inquiry convinced me that Malacca was not the place for me, and without a moment's unnecessary delay I changed my programme entirely. The little steamer *Telegraph* was already getting up steam to go to Selangore and I hastened aboard. In the person of the chief engineer, Mr. J. M. Hood, a Scotchman, of course, I met a "jolly good fellow," who, from first to last, did everything in his power to make my trip to Selangore agreeable. But for his thoughtful kindness from time to time, I would not have fared nearly so well as I did. He was another of those good fellows one meets in knocking about the world, who are so free with their favors that it is hopelessly impossible for any but the wealthy traveller to fully requite them.

We left Malacca at 5 P.M.; and at daybreak the next morning, were in a narrow strait which separates a chain of islands from the mainland of the Malay Peninsula. I thought at first we were in a river; but after steaming smoothly along for a few miles we made a turn toward the mainland, passed a stockade and a white house on a point, showed our colors, and entered the mouth of the River Klang, two hundred miles from Singapore.

Although this is the largest river in Selangore, it is only a hundred and fifty yards wide at the mouth. The water is brown and thick with mud, and looks bilious. The banks are low and swampy, and covered with mangroves and nipa palms growing in the soft mud. Twelve miles from the mouth, the ground suddenly rises high and dry, and we come to Klang, the capital.*

On a stretch of level ground about as large as a race course, on the left bank, are about fifty gray houses covered by roofs of weather-beaten thatch. This is the town. Near the rather insecure wharf stands a good-sized modern building of masonry, painted white, which we know, instinctively, is the public building of the place, the court-house, treasury, post-office, and the like. Near the river bank, just below the town, we see a smoothly shaven hill, the top of which is encircled with a grassy earthwork and shallow moat, minus water. There is a dusky sentry at the gate and two others on the embankment, so that must be the fort. A short distance back of the fort, at the top of a higher hill, stands a spacious and comfortable modern residence overlooking the town and fort, as if to keep a watchful eye over all. This is the British Residency, and it does not belie its looks.

I went ashore with Mr. Hood and up to the fort, where he introduced me to Mr. H. C. Syers, Superintendent of the police and military force of the Territory, who forthwith gave me a cordial invitation to "put up" with him at his quarters in the fort. Finding there was neither hotel nor boarding house in the town I accepted the offer with a sneaking sense of thankfulness that I was really obliged to do so, for I hate hotel life.

Mr. Syers and I became friends directly, for I greatly admired his strength of character and he was not averse to the companionship of one interested in shooting quite as much as himself.

---

* The seat of government is now at Quallah Lumpor.

He was a character fit to do duty as the hero of a vigorous romance, and I found great interest in drawing him out. He was a young Englishman from London, only a little older than I, frank, big-hearted, fearless as a lion-tamer, and tenacious as a bull-dog. He had been a soldier in the British army, but purchased his discharge in order to enter upon a wider field of usefulness in his present position. No officer could be better fitted by nature to fill a position than he to fill his. He has built up out of very suspicious materials, and solely by his own efforts, the present military force of Selangore, which is now well-armed and equipped, and well-drilled, and his grip upon the law-breaking element is so firm, so severe, and so certain, that outbreaks are now extremely improbable. The vigilance with which murderers are hunted down and executed, has rendered crime of that sort very rare.

From Klang I made one short shooting trip up the river, another down it, and another into the hilly jungle back of the town, all of which were rather barren of results, I thought, and convinced me that I must look elsewhere for good collecting ground. Mr. Syers and I planned a trip into the interior after large game; but just then, the Resident, Captain Douglas, was in Singapore and the execution of the plan had to be deferred till his return. Acting on the information and advice of Mr. Syers, I packed up and hired a Malay boat and crew to take me down the river, and thence up the coast, about fifteen miles, to a little Malay hamlet called Jerom.

We started from Klang with the ebb tide, about two o'clock in the afternoon, passed out at the mouth of the river just at sunset, and, hoisting our sail, to catch the gentle breeze, bore away up the coast. We were soon clear of islands and on the open sea. It was a beautiful moonlight night, of the kind made especially for boating, and I think even the stolid Malays enjoyed it.

We reached Jerom at one o'clock, and all the Malays went ashore while I slept in the boat until morning. I went to sleep with the water patting the side of the boat and tumbling in tiny breakers on the shore in front of the house, but when I awoke in the morning all was still and silent as the grave. The boat lay helpless upon the sand, and the sea had quietly stolen away from the shore, leaving between itself and us a barren bank of mud and sand more than half a mile wide. No wonder it was still. It was well for us we made the shore during the high tide, for otherwise we would have been compelled to wait several hours.

The only house in the hamlet which could afford me shelter was that of Datu Pudeh, the Malay headman of the place, and having been confided to his care by Mr. Syers, he took me in, and gave me a corner of his front room, in which I hung up my hammock and *musquitero* without further ceremony. When the tide was in, the house stood almost at the water's edge, rather low upon its posts, with slatted floor, and roof of thatch which had in it several holes large enough to have thrown a dog through. I suppose that, like the man of Arkansaw, when it rained they couldn't fix the roof, and when it did not rain they didn't need to. We had no sooner moved in with our belongings than it began to blow and rain very hard. The bamboo curtains outside were let down over the windows, and the place made as snug as possible, but the wretched old roof leaked like a shower-bath.

A mile above Jerom, a muddy little creek, called Sungei Bulu, runs into the sea between two wide banks of soft mud which are submerged at high tide, and left four feet out of water when the tide is out. A little way up from the mouth is a village of Chinese fishermen who are engaged in catching prawns and making them up into a stinking paste called *blachang*. Every house in the village is tumble-down, rickety and dirty beyond description, and the village smells even worse than it looks. The Chinamen live more like hogs than human beings; and, for my part, I would rather take up quarters in a respectable pig-sty than in such houses as those are.

At high tide there is no ground visible along the banks of the creek, but, when the ebbing tide empties the murky little stream, the channel flows between sloping banks of soft, slimy, gray mud. I never before encountered mud having such a nasty, putrid smell as that emitted when exposed. It smelled like sulphuretted hydrogen, and was, at times, almost overpowering. If I were making up a hell out of the most disagreeable elements on earth, I would put in it the Sungei Bulu at low tide, as being the most dismal, wholly repulsive and sense-offending stream on the earth. Its water is a kind of mud gruel, seasoned with salt, dead leaves, and rotten wood finely pulverized. One would think that even the meanest living creature would find life unendurable in such a place ; but nevertheless the creek is swarming with salt water crocodiles (*Crocodilus porosus*), all of which deserve to be shot for living in such a vile place.

At low tide they crawl out and lie among the mangroves, wallowing in the soft, hot mud until the water rises again. I got several specimens by floating quietly down the stream and shooting them before they were aware of our proximity. The largest ones however, were too smart to be taken in that way, and having become convinced of this fact by the failure of several attempts to shoot a well-known individual of large size, I determined to go a-fishing for him.

Acting under the advice of a Chinese fisherman who seemed to know how to catch crocodiles with a hook and line, we got a rattan about forty feet long for a line, and a dry cocoanut to tie at one end as a float. The Chinaman then proceeded to make an "alir," such as the Malays use in Sarawak, by whittling an inch piece of tough green wood ten inches long into a shape something like a crescent, sharp at both ends and with a groove running round the stick at the middle, which was the thickest part, where the line was to be attached.

Some soft but very tough green bark was then procured from the jungle, and braided into a line six feet long, which was at one end fastened firmly round the middle of the alir, and at the other to the long rattan rope. This bark line was supposed to be so soft and tough no crocodile could bite it in two. The bait used was the body of a sting ray caught by one of the fishermen, which was lashed securely to the alir, one end of which was then bent up close to the bark line and tied to it with a bit of string that could be broken by a slight pull. The intention was that the alir should be swallowed point foremost, and when we pulled on the line the upper point would catch in the side of the stomach, break the string and instantly bring the alir crosswise in the crocodile's interior.

The crocodile we wanted to catch was well known by his repeated appearance at the village, within stone's throw of the houses, and he was described as being a perfect monster, with a throat large enough to swallow a large-sized man instantly. The villagers manifested great interest in our effort, and helped us in every possible way.

We took our tackle just far enough above the village to be out of sight, for we wanted our victim to have so good an opportunity that he would not feel bashful. Following the custom of the Malays we found an overhanging branch, quite low down, over the end of which we threw our line so that the bait hung within six inches of the water at high tide, and so adjusted that a very slight pull would bring it down. The rattan line we threw into the stream with the cocoanut buoy at the end, and quietly retired to the village to await developments.

At the close of the day the bait still hung there undisturbed, and I walked home to Jerom hoping for better luck on the morrow. The next morning we were there soon after sunrise, and the Chinaman joyfully informed us the bait was gone. We got into a small Malay sampan and paddled up the creek at once to investigate. We found the cocoanut moving slowly through the water against the current and upon laying hold of the line we felt there was big game at the other end. We gave a vigorous pull, and the next instant were almost capsized in mid-stream by a pull we got in return. We then passed the line over the stern of the canoe and while I held it, the rest began to paddle down stream toward the village where we proposed to land our catch.

Then he showed himself. He rose to the surface apparently to see what was the matter, and, after giving a good look at us, started forward and began to turn as if about to go up stream. Before he had turned half round he fetched up with a violent jerk which must have given one point of the alir a vicious dig into the side of his stomach; for he began to plunge and thrash around with great violence, sending the water circling around him in huge waves. There was also considerable excitement at our end of the line, for the sampan was small, light, very tipsy, and contained three men of good weight. Chinaman, Malay, and Anglo-Saxon, each shouted at the other two in his own language. Had we been capsized I scarcely know which would have disgusted me most, the ducking in that dirty creek, full of crocodiles, or the loss of my rifle. As soon as we could I tied the weapon fast to the boat so that in the event of a mishap I would not lose it.

After this struggle the crocodile seemed to give up the fight, for he allowed himself to be towed down to the village without further resistance. But as we neared the landing place where we intended to haul him out, he made a final and still more vigorous struggle to get free. He snapped his jaws angrily together in an effort to cut the line, but it was no use, so shutting them together like a vice he plunged first to one side and then the other, striking out with tail and legs, diving deeply one moment and suddenly thrusting his ugly snout far out of water the next.

Another boat came to our assistance at this point and the huge old reptile was dragged shoreward by main force. The men landed

CATCHING A CROCODILE WITH HOOK AND LINE. (*From a drawing by W. M. Carry.*)

and dragged him close up to the shore without further resistance on his part, whereupon I fired a bullet into his neck from the side which cut his spinal marrow so neatly that the vertebra was but very slightly injured. He was the very crocodile we wanted, and his death occasioned no sorrow. He measured exactly twelve feet in length, and his weight was four hundred and fifteen pounds. He was so old, so dingy, dirty, and ugly every way that I concluded to take his skeleton instead of his skin, and spent a day in roughing it out neatly.

Encouraged by this venture, and a satisfactory offer of hard cash, my Chinaman caught for me (on his own hook) two other fine crocodiles, one being eleven feet in length and the other nine, both of which were skinned. I got altogether ten crocodiles out of the Sangei Bulu, which yielded four skins, four skeletons, and one skull.

I was greatly surprised one morning at seeing two crocodiles swimming out in the open sea, directly opposite Jerom, fully a mile from the shore, and three miles from the mouth of the Sungei Bulu. It was a calm, clear day, and I watched them for half an hour with the glass as they floated at the surface of the water, or swam slowly about with their entire length visible the most of the time. One was very large, probably twelve feet in length, and the other was apparently eight feet long. At length they disappeared and we saw them no more. It is not unusual for crocodiles to live in salt water, but I never before saw one out in the open sea.

The mud flats at the mouth of the Sungei Bulu were excellent collecting ground, both when under water and out. Water birds were really numerous when the conditions were favorable for their appearance. Some came to fish in the shallow water and others to pick up a living on the flats when the tide was out. I saw several pelicans (*Pelecanus rufescens?*) perching on some dead trees near the shore, small white egrets (*Herodias garzetta*) and a solitary booby (*Sula piscator*). On a little islet of igneous rock opposite Jerom I saw stone plovers (*Esacus recurvirostris*), two species of tern (*Sterna caspia?* and *Sternula minuta?*), two of ibis, snipes, sand pipers, etc. At low tide many small shrimps were left stranded on the mud, and I often saw troops of small gray monkeys, called krahs (*Macacus cynomolgus*), wading about in the mud among the mangroves, picking them up. At such times it was easy to shoot them, but difficult to get them afterward.

Once we discovered a fine, large kabra goya or iguana (*Hydro-*

saurus salvator), wading about on the mud banks, also looking for food. At my solicitation my young man Francis at once jumped out into the mud and gave chase. He sank almost to his knees at every step, and the race was certainly the slowest on record. The official time was one hundred yards in twenty minutes ; but the kabra goya got beaten, although usually a swift runner ; the soft mud so impeded its progress that it was finally overhauled and killed with a stick. Its length was just six feet. We often found small crocodiles lying hidden in the little gullies which the receding water cuts in the mud banks, and shot several as they came charging out toward the deep water.

The most interesting animals we found on the mud flats were some fishes whose actions were really remarkable. Although apparently stranded there, they seemed to feel perfectly at home, and went jumping round over the mud in every direction with the greatest indifference to their sudden change of element. In reality they were feeding upon the tiny crustaceans left on the bank by the receding tide. They were very lively considering the nature of their play-ground, and when I tried to beguile my Malay boatmen into catching some specimens for me, they declared it would be impossible to catch them on account of the deep mud, and the swiftness of the fish. Neither was my young man Francis to be tempted into such a muddy enterprise, and as I make it a rule never to ask a servant or assistant to do anything I would not be willing to do myself, I saw that I would have to lead the attack in person.

The Malays were thunderstruck when I pulled off my shoes and told them to put me ashore. Seeing that I was really going, Francis, like a good boy, did not hesitate to follow, and we stepped out of the sampan into mud and water hip deep.

We will never know the actual depth of the mud on that bank, but we sank into it to our knees at every step, and were fortunate enough to stop sinking at that point. What a circus it must have been for those who looked on ! But, in for a penny in for a pound, and, bidding Francis choose the largest fish when possible, we went for them. There were probably a dozen in sight, hopping spasmodically about, or lying at rest on the mud, but when we selected the nearest large specimens and made for them, they developed surprising energy and speed, and made straight for their burrows. They progressed by a series of short but rapidly repeated jumps, accomplished by bending the hinder third of the body sharply around to the left, then straightening it very suddenly, and at the

THE JUMPING FISH.—(PERIOPHTHALMUS SCHLOSSERII.)
(Drawn by F. A. Lucas, from a specimen.)

same instant lifting the front half of the body clear of the ground by means of the armlike pectoral fins which act like the front flippers of a sea lion. These fins are almost like arms in their structure and use, the bones being of great length, and thus giving the member great freedom of movement. Owing to the soft and yielding nature of the mud the leaps were short, about six inches being the distance gained each time, but they were so rapid, the mud so very deep and our progress so slow, the fish always succeeded in getting into their holes before we could reach them. Their burrows were simply mud-holes, going straight down to a depth of three to four feet, large enough in diameter to admit a man's arm easily, and, of course, full of water. Although the mud was soft it was not sticky, and we were able to use our hands for spades very effectually. By digging a big hole two feet deep, and standing on one's head in the bottom of it, we were able to reach an arm down two feet farther and seize our fish at the bottom of the burrow. Lucky it was for us that they had no sharp and poisonous spines, like the mud-laff which stung me in Singapore and paralyzed my right hand for some hours.

My first fish was hard to get and hard to hold, but, in the immortal words of "The Shaughraun," "begorra, 'twas worth it."

The species is known scientifically as *Periophthalmus schlosserii*, (Pallas, Bl. Schn.) a member of the family *Gobiidæ*, whose expanded ventral fins serve as a foot, the lengthened pectorals as organs of locomotion, while the small gill opening allows the retention of sufficient moisture to sustain the fish for a considerable period on land.

Adult specimens are nine inches long, of a uniform slaty color.

As I remarked before, our living specimens were hard to hold. When I was trying to pass a string through the gills of my first fish, he struggled out of my grasp, and the moment he touched the mud started at his best speed for the water twenty yards distant.

I was horrified at the thought of his getting away, and instantly falling upon my hands and knees I pursued him frantically "on all fours." It must have been a sight fit for the gods, for even my stolid and ever respectful Malays actually shouted with laughter to see the tuan go over the mud like a "buaya" (crocodile). My change of base was successful, however, for I was able to go over the mud instead of through it, and I overhauled my fish in fine style. A few minutes later I saw Francis execute the same brilliant manœuvre for the same cause, and it certainly was a most laughable spectacle.

We got seven fine specimens altogether, one of which is figured herewith, and of all the muddy human beings you ever saw—but I will draw the veil.

We were fated to have another adventure in mud which was not down in the programme. We left the mouth of the Sungei Bulu very late one evening with the tide at the ebb, and did not arrive opposite Jerom until after sunset. To my horror, our boat grounded in the mud three-fourths of a mile from shore, and stuck fast, leaving us to choose between staying in the boat, with the mosquitoes biting vigorously, for five hours, until the tide came in, or wading ashore through that sea of mud. Of course we chose the latter. It is easy to imagine mud knee deep; but it is a different thing to go through it, when one actually sinks to the knee at every step. We had a quarter of a mile of that, floundering along, slowly and painfully, the dim lights on shore seeming farther away every time we looked. At last we emerged from this slough of despond upon firm ground of shells and sand, and the last half of the distance was quickly accomplished; but we were never caught in that way again.

But for a clean sandy shore line, Jerom would be intolerable, for it is entirely surrounded by mud. No prospect could be more dreary than the vast mud-flat left bare all along the shore at low tide. But even the sandy shore is being rapidly eaten away by the sea. The beach is thickly strewn with the trunks of cocoanut trees which have been undermined and overthrown by the waves, and many more are doomed. Back from the beach, for an unknown number of miles, extends a swampy wilderness inhabited at present only by wild beasts. Mr. Syers once penetrated it a short distance, with a French count as a companion, in search of wild cattle (*Bos sondaicus*). After proceeding a little over a mile, the Gallic sportsman made his attendants construct a litter and carry him back to Jerom. Mr. Syers proceeded, but found no game, and returned in disgust. Along the banks of the Sungei Bulu I saw where the high grass had been trampled down quite recently by wild elephants.

Besides the specimens of *Macacus cynomolgus*, the only other mammal species I obtained at Jerom was an otter (*Lutra leptonyx*), brought in by a Chinaman, who killed it with his parong.

Half a dozen small box-turtles (*Cuora Amboinensis*) were brought to me, and one large tortoise (*Emys trijuga*), which was caught near Jerom. The fishermen catch and eat a good many spiny-backed rays (*Urogymnus asperrimus*) of large size, the dry backs of which lay all about Jerom. One was caught during my stay there, but the stupid Chinaman ruined it as a specimen by cutting off the skin of the back, which he brought to me instead of the whole fish I had called for. It was a very large specimen, measuring 2 feet 9 inches across the back, and I exceedingly regretted its destruction.

A collector of insects could have made quite a collection in the house which (partially) sheltered us. On putting on my clothes one morning, I found a fine healthy centipede in my trousers-pocket, along with my knife and keys. I took this warning rather carelessly, and paid for it the very next day by putting on my shirt with a four-inch centipede in the shoulder. Feeling something crawling vigorously on my flesh, I reached up and made a grab for it, but unfortunately seized it in such a way that the head was left free, and it instantly bit me. Before I could catch its head it bit again, but it never bit any more. When Francis had helped me out of my shirt, and I loosened my grip on the insect, it looked as if it had been through a clothes wringer. After all, its bite was not so terrible as I had been taught to expect. The sensation was similar to what I would have felt had three or four hot needles been thrust into my shoulder a quarter of an inch or so. I bathed the bite directly with tincture of arnica, my favorite remedy for all such ills, and, after several applications, the pain ceased entirely at the end of about two hours.

Just before I left Jerom one of the Malay fishermen living there was badly hurt by a sting-ray. While reaching down in the water to pull up one of his fishing stakes, he disturbed a large ray, who instantly struck at him and drove the ragged, bony spine on his tail completely through the poor fellow's hand, making a dreadfully ragged and painful wound. Datu Pudeh came for me to doctor him, saying that he was about to die. Catching up my little tin box of medicines I went to the injured man, and found him lying limp and helpless in the arms of his friends, surrounded by a sympathizing crowd, not one of whom knew what to do for him. "Will he die, tuan?" was the universal question. "Certainly not," I replied, with assurance that would have astonished an Abernethy, I dare say. I dreaded lock-jaw, but he had no symptoms of it then. Calling for cold water I kept a stream running on the man's hand for fifteen minutes, and then steadily bathed the wound with arnica for half an hour. After that I saturated cotton with the same divine stuff, and bound it upon the wound, with the repeated assurance to the patient that he would not die.

The next day, while I was busy packing up to leave, in walked my patient, so briskly as to take me by surprise, to express his gratitude. He certainly did recover much quicker than I expected. Datu Pudeh begged me to give him some of that wonderful "obat" (medicine); and, having used up my supply, I earned his gratitude by sending him some from Klang on my return.

At Jerom I had a very good opportunity to study Malay character, in one phase at least. I had to respect them for their sobriety, their quiet, dignified manner under all circumstances, their entire disinclination to loud-mouthed brawling, and their freedom from all symptoms of the offensive and impertinent curiosity so characteristic of the higher races of men. I was constrained to regret their characteristic indolence, and lack of enterprise, for this national failing, and this alone, has kept the Malays from holding all Malasia securely in their grasp. Procrastination is the evil genius of the Malay, and the exasperation of whoever looks to him for help in time of need.

The people of Jerom treated me well from first to last, but their ways were too slow for me. Somehow they seemed never ready to start, and delay was ever the order of the day. Being totally unused to their deliberate ways, I lost my temper more than once when depending upon them as boatmen and guides. Even when we were ready to return to Klang, and the boat and crew engaged well in advance, neither were ready on the day appointed, nor had a move been made except by ourselves. At last, when we got the boat all ready to load, the Datu declared it had no sail, and we must wait a day, or until one could be procured. After we had given up in despair, the Datu bestirred himself and enabled us to get off with a loss of only two days. And what are two days to a Malay!

Before leaving I gave the Datu's wife a very nice figured sarong, which pleased her mightily, and called forth from her most earnest apologies for their inability to entertain me in better style during my stay. She insisted on cooking a hot dinner for me just before we were to start, to which I finally consented, to please both the lady and myself. There was presently forthcoming a very nice and highly palatable meal of fried bananas, preserves of nutmeg and pomegranate, and a dry short-cake to eat with butter and sugar, made by the Datu's mother-in-law. In one sense it was not much, all told, but in another it was a feast, for it was the very best the house could offer.

The mother-in-law and daughter had often peeped through the crack of the door at me, but never had shown themselves until I sent in to the old lady a knife, fork, and spoon as a present, instead of the spoon she had craved as a curiosity; whereupon she forthwith donned her best sarong and jacket, and came into the room where I was, to thank me for her presents and her daughter's. (Nothing makes a man feel meaner than to give a poor present and see it appreciated far beyond its worth.) But her daughter's face I never saw.

We got off about an hour after dark, spread our huge matting sail, and glided slowly along the shore. Francis spread a bed for us under an extemporized roof, and we slept well. In the middle of the night I was rudely awakened from a dream of bison-hunting by my bedfellow, who sprang to his feet, clawing violently at the back of his neck, and "uttering strange oaths" as well as familiar swear words. He had been bitten by "an awful big centipede," and advised me, for my own safety, to get up quickly. Being a firm believer in the truth of the saying that "lightning never strikes twice in the same place," I lay still and went to sleep. At noon of the next day we reached Klang again.

CHAPTER III.

HUNTING IN THE INTERIOR OF SELANGORE.

A Trip to the Interior.—Road to Kwala Lumpor.—The Town.—"The Captain Cheena."—A Bonanza in Champagne.—Sungei Batu.—A Foolish Feat.—Our House.—Feasting on Durians.—A Jacoon House and Family.—Resemblance to the Dyaks.—An Impromptu Elephant Hunt.—Attack in a Swamp.—Death of a Young Tusker.—Plague of Flies.—Another Elephant Hunt.—A Close Shave and a Ludicrous Performance.—Discovery and Exploration of Three Fine Caves.—Cathedral Cave.—Mammals. —Visit to a Tin Mine.—Chinese *versus* Malays.—Political Condition of Selangore.—Statistics.—Snakes.—Good-by to Klang.—Mr. Robert Campbell, my Good Genius.

On again reaching Klang I found there Captain Douglas, the British Resident, who, much to my advantage, was kind enough to interest himself in the object of my visit. Through his co-operation Mr. Syers obtained fourteen days' leave of absence for the trip we had planned to take into the interior, and, on the evening of June 27th, we started up the river in Mr. Syers' boat. Four Malays pulled the boat, while we lay down and slept comfortably until we reached Damensara, eighteen miles up, where we tied up till morning. From the Police Station at that point a good carriage road leads east seventeen miles to Kwala Lumpor, the largest town in the territory, in the centre of the mining district.

After our cup of coffee at the police station, I hastily skinned a *Macacus nemestrinus* (broque monkey), which I bought alive of one of the policemen, and then we started for the other end of the road. Mr. Syers had his two ponies in readiness, and we rode them, leaving our luggage to follow on a cart.

The road lay through very dense, high forest, composed of large and very lofty trees (among which the camphor was often noticed), growing very thickly together, while the ground underneath was choked with an undergrowth of thorny palms, rattans and brush so thick it seemed that nothing larger than a cat could get through it. Nowhere was there the smallest opening in this dark and damp mass of vegetation, and it made me shudder to think of attempting to go through it. Surely, I thought, we will not attempt to hunt in such forest as that.

Six miles from the river, we came to another police station, Kooboo Ladah, where we halted to wait for the baggage to come up. Two miles farther on we reached the end of the road,* where we found a gang of government coolies waiting to carry our luggage the remainder of the distance. Without these men, whose services were thoughtfully supplied by Captain Douglas, we should have been obliged to pay a ruinously exorbitant price for coolie hire, almost as much as our baggage was worth.

For the remainder of the way, we had only a very rough bridle path through hilly jungle and across many muddy little streams. At the twelfth mile we passed the Sungei Batu police station, very prettily situated in a highly romantic spot.

After passing two or three clearings, we reached the top of a long, steep hill, and, at its foot, Kwala Lumpor lay before us, on the opposite bank of the river Klang, here reduced in size to a narrow but deep creek. A sampan came across to ferry us over, while our ponies swam beside it, and at 5 P.M. we were at our resting place for the night.

All along the river bank, the houses of the Malays stand in a solid row on piles ten feet high, directly over the swift and muddy current. The houses elsewhere throughout the town are walled with mud, and very steeply roofed with attaps (shingles made of nipa-palm leaves), so that a view of the town from any side discloses very little except high, brown roofs slanting steeply up. In the centre of the town is a large market where fruits, vegetables, meats and various abominations of Chinese cookery are sold. The vegetables are sweet potatoes, yams of various kinds, beans, melons, cucumbers, radishes, Chinese cabbage, onions, egg-plant and "lady's fingers." The fruits were the durian, mangosteen, pineapple, banana, and plantain, oranges (of foreign growth), limes, "papayah," and other small kinds not known by English names.

In the centre of the market-place are a lot of gambling-tables, which, a little later in the evening, were crowded with Chinamen earnestly engaged in the noble pastime of "fighting the tiger." The principal streets are lined with Chinese shops, and are uniformly clean and tidily kept. The streets inhabited by the Malays

---

* This road was completed soon after to Kwala Lumpor.

can be recognized at sight by the accumulation of dirt and malodorous rubbish, and the dilapidated appearance of the houses.

We went straight to the house of the Captain China (pronounced Cheena), the man of importance in the district, who is governor of the Chinese in every sense of the word. His title is Sri Indra Purkasah Wi Jayah Bucktie ("Fair-fighting Chief and Hero"), and his name, Yap Ah Loy, commonly called by Europeans the Captain China. In return for his services to the district in opening new roads and preserving good order, with his own police force, the government allows him a royalty of $1 on every bhara (which equals three piculs, or four hundred pounds) of tin exported, and from this source, and also from his eleven tin mines, he is said to be the wealthiest man in the territory. He has in his employ sixteen hundred and twenty-seven men, and entertains at his house, in true European style, every white man who visits Kwala Lumpor. Unfortunately he was absent at that time, but his people received us quite as if he had been there, and made us comfortable with a fine dinner, an abundance of excellent champagne and good beds.

The next morning, while in the largest Chinese store in the place, buying provisions for our stay in the jungle, we struck a bonanza. We found Mumm's champagne for sale at sixty cents a quart, and India pale ale at fifteen cents per pint! How they ever managed to sell either at such ridiculously low prices we could not understand, and, to ease our consciences before victimizing the dealer, we told him he must have made a mistake in marking his goods. No, that was the price, and we could have all we wanted. It would have been flying in the face of a kind Providence to have neglected such an opportunity as comes but once in a lifetime.

Engaging the strongest coolie we could find we loaded him with champagne (at sixty cents per quart!), and marched him ahead of us into the jungle. It was the proudest moment of my life. I may never strike oil, or gold-bearing quartz, or draw a prize in the Louisiana lottery; but I have struck Jules Mumm's best at sixty cents a quart. My only regret is that I did not fill a tub and take a bath in it, for champagne is the only artificial drink I really like.

Having slept and breakfasted at Kwala Lumpor, we saddled our ponies, and prepared to move on six miles farther to Batu. Not having enough government coolies, we had to hire two Chinamen, who charged us $2.00 for carrying a sixty-pound box six miles.

We crossed the river again, rode along a bridle-path through some dense jungle and one or two clearings, and presently reached Batu, on the Klang River, our journey's end. And right there we did the most foolish thing we could possibly have done, for attempting which we both deserved to have our necks broken. There is a narrow foot-bridge across the river, a single line of planks a foot wide, supported on posts about eight feet high over the bed of the river, and without any railings whatever. Mr. Syers asked if we should ride our ponies over the bridge instead of fording, and I told him to do as he liked, and I would follow. Fool that he was, he started to ride across the bridge, "just for a lark," and, fool that I was, I followed. The least nervousness, or a mis-step on the part of either pony, would have thrown us all over pell-mell, and, considering everything, it is a wonder we got safely over. Not satisfied with this, and to tempt fate still farther, we presently recrossed in the same way. The next day we were amazed at our folly, and ascribed our safety to the Providence which watches over fools and drunken men.

At Batu there are four Malay houses and two Chinese. The headman was absent in Klang, but his wife proved herself a woman capable of meeting an emergency, and forthwith had one of the Malay families vacate their residence, which stood a good distance away from the others in a very pretty grove of durian trees on the high bank of the river. The family moved out, bag and baggage, in twenty minutes, and we moved in with quite as much furniture and general luggage as the dispossessed. The floor was of bamboo slats, tied down to the sleepers, an inch apart, and raised on posts five feet above the ground. The walls were of bark, and the roof of attap. The principal room, in which Mr. Syers and I hung our hammocks, was cool and comfortable, but rather dark from lack of windows. In the other room were quartered our companions, consisting of two Malay policemen, one of them a smart, active young fellow named Yahop—a keen sportsman withal; my boy Francis, Syers' Chinese boy, Cat's Face, cook and servant, and also his Malay horse-keeper, a good servant at all times. The ponies were stabled very comfortably underneath the house.

The jungle all around Batu, although swampy in places, was so open that one could go through it on foot with tolerable ease. Here and there were patches of low and thin forest, broken occasionally with fine grassy glades, such as large animals love to visit for a sight of the sun and sky. But we soon found that beyond this fine ground lay a wide tract of swampy forest, very difficult to traverse, and very bad ground on which to attack dangerous game.

The day of our arrival we did nothing; but set out bright and early the following morning with a Malay guide who knew the locality well. We went to look the ground over, and if possible find wild cattle.

For an hour, our guide led us along a muddy path, through very thick jungle, and finally we halted at a place where there were a number of durian trees, and a party of Malays gathering the ripe fruit as fast as it fell. Being an animal of largely frugivorous habits, I have marked that day with a white stone as being the one on which I ate my first durian.

It is said that most Europeans have to learn to like this celebrated fruit. Ye gods! Learn to sip nectar from a blushing maiden's lips, if you must, but if you are fond of fruit at all, you will not need to be taught to eat what is at once the most delicate in substance, and delicious and aromatic in flavor, of all the many good fruits of the tropics.

This remarkable fruit (*Durio zibethinus*) grows upon a tall forest tree, sixty to eighty feet in height, having a smooth, naked trunk, and otherwise a general resemblance to our hickory. The fruit is very much the same in size and shape as a pineapple, but the entire outside is a bristling array of dark-green, conical spines, three-fourths of an inch high and very sharp. Sometimes, however, the fruit is smaller, and quite round. It is a painful matter to hold a durian except by the stem, and I would about as soon have a six-pound shot fall upon me as one of them. This wholly abominable pod smells even more offensive than it looks, the odor given off being like that of a barrel of onions at its most aggressive stage. Many people are unable to eat durians at all, on this account, but my first one disappeared so suddenly as to greatly astonish and amuse the spectators.

The fruit hangs upon the tree until it ripens and falls of its own accord, and then the husk is pulled open very easily from the blossom end toward the stem, which discloses five longitudinal compartments or cells, in each of which is a row of large chestnut-shaped seeds, about five in each shell, each of which is thickly coated with a soft, grayish, pulpy mass, which is the edible portion. In consistency it resembles flour paste, but in flavor it resembles nothing under the sun. There are, indeed, faint suggestions of black walnuts and rich cream, chocolate and sugar, but all these

A JACOON HOUSE.   (*From Author's sketch.*)

are lost in the flavor peculiar to the fruit itself, indescribable both in delicacy and richness. If there are no durians in heaven it will be the fault of the husk, not the kernel.

The Malays had built a lofty platform of poles to which they could retreat from wild beasts, and also sleep upon at night, and as fast as the durians fell they gathered them. They sold them on the ground, seventeen for a dollar, at which price I invested a dollar forthwith. No Anglo-Indian is half as fond of "brandy-and-soda" as I am of fruit, and I am sure the number of durians exported that week must have fallen off considerably.

While hunting through the forest in search of wild cattle or rhinoceros spoor we came upon the strangest human habitation I ever beheld. It was a Jacoon house, if we may dignify such a structure by that name, and the family was at home. The site had been selected with reference to four small trees, which grew so as to form the four corners of a square about nine feet each way. Twelve feet from the ground four stout saplings had been lashed to the trees to form the foundation of the house, and upon them was lashed the flooring of small green poles. Six feet above it was a roof of green thatch, sloping shed-like from front to back. There were no walls whatever to this remarkable dwelling, which was reached by means of a rude ladder. Upon this platform we found three men, two women, a nursing baby, a miserable little dog, two or three old parongs, some sumpitans and poisoned arrows, and a fire smouldering on a bed of earth at one corner. There were no mats of any kind, and the people slept on the bare poles. The men were naked, with the exception of a dirty loin-cloth, but the women were satisfactorily covered with mantles of dingy cotton cloth.

In physique, physiognomy and habits the Jacoons so closely resemble the forest people (Dyaks) of Borneo as to lead one to believe they have descended, and that, too, by no very long line of ancestry, from some of the numerous sub-tribes now flourishing in that great island. Judging from Mr. Bock's admirable portraits and description of the Poonans, the Jacoons are as much like them as it is possible for two separated tribes to be like each other. The Poonans, like all the Dyaks, have progressed through Borneo from south to north, and it is more likely that the Jacoons are accidental, perhaps involuntary, emigrants from Borneo than that the reverse has been the case.

The Jacoons are a very peaceable, almost timid, people, very ignorant, and wholly averse to living in villages, however small.

They are nowhere numerous, the total number in Selangore being estimated at only seventy. They subsist wholly upon the fruit and vegetable products of the jungle, and the game they kill with their sumpitans, or blow-guns and poisoned arrows. Some of them are said to be very expert in the use of this singular weapon. The present Rajah Brooke states that he once saw a Jacoon drive an arrow into a single crow-quill at a distance of fifteen yards! We learned accidentally, a few days later, that the Jacoons are very fond of bats, and were stopping at that place in order to capture them in some large caves near by.

They were very accommodating people, and our party held quite an animated conversation with them upon the subject of wild game, as they sat perched aloft and looking down upon us. Fortunately they knew the value of money, and we engaged two of the men to act as our guides when we went in quest of wild cattle, rhinoceros, and other animals. One of them came down forthwith and led us a long tramp through the silent and gloomy forest for the remainder of the day, but we saw nothing worth shooting. Much to our disappointment, the Jacoons said there were, at that time, no rhinocerous in that region, but plenty of elephants.

The next morning about daybreak, as we were dozing comfortably in our hammocks, our sleepy ears were suddenly saluted by a clear, ringing note, like a blast of a hunter's horn, coming from the thick jungle half a mile away. We were instantly galvanized into action.

"Elephants!" we both exclaimed in the same breath, as we sprang out of our hammocks, and into our clothes. Never was a reveille responded to with more alacrity.

We swallowed our coffee, albeit rather hastily, crammed down a substantial breakfast, buckled on our hunting-gear, and mustered the men, who were ready as soon as we were. The Jacoons were not there yet, but no matter; I knew we could track up a herd without them. Leaving orders for the Jacoons to track us up if they came, and overtake us as soon as possible, we hurriedly set out.

To our surprise it took us nearly an hour to find the trail of the herd, and even when we did it was apparently two to three hours old. Evidently we had lost our bearings, to begin with. There was nothing to do but follow up the spoor as we found it, so away we went. Our whole party was there, except Mr. Syers' cook, Cat's Face.

My weapon was a rather ancient Sneider rifle, and Syers was

armed with a double rifle carrying the same cartridge, good enough for deer, but very light for elephants.

The trail led us through thick forest for a while, but very soon entered a clearer tract and passed through the very grove of durian trees we had visited the day before. Our Malay friends, the durian gatherers, hailed our warlike appearance with delight, and gathered in an excited group around the ruins of their pole platform, which the rascally elephants had torn down with their trunks just before daybreak. They pulled it down as a sort of elephantine joke on the Malays, just to show them they had not built beyond their reach. The Malays, however, regarded it as anything but a joke to be compelled to quit their platform, climb up into the tree-tops and sit there for several hours in a badly scared condition. No wonder they begged us to shoot all the beasts, one by one, which we solemnly promised to do.

Within the next hour, the trail led us up and down through the more open jungle, four times across the river, and for some distance along its pebbly banks. At one time, nearly an hour was lost in trying to carry the trail across a stretch of hard, bare ground, where it got inextricably mixed with a number of other trails made by elephants which had fed about at random. Dispersing, we searched carefully, scrutinizing every broken twig and blade of grass in our effort to find the direction finally taken by the herd. At last we found where our elephants had marched off into the grassy jungle along *an old trail* for some distance. No wonder we were at fault.

At this juncture up came the Jacoons. "You vagabonds," exclaimed Mr. Syers in Malay, "why didn't you come up an hour ago and save us all this trouble?"

"The white gentlemen walked so fast we thought we would never come up with them," they answered very frankly.

The trail then led straight away for a tract of low, swampy forest, and the character of the jungle changed entirely. Near the edge of the swamp huge, spreading clumps of thorny palms grew in great abundance, and rendered our progress difficult and painful. Strangely enough, however, the farther we got into the swamp the thinner became the undergrowth, until presently it almost entirely disappeared, and in its stead we found uprooted trees, decayed tree-trunks, dead branches, and gnarled surface-roots. The trail had disappeared entirely under a foot of water, save when it crossed a bit of dry ground. We were wading along in water half way to our knees, with slow and tiresome progress, when suddenly the old Jacoon ahead of us stopped, and with his parong pointed through the forest.

"There they are, boys!" exclaimed Syers, in an excited whisper.

A hundred yards away across the tangle of fallen trees and dead branches we plainly saw the massive dark-gray forms of nine wild elephants. They were standing in the water, leisurely browsing upon the juicy aquatic plants that grew here and there, and wholly unconscious of our presence. It was a fearful place for an attack, either upon them or by them. Greatly to our amusement our brave Jacoons immediately swarmed up the nearest saplings, and the other members of the party fell back in good order and concealed themselves.

As the reader is possibly aware, I had had trouble with elephants before, but this was my friend Syers' first experience with such colossal game. Like a true sportsman and green hand at elephants, he was for attacking the herd instantly, before it took alarm and ran away, and I had great difficulty in even partially restraining him.

We quickly looked the herd over and saw that the only tusker in it was a rather small one, with short tusks, but fortunately he was the one nearest us. It seemed like an utter impossibility to get near enough for a sure shot through that open swamp; but, selecting our line of attack, and keeping carefully behind the tree-trunks as long as possible, we crouched low and stole forward. In spite of our caution, a stick would snap every now and then, and our feet make a noisy disturbance in the water. Mr. Syers, who was eager and excited, took the lead, altogether too rapidly I thought, and I followed, almost upon his heels.

At last we reached a large tree at the foot of which was a bit of bare ground. Syers stepped up on it and cocked both barrels of his rifle. The elephant was in clear view forty yards away, but his hind quarters were toward us and his head was hidden by the root of an upturned tree. Syers threw his rifle up to his cheek with a look that meant business, and was glancing along the barrels for a shot, when I gave him a dig in the ribs and hurriedly whispered:

"Confound it, man, don't fire yet!"

"Why, I can hit him here well enough," he protested, in an excited whisper.

"But you couldn't possibly kill him. We must get up to that root close by his head before we fire."

I hardly knew whether to be vexed or amused at my good friend's impetuosity, for I felt that as an old elephant hunter of four months' standing (and running also!) he should have allowed me to lead the attack. I shall always regard it as a hunter's miracle that we succeeded in approaching that animal when making so much noise and going ahead so precipitately in open cover.

With every nerve strained to highest tension, we crept out recklessly toward the upturned root, crouching almost into the water, and after a few moments of breathless anxiety we reached it and were within twelve paces of our elephant. I was totally surprised at his not seeing, hearing, nor scenting us. He was utterly unconscious of our presence until we both stepped from our cover, aimed quickly at his temple and fired together.

The great beast gave a tremendous start as the bullets crashed into his skull, threw his trunk aloft with a thrilling scream and wheeled toward us.

Before he had time to make a single step forward we aimed for the fatal spot over the eye and fired again. Down sank the ponderous head, the legs gave way, and the huge beast settled down where he stood and rested in the mud, back uppermost, with his feet doubled under him.

We instantly reloaded and came to a "ready," just as the tough old pachyderm began to slightly recover and struggle to regain his feet. Choosing our positions this time, a couple of shots behind the ear penetrated his brain and settled matters. With a convulsive shudder and a deep groan the great creature slowly sank back upon the ground, moved his trunk feebly a few moments, fetched a deep sigh and expired.

Of course all the other elephants had bolted at the first alarm, and were by that time far away. Our followers came running up, grinning from ear to ear at our success, and when they surrounded the fallen giant their exclamations of astonishment were loud and fervent. We could not measure our game, but according to the circumference of his fore foot, and his general appearance, he was about eight feet in height at the shoulders. His back was thickly encrusted all over with a half-inch coating of dried mud, the wise provision of a sagacious animal against the attacks of the swarm of huge gad-flies which buzzed about him. They bit the blood out of us more than once, and annoyed us exceedingly while we were at work on the dead elephant.

In a pouring rain, we cut off his head and took his skull, cervical vertebræ, and feet—quite enough of that sort of thing in that pestilential swamp. We carried home all except the skull, which we left to be brought out the next day by a party of Malays.

We reached home thoroughly tired, hungry, and bedraggled, but Jules Mumm and Cat's Face came to our rescue, and as Syers and I sat on the slatted floor and banqueted from the top of our camp chest we ran the chase all over again.

The next day the elephant's skull was carried out of the jungle, and I stayed at home to clean it carefully with knife and scraper, while Mr. Syers went off on an unsuccessful hunt after wild cattle.

The day following that we had another go at elephants. We overtook a herd, and attacked it in thick cover, bareheaded, in a pouring rain which half blinded us. The only tusker in the herd was small and young, and I was for letting him go, but my eager companion insisted that elephants were a nuisance in Selangore, and ought to be killed off for that reason if no other. We fired at the young tusker, but failed to bring him down, and the herd made off very deliberately. They thought our firing was thunder, or at least a part of the storm. I was willing to let them go, but Syers voted to follow them up, so I assented with every appearance of satisfaction. For three mortal hours we went at our best speed along that trail, through mud and water a foot deep, through bog and brake, over fallen trees, and through thickets of thorny palms, until finally, when quite tired out, we came up to the elephants in the densest of cover.

As we were advancing promptly to the attack, across a bit of open ground with the herd on our left, we heard a sudden crashing in the bushes on our right, and in another instant saw a young seven-foot elephant coming full tilt, straight toward us, and not twenty yards away. I thought, "Merciful heavens! The beast is charging us!" and we instantly threw up our guns to fire. I took a quick aim at his forehead, and was in the act of pressing the trigger, when the elephant, then within twenty feet of us, suddenly sheered off at a right angle to his former course, and fairly humped himself to get safely away. He went at a splendid gait, directly away from us.

"All right, my young friend, its a bargain!" thought I, thankfully. "You let me alone and I'll do the same by"——bang! went Syers' rifle, with an infernal roar just beside my ear, aimed at the fast retreating elephant. Had he shot him in the hind quarter? The animal gave a shrill little scream, humped his back still higher, pulled his throttle wide open, and rushed off through the jungle like a runaway locomotive.

I turned to Syers in astonishment.

"What on earth did you shoot for, and where did you hit him?"

"Why, confound it, I thought he was going to run over us, and he scared me so I put a ball through the butt of his ear to pay him off."

I enjoyed a good laugh at my vindictive friend's expense, in which he joined very heartily, for I certainly never saw a more absurd performance in the hunting field. The idea of his firing a ball at that little elephant, who was already doing his best to get away from us, was comical, to say the least, and the joke lasted many a day.

On the way home we made a very interesting discovery, quite by accident. We fell in with an old Malay and some Jacoons, who walked along with us for some distance. As we were going through the forest, a short distance from the foot of a gray limestone cliff about two hundred feet high, covered on the top with forest, we noticed in the air a very curious, pungent odor, like guano, the cause of which we could not divine. Mr. Syers turned to the old Malay, who was familiar with the neighborhood, and inquired:

"What is it that stinks so?"

"Bats' dung, sir."

"Bats' dung! Where is it?"

"In the cave yonder in the rocks, sir."

"Why did you not tell us of it the other time we were here, old simpleton?"

"I didn't know you wanted to know about it, sir," said the old fellow, innocently.

We turned about directly and made for the cliff, under the old man's guidance. The cave was soon reached. We climbed up forty feet or so over a huge pile of angular rocks that had fallen from the face of the cliff, and on going down a sharp incline found ourselves underneath a huge mass of bare limestone rock, leaning at an angle of forty-five degrees against the side of the cliff, forming a cavernous arch, open at both ends and a hundred feet high. It was hung with smooth, dull-gray stalactites, which, when broken off, showed such a clean white limestone formation that it might almost be called marble.

From near the bottom of this curiously formed arch a wide

opening led into the cave proper. We procured a torch of dry bamboo and entered forthwith. This cave, which it seems is called Gua Belah, or the Double Cave, is about sixty feet wide, a hundred and fifty feet long, to where it terminates in a narrow cleft in the rock, and about forty feet high at the highest point. The ground plan of the cavern is therefore an isosceles triangle. The walls were smooth, of a light-gray color, and without stalactites. The floor was covered to an unknown depth with a layer of loose and dry bat guano, which gave off the odor we had noticed half a mile away.

The cave was full of bats (*Eonycteris spilla*) which left their resting places on the walls as we entered, and flew round and round above us in a roaring swarm, at times coming within a foot of our faces. Our footsteps fell noiselessly on the soft and spongy bed of guano, and had we been provided with sticks we could have easily knocked many bats from the walls. There must have been two thousand of them there. In the outer cavern we easily shot a number of specimens as they clung to the rocks high above us.

Not far from that cave was another in the same mountain, which we visited on the following day. The mouth was simply a hole in the base of the rocky wall, leading straight into a low, but very extensive, cavern, which must have been an acre and a half in extent. The low roof reminded me of a mine, and the numerous galleries and narrow passages leading off on either side rather heightened the resemblance. In the light of our torches the roof was yellowish-white and very clean looking, generally smooth, and without stalactites. The floor also was bare rock.

We found the mouth of the cave entirely stopped with branches —excepting one opening about a foot square—and were informed that, after thus blocking the mouth, the Jacoons send two or three men inside to scare the bats out so they can be knocked down by the sticks of those who stand outside at the opening. We tried the same dodge in order to get a few more perfect specimens, and easily secured five by this knock-down process. The scheme is so easy to work, however, and so successful that the Jacoons have almost entirely depopulated the cave of its winged inhabitants.

After leaving this cave, which is called "Gua Lada," or Chilli Cave, we were conducted through a mile of very wet jungle to a third cave, called "Gua Lambong," which is really a very fine cavern. At the mouth there is a perfect little vestibule scooped out of the solid rock by the hand of nature for the express accommodation of the party who will keep a stand there for the sale of refreshments, photographs, and torches to the tourists who will visit the cave during the next century.

On entering the cave at the yawning black hole, we found ourselves in a grand cathedral, whose floor, walls, and roof were of smooth white limestone rock. Descending for a few yards from the mouth we came to a clear stream of water rippling across the rocky floor and seeking an exit near the mouth. Crossing this, we

walked forward along a grand gallery, with clean and level floor, perpendicular walls and gothic roof, like the nave of a cathedral, fifty feet wide and sixty feet high. At the farther end of the gallery—which was by our estimate about three hundred feet in length—the roof suddenly rose in a great round dome ninety or a hundred feet in height, completing so perfectly the resemblance of St. Peter's, at Rome, that had I the privilege of naming the cavern I could call it nothing else than Cathedral Cave. The accompanying diagram represents a vertical section, as nearly as could be obtained without measurements.

We stood for some time gazing in silence about us, quite awed by the grandeur of the natural rock-temple we had discovered.

Remembering the Baptistry at Pisa, and, recalling its beautiful echo, I sang out clear and strong,

Sol mi do.

The echo of the three notes mingled directly in a beautiful chord, wonderfully prolonged, like the sound of three voices winging their way upward until they were lost in the distance. The illusion was perfect and the effect of the echo highly weird and impressive. It seemed fully a quarter of a minute that the echo reverberated in the top of that rocky dome. As a further experiment, Mr. Syers discharged his rifle, and the report sounded like a deep boom of thunder, prolonged and rolling, echoing in the dome and at the farther end of the long gallery with a long-continued roar.

Under the dome the floor began to rise as we progressed, and sloped up all the rest of the way to where the cavern terminated in a narrow cleft. This portion of the floor was covered with a thick deposit of bat guano, loose and dry, but there were very few bats in the cave.

All these caves are about three miles east of Batu, and nine from Kwala Lumpor, in a northerly direction. The whole hill is a solid mass of white crystalline limestone, and its greatest height is about three hundred feet. Besides catching bats in the caves, the Jacoons say that they often retreat to them for safety at certain seasons when the woods are overrun by wild elephants and other dangerous animals.

We made several other hunting excursions in different directions from Batu, always under good guidance, but, although we often saw the tracks of wild cattle, we were never fortunate enough to fall in with the animals themselves. The inevitable krah monkey (*Macacus cynomolgus*) was often seen and sometimes shot.

Squirrels were plentiful, and besides two other species (*Sciurus ephippium* and *bicolor*) we shot several specimens of the beautiful black and white *Sciurus Rafflesi*.

The Malays and Jacoons brought us many specimens of the pretty little mouse-deer (*Tragulus napu* and *kanchil*), several small Felinæ (*Felis marmorata* and *Bengalensis*), and two species of civet cat (*Viverra*), all of which they caught in traps for our especial benefit. We collected a few bright birds also, and one rhinoceros hornbill.

Having spent a week at Batu with both pleasure and profit, we sent our elephant bones, rock specimens from the caves and other dead weight down to Klang by the river, while we packed up and returned to Kwala Lumpor. On the ride back Mr. Syers' pony went down when at full gallop and gave him a terrible fall, which, but for the protection of his thick pith helmet, might have resulted very seriously. It would have sent almost any other man to bed for a week, but my plucky friend insisted on his ability to carry out the programme, and would scarcely let me rub him with my favorite remedy.

On reaching Kwala he took me off four miles south to see a number of tin mines. The road was good all the way, and lay through open uplands of dark alluvial soil. We passed several fine fields of sugar-cane, two of tobacco, and my guide pointed out several coffee bushes hanging full of berries. There were houses and huts of both Malays and Chinese scattered along the road, and the two could always be distinguished at a glance. Those of the Chinese were always in good repair, and surrounded by flourishing and beautifully-kept vegetable gardens of one to two acres in extent. The houses of the Malays were always in bad repair, and their gardens, when they had any, were neglected and weedy. Every Chinaman we met or saw was carrying something, or else at work in his garden. Every Malay was either strolling along empty-handed, or else loafing in the door of his hut. If Selangore were my territory I would give it to the Chinese. Before returning, however, we were astonished beyond measure at seeing two Malays actually at work in a garden, and we stopped and gazed at them in incredulous amazement.

The first tin mine is about four miles from Kwala, situated in the middle of a "flat," near the foot of a range of hills.

The tin is found in the form of dark-colored sand or fine gravel about fifteen feet below the surface, and is reached by simply removing all the over-lying strata of soil, clay, and gravel. The tin lay in a bed, like a vein of coal, about two feet in thickness. The water which runs into the excavation is pumped out by an overshot water-wheel and an endless chain, a very ingenious contrivance which I cannot take time to describe. In the smelting-shed near by the tin is simply melted out and run into ingots of a size and shape convenient to handle.

On reaching Kwala again we found the "Captain Cheena" at home, and he sat us down to a superb dinner, consisting of soup, fish, roast capon, roast duck, green peas, potatoes, cucumbers, pork chops, curry and rice, a monster tart, mangosteens, durians, bananas and champagne. The captain does not speak English, so I lost the benefit of a conversation with him.

The next day we returned to Klang, and after a day's rest I began to get ready to "move on."

We were again entertained at dinner by Captain and Mrs. Douglas at the Residency, and spent a most enjoyable evening. Although the country is perfectly tranquil, the Malays are a trifle uncertain and the Chinese also, as the murder of Europeans not long since in Perak, and later at the Dindings, has rendered painfully evident. A body guard of six stalwart policemen from Mr. Syers' force watches over the Residency night and day, so that there is little to fear from foes without. Captain Douglas has entered, heart and soul, into the development of the territory of which he is virtually the governor; and it is gratifying to see such a promising country in such good hands. Under the control of the shiftless Malays its resources would never have been developed.

It takes the British Government to rule such places and make them habitable for producers, and worth something to the world.

Nominally, the old Sultan of Selangore is still a sultan, and ruler of the country, but actually he is a mere figure-head, living off in a corner at Selangore, and quietly enjoying the royalty of $2,000 per month, which is paid him out of the revenues of the country which he is not competent to govern and develop. His son, the heir apparent to the figure-headship, has a much larger harem than his sultanic papa, and also some notions of his own about government, which may result in giving the country a backset if he ever acquires the power to put them in force.

The Territory of Selangore has a coast line of one hundred and twenty miles, and it extends into the interior about fifty miles, where it joins Pahang, another territory of the same political complexion. Its population in 1880 was fifteen thousand. The chief productions of the country are tin, gutta, rattans, rice, gambier (pepper), and tobacco. The principal industries are tin-mining, gardening, and gambling. The average monthly production of tin is six hundred bharas, or two hundred and forty thousand pounds. The soil of the interior is certainly very rich, and I should think could be made to produce sugar-cane, tobacco, and perhaps coffee also, with great profit.

As a sort of parting send-off, we were dined the last evening of our stay by Mr. Turney, Treasurer of Selangore and his estimable lady. This is what the Klang people mean by being "civil" to strangers. Healthy civility surely, but the odds are every time in favor of the stranger.

Almost my only disappointment in Selangore was that, from first to last, we found no snakes in the jungle. I fondly hoped to meet a python in his native wilds and see what he would do, or at least an *Ophiophagus elaps*—snake-eating cobra—but neither did we see. My imagination had pictured the forests of the East Indies as producing a big snake for every square mile, but they are almost as

HUNTING IN THE INTERIOR OF SELANGORE.   41

scarce as snakes in Ireland. In all my jungle wanderings in the far east I did not encounter a snake four feet long, although I looked for them very hopefully. It was disgusting after all the big snake stories I had heard. The only snake I saw in Selangore was a vicious little viperine affair, eight inches long, which I killed with a prayer-book in Captain Douglas' drawing room at the Residency, while kneeling at prayers one Sunday evening. He came wriggling toward me across the matting, and I took him in. Just before my visit Mr. Syers killed three cobras in his house in the fort, which had taken up quarters under the floor. Fortunately I am not at all nervous, and this discovery did not disturb my slumbers in the least.

On the last day of my stay, an old Malay came into the fort dragging the headless body of a python which measured twelve feet six inches. He was walking through the jungle, and in passing by a hollow tree, the snake thrust its head out of a hole near the bottom. He whipped out his parong and very neatly decapitated the reptile at a single blow. I bought the body and sent him back for the head, which he presently produced, and at the last moment we removed the skin and preserved it for mounting. The jungle had relented and given me a snake after all.

A few months later I saw in Singapore a fine living *Ophiophagus elaps*, about seven feet long, which Captain Douglas had sent down to the Museum—the third specimen of that species he had secured.

When the time came for me to leave Klang I was in no way thankful to go. My visit had been so pleasant that I was really sorry that I could not stay longer. My collection made a very satisfactory showing for six weeks' work, and Mr. Syers' hearty hospitality had made the place seem like a home. He himself was the most interesting specimen I found in this territory, and as a character study he was "immense." In point of modest reminiscence of "dangers he had passed, and moving accidents by flood and field," he was another Othello, a fit type for the hero of a stalwart romance.

But my time came, and I had to leave his rambling, roomy, and cool bungalow in the fort; the Malay bugler who used to practise the "Dead March in Saul" every morning; the drills and parades; and the jolly friend who entertained me so patiently to the last. At parting, he gave me a Malay kris, and a "pig-tail" which he cut from the head of a Chinese murderer just before hanging him, as souvenirs of the visit.

Three days later I reached Singapore once more, and prepared to depart for Borneo.

At this point I desire to mention the kindness of Mr. Robert Campbell, now, alas! numbered with the silent majority, who was my good genius all the time I remained within his reach. I was a total stranger to him until a London firm placed a sum of money to my credit with the firm of Messrs. Martin, Dyce & Co., of which he was the head. When the time came for me to start to Borneo the balance remaining to my credit was not at all sufficient for the trip, and my good friend insisted upon advancing all that I needed. From that time until I started home I spent my funds faster than they came, and every time I became embarrassed Mr. Campbell generously came to my relief. But for his self-forgetful generosity I should more than once have found myself in most unpleasant straits, due, I admit, to my own fault in disregarding Professor Ward's instructions, and going ahead full speed with my work instead of resting and waiting for funds. All thanks to Robert Campbell, and the firm of Martin, Dyce & Co. Thank heaven that my faith in humanity is so often and so handsomely justified!

But it passes my understanding how any stranger, who under such circumstances is trusted without any security, can be so unspeakably contemptible as to defraud his benefactors, as I have known some to do.

PART II. — BORNEO.

CHAPTER IV.

SARAWAK, PAST AND PRESENT.

Geographical Position and Area of Borneo.—Explorations.—From Singapore to Sarawak.—The Finest City in Borneo.—Historical Sketch of Sarawak Territory.—Sir James Brooke.—Anarchy and Oppression.—Cession of the Territory.—Order out of Chaos.—Evolution of a Model Government.—A Wise and Good Rajah.—Justice in Sarawak and the United States.—Present Prosperity.—A Lesson for Political Economists.

THREE hundred miles east of Singapore, directly under the equator, lies a vast island clad from centre to circumference with a wonderful and luxuriant growth of unbroken forest, and peopled with the strangest men and beasts to be found in all the East Indies.

Rich in both vegetable and mineral products, teeming with animal life, and filled with both social and scientific problems, Borneo is a most inviting field, interesting alike to the naturalist, the anthropologist, and the student of political economy. In time, also, when its vast agricultural resources are properly developed, it will offer a chance for life, liberty, and happiness to the overcrowded millions of China, Hindostan, and even Europe.

With an area of one hundred and ninety thousand square miles, and a coast line of over three thousand miles, Borneo is the second largest island in the world. When we look at its proportions on a map which compresses the whole of Asia or Australasia into the limits of a single atlas page, we fail to realize its actual immensity. The whole of New England, the Middle States, and Maryland could be set down in the forest which covers Borneo, and still be surrounded by a wide belt of jungle. The length of the island is eight hundred and fifty miles, and its greatest width six hundred and twenty-five.

Politically, the island is divided into the Dutch Territory, which embraces the whole southern, central, and western parts of the island, fully one-half its entire area; the Territory of Sarawak on the north coast, ruled by an English rajah; the sultanate of Brunei, or Borneo Proper, northeast of Sarawak; and beyond that a fine tract of territory, now called Sabah, almost as large as Sarawak, which has had the good fortune to pass from the protection of the sultan of Sulu into the hands of a new mercantile organization called the British North Borneo Company. This territory has the Kimanis River (between Gaya Bay and Labuan Island) for its western boundary, and the Sibuco River on the east coast, for its southern boundary. Its area is between twenty and twenty-five thousand square miles. Its five hundred miles of coast line include a great many finely sheltered bays and harbors, and its interior has not only a number of large rivers, but, also, the highest mountains in Borneo, including Kina Balu. It is extremely gratifying that such a naturally rich and promising country should have fallen into such good hands as those of Sir Rutherford Alcock, and Messrs. Dent, Martin, Read, and Mayne. Success and long life to the British North Borneo Company!

South of Brunei lies Kotei, a large triangular territory, ruled by a Malay sultan, under Dutch protection, but as independent of the Dutch Government as Nicaragua is of the United States, and which should have boundaries and a color of its own on every map. Above Kotei lies another independent territory of similar shape, also under Dutch protection, but about as little known as the Kina Balu country which joins it on the north.

Even in this age of venturesome and persistent travellers, no white man has crossed Borneo from side to side, and its interior remains in great measure a sealed book. No European has ever succeeded in doing more than to ascend one river to near its source, cross a narrow water-shed and descend a contiguous stream to the same coast from which he started. In this way Von Gaffron ascended the Barito and descended the Kapooas, Bock journeyed up the Mahakkam and down the Barito, and Wallace traversed the Sadong and the Sarawak. An energetic Scotchman, prospecting for diamonds, also crossed from the Kapooas River to the Sarawak, St. John thoroughly explored to their sources the Limbang and Baram Rivers on the north coast, and both he and Hugh Low ascended the great mountain of Kina Balu, near the northeastern extremity of the island.

Nothing could be more arduous and full of risk to life and limb than overland travel in the interior of Borneo, where the traveller is confronted by dense, dark forests and rugged mountains from the beginning to the end of his journey. The interior is practically an uninhabited wilderness, destitute of nearly everything fit for human food, and he who would explore it must carry on his back, through forests and rivers, and over mountains, sufficient food, clothing, and medicines, to last to the end of the journey. The heart of Africa is not nearly so inaccessible as the heart of Borneo. The difficulties of overland travel in the interior are almost beyond belief.

Even in the extreme northeast, accessible from the coast on three sides, there is said to be a great lake and a mountain-peak higher than Kina Balu, never yet visited by a white man, which beckon to the explorer with whispered promises of undiscovered wonders. From the remote interior of the island come wonderful stories of a race of men with tails, with descriptions of their form and habits, stories implicitly believed by many intelligent natives, but which even the most skeptical white men are powerless to disprove.

The dense ignorance which prevails in Singapore regarding Borneo is quite phenomenal. Although so near and in regular steam communication with the island, I found it utterly impossible to obtain there any definite information regarding the distribution or abundance of the orang-utan. At last, when on the point of buying a steamer ticket for the Dutch settlement at Pontianak, I was introduced, quite by chance, to the late A. R. Haughton, Esq.—His Highness' resident of the Rejang District, Sarawak—which piece of good fortune led to an immediate and important change in my plans. From this most agreeable and obliging official, who, from his eighteen years of service in the Sarawak Government, was prepared to answer any question regarding Northern Borneo, I learned that the orang-utan had not yet been exterminated in the rajah's territory, and that the valleys of the Sadong and Batang Lupar Rivers abounded in animal life. I forthwith purchased a ticket for Sarawak, and prepared to accompany my new friend, who was returning from leave of absence to England to regain his shattered health.

I often think how differently I might have fared in my visit to Borneo had I not met Mr. Haughton at the critical moment. Thanks to his courtesy and friendly interest, my introduction to the island was a very agreeable one ; and I shall always remember that but for him I should have gone further and fared worse, for I learned later that Pontianak would not have been the place for me. Since my return to America, the sad news has reached me that my genial friend has gone forever from the land he helped to govern both wisely and well. In his nineteenth year of service his health failed utterly, and on the voyage home he died on the passage up the Red Sea. The rajah lost a valuable officer and the Dyaks a valuable and trusted friend.

The trim little steamer *Rajah Brooke*, belonging to the Honorable Borneo Company, makes tri-monthly trips between Singapore and Sarawak (pronounced Sar-*ah*-wok), carrying to the latter Chinese emigrants, cloth, brass. and ironware, crockery, opium, tobacco, sugar and manufactured sundries, and returning with sago, flour, gutta-percha, dried fish. rattans, edible bird's nests, timber and other jungle products, and also a very considerable quantity of antimony and quicksilver from the mines of the Borneo Company.

On August 7th I embarked myself, a first-class Chinese servant named Ah Kee, a half-caste Portuguese lad named Perara to assist in hunting and preparing specimens, and a complete jungle outfit, with provisions for three months.

At three o'clock we left the Singapore Roads, and, while at our six o'clock dinner, steamed out between Horsburgh Light and Point Romania, the extreme southeastern point of Asia, heading "east-b'-north" for Sarawak. The day following was one of smooth, uneventful sailing o'er a "sultry summer sea," with here and there a pretty green islet in sight, but the cloudless sunrise of the third day out found us running close along the coast of Borneo. Cape Datu lay directly astern, Cape Sipang stood out directly ahead, while all along the south stretched the yellow, sandy beach and evergreen forest of my new land of promise. Borneo at last, the land of apes and monkeys, the home of the orang-utan, the country of the head-hunter, perhaps the sepulchre of the mysterious Missing Link !

Far in the interior there loomed up the rugged masses and isolated peaks of the Krumbang range, clad with tropical verdure, looking dreamily blue and hazy in the distance. As we proceeded, the view disclosed still more lofty and extensive ranges farther inland, until at last the whole interior seemed to be composed of mountains only, between which and the sea there stretched a wide expanse of level forest. A lofty, flat-topped mountain called Penrissen, elevation four thousand four hundred and fifty feet, lying directly south from Cape Sipang, was pointed out as the site which had been selected by the Government of Sarawak for a sanitarium.

The Sarawak River has two main entrances, one called the Santubong, which forms a northwest pass, while the Moritabas is the northeast pass. On the triangular island thus formed, Santubong Peak rises grandly up, like a nearly perfect cone, to a height of two thousand seven hundred and twelve feet, and forms a noble landmark at the river's mouth, visible forty miles at sea.

The Santubong entrance is difficult and dangerous to navigate on account of its sand banks and shoal water, and the *Rajah Brooke* always acts on the principle that the longest way round is the shortest way to Sarawak. We passed Cape Sipang and presently rounded Po Point, upon which rocky promontory sits a dumpy little light-house. From the flag-staff floats the flag of His Highness, the Rajah of Sarawak, a St. George's cross half black and half red on a yellow field. The face of Po Point is a smooth cliff of brownish limestone, which shows pale yellow in places where masses of rock have been freshly broken away by round shot from British gunboats and men-of-war. These vessels are in the habit of using the cliff as a target for cannon practice whenever opportunity affords.

At the mouth of the Moritabas entrance, the river is about three hundred yards in width. The west bank rises in a considerable hill, but the eastern shore is a level, alluvial plain of soft mud, scarcely above tide level. At the foot of the hill is the village of Santubong, inhabited by Malay fishermen. The tide is at the ebb as we enter, and the smooth surface of the river is covered with dead leaves and stems of the nipa palm, decayed logs, dry bamboo stems, chunks of wood, sticks, leaves, and trash—in short, a level plain of driftwood floating swiftly out to sea. We wondered which of those logs would be the one to drift far out past Point Po, into the great equatorial current of the East Indies corresponding to our Gulf Stream, and be borne along on the bosom of the Black River, past Japan, until finally cast ashore on one of the Aleutian Islands to serve some islander as firewood, or timber for a new harpoon handle. The river needed skimming, badly, and like most equatorial streams, it needed straining and filtering also, for it was brown and murky with decayed vegetation and vegetable mould.

The banks are covered with low mangroves and nipa palms (*Nipa fruticans*) growing in the soft mud, the latter sending up their tall, feathery leaves so thickly in places as to exclude the monotonous mangrove entirely. The nipa palm resembles a bunch of cocoanut leaves growing stiffly up, and a cocoanut leaf looks like a huge, uncurled ostrich plume dyed a deep green.

The scenery of the Sarawak River below the capital is decidedly monotonous, and uninteresting except for the distant mountains; but I venture to assert the same may be said of any equatorial river for the first twenty miles up. The banks are of soft mud, the jungle is low and swampy, and the trees are so small and straggling that even the monkeys disdain to inhabit them. We must get farther from the coast to find the grand forests which are fairly alive with wonderful monkeys, and apes, deer, wild "pigs" (fancy a "pig" standing thirty-seven inches high at the shoulders!), civet cats, flying squirrels, hornbills, and argus pheasants. On the way up the Sarawak we saw not a single monkey nor other mammal, and only one or two stray birds.

We followed the tortuous windings of the river for nearly fourteen miles before we came to any signs of civilization; and, for a time, we were in a quandary whether or not to class as such the first Malay houses we saw. The Malay loves water like a duck, and, if possible, he builds his house on piles over a running stream. Failing in that, he builds over stagnant water; and, failing in that, he builds over the softest mud he can find.

He cannot build over the Sarawak River suitably for various reasons, so, leaving thousands of dry acres tenantless, he builds over the soft mud on the river-bank. His boat-house is a pole stuck in the mud, and his wharf is a slimy, slippery, slanting log, reaching down from the top of the bank, across the mud, and into the water indefinitely. If your Malay is really industrious and enterprising, he may even go so far as to cut a few rough notches along the top of his landing-log; but even then it is a difficult and perilous feat for a booted European to make a landing just after the tide has gone out and left a good thick deposit of slippery mud all along the top of the wharf.

As we neared the capital a lofty green peak seemed to rise from just behind the town, but in reality it was several miles beyond. It was Matang Peak, three thousand one hundred and sixty-eight feet in height. We passed a number of Malay houses and straggling villages strung along the banks, passed a flourishing pottery, a warehouse containing a million rattan canes, a number of small boats and a few large ones, came to some airy European

MALAY HOUSES ON THE SARAWAK.

(*From a sketch by the Author.*)

houses, rounded a little promontory and came in sight of the snow-white walls and battlemented tower of the new prison. We passed the point, the clean white "go-down" (business house) of the Borneo Company, and next to it the long sheds in which the racing-boats are housed from one New Year's Day to the next. Wherever an Englishman goes he takes with him all his national institutions, and from Nova Zembla to New Zealand, wherever two or three Englishmen are gathered together, there will they have their annual races and regatta; their club, theatricals, and athletic sports; their *Times*, *Punch*, and Bass' pale ale. Forty-six hours from our starting finds us at Sarawak, here known only as Kuching—the Malay for "Cat"—sixteen miles from the sea and four hundred and twenty miles from Singapore.

After the Borneo Company's "go-down" came the Chinese bazaar, a long regular row of two-story Chinese shops built solidly together, designed and executed in the most substantial style of Chinese architecture. On the opposite side of the river, which is here about one hundred and fifty yards wide, is the new fort perched upon a hilltop, a substantial brick structure, rather better calculated to withstand an attack than the flimsy wooden stockade which the Chinese assaulted and carried so easily during their insurrection in 1857.

Just above the fort, at the top of a grassy slope which sweeps up from the riverside and overlooks the town, is the Astana, the residence of His Highness the Rajah, the palace, in fact. It is really three complete houses such as Europeans build in the Straits Settlements, differing from the regular Indian bungalow in being much higher and possessing two stories instead of one. The basement floor contains the dining-room, billiard and store rooms, while the more spacious upper floor, being well above the malarious dampness of the earth, contains the drawing-room, library and sleeping apartments. Along the entire front of the main building runs a cool and roomy verandah, furnished with tables, easy chairs, and newspapers. Long strips of striped black and white matting hang between the pillars which support the roof, and, when let down at full length, they form for the verandah a continuous ventilated screen to protect the interior from the dashing of rain, the glare of the sun and the inquisitive gaze of the passers-by.

An ancient-looking square tower with battlements forms the entrance to the Astana, which, together with the coat of arms over the door and the swarthy sentry in the doorway, gives to the edifice the air of a feudal castle. But it is a very modest residence for a man who is absolute monarch over such a large territory, and who, were he avariciously disposed, could plunder his subjects sufficiently to enable him to maintain his position in truly regal style.

The river is well filled with craft, including decent schooners of modern type, Malay trading praus, Malay and Dyak "sampans" —every small canoe is a "sampan" in Malayana—Chinese junks, clumsy coasting vessels, a number of large sailing ships, and the steam vessels *Aline* and *Firefly* of H. H.'s Navy.

As soon as we touched the wharf, my fellow-passenger was surrounded by a crowd of good-looking young Englishmen, in corded white uniform coats and cork helmets, who welcomed him back with enthusiasm. Meanwhile, I was busy with my two servants, and in a very short time we hired a cart and loaded it with the boxes, bags, and parcels containing our jungle outfit, which included canned provisions, kitchenware, guns, ammunition in great variety, preservatives, tools, alcohol cans, bedding, clothing, and books, and—last but not least—two bags of Spanish dollars.

We took our way up a broad street which leads from the handsome new jail, passed the south side of the bazaar, the courthouse and public offices in the centre of a square, the hospital, the government dispensary, the library, European residences in plenty, and at last came to the hotel of the place, the Rajah's Arms. Just above this hotel, on a pretty knoll, stands the handsome residence and grounds of the Resident of Sarawak proper, an office filled at that time by Mr. William M. Crocker.

In front of the court-house I noticed nearly a dozen extremely long and wide-mouthed brass cannons, all of small calibre, however, but each had a history. Some had been taken from pirates, others from the stockades of rebellious rajahs in early days, while others represented fines imposed by the government and paid by native chiefs who had violated the laws. It sounds oddly enough to be told that "Nipah Tuah, of Tatu, has confessed to having murdered a Mukah Dyak, supposing him to be under arms against the government, and had been fined six piculs" (about eight hundred pounds of *brass guns*)!

A tour of observation through the bazaars and the town is full of interest. One first notices that the streets are scrupulously clean, the drainage good, and that the town has been laid out with European regularity. There is nothing slip-shod or loose-jointed about Kuching. The principal business street is that facing the river for about half a mile. The shops, which are kept almost exclusively by Chinese and Klings (Hindoos), are filled with a moderate assortment of European sundries, which include a gaudy array of colored cotton cloth, cheap cutlery, fancy mirrors, tin boxes, combs, glass beads, perfumery, belts, handkerchiefs, Malay caps, tools of many kinds, thread, needles, buttons, brass wire, paddles, spectacles, ammunition, etc. In the provision shops were the usual food staples; and also quantities of alum, blue vitriol, washing-soda, soap, indigo, and various kinds of roots, herbs and seeds "for the healing of nations."

Fruits were abundant, but vegetables were scarce. I noticed quantities of bananas, jak fruit, custard apples, watermelons and dates; also hundreds of fresh turtle eggs from an island near the coast, and poultry in plenty, but in the fish market the supply of fish was very scanty.

Unlike all the other cities and towns in Borneo, Sarawak is high and dry, and quite substantially built. The houses are nearly all of brick, neatly whitewashed, and those of the European residents are nearly always surrounded by spacious ornamental grounds full of trees and flowering shrubs. The houses of the Malays line the river-banks for a considerable distance both above and below the bazaar, but there is not a Dyak residence in the place. They prefer the freedom and seclusion of the jungles.

When we compare the present condition of Sarawak Territory and its people with the state of affairs which existed prior to the year 1841, we are lost in wonder at the mighty changes which have been effected, and admiration for the agencies by which they have been wrought.

In the year 1839, there landed at the town of Sarawak an English gentleman of fortune with a heart full of good-will to men, in short, a real nobleman of the highest type our modern civilization is capable of producing. He found the country in a state which must have awakened sympathy in any but a heart of stone. As a study in political economy it is interesting to note the principal features of the condition of Sarawak then and now.

When James Brooke, Esq., arrived from England in his little vessel, the *Royalist*, he found the territory in an almost indescribable state of anarchy, oppression, and murderous confusion. Forming, as it did at that time, a part of the Kingdom of Borneo proper, and under the dominion of the Malay Sultan of Brunei, Sarawak was ruled, or rather misruled, by the Rajah Muda Hassim and his prime minister, Pangeran Makota, the greatest villain who ever wore a sarong. Attached to these worthies and their immediate relations was a swarm of reprobate Malay nobles (?) and lesser followers, representing every degree of worthlessness and profligacy, most of whom lived solely by officially plundering the people, and not a few by covert piracy. The Dyaks were the only producers, and, as such, the Malays considered them their lawful prey. Upon those wretched jungle-dwellers were practised every species of oppression, extortion, and open robbery from the most brutal to the most refined. To prevent any attempt at a combined resistance, the various tribes were encouraged to wage murderous wars with each other, which often led to the utter extermination of whole villages at a single blow. In this way the short-sighted Malays more than once destroyed their own sources of revenue. Head-hunting was the chief business of life with the Dyaks; and robbery was that of the Malays.

The degree of oppression patiently endured by the poor Dyaks is almost incredible. The Malays, from time immemorial, have regarded them as their natural bondsmen, heathens with no more claims to consideration than oxen, with no inalienable rights even to life. Therefore, in the first place, they were taxed first by the local officers on account of the rajah, and then for the benefit of the officers themselves. The jungle produce collected by the Dyaks was monopolized, *i.e.*, taken at a fixed price by the patingi, who also claimed their mats, boats, fowls, and fruit at his pleasure, and had the power to claim their services at whatever price suited his convenience. When the rajah or the patingi had received all they cared to extort, their relatives and immediate followers claimed the right of forced trade, and gradually this privilege was extended to every Malay in the territory.

To the Dyaks this was a two-edged sword, which was wielded in a very simple manner. The Pangeran Makota, for instance, would send to a Dyak village an invoice of rice, cloth, gongs, iron, or salt at a price from six to eight times their real value, and in payment he would demand, at one-eighth of its value, any produce the Dyaks possessed. The profits from these transactions sometimes reached as high as one thousand five hundred per cent. of the amount invested. If the Dyak declared himself wholly without property, starving, and unable to pay, the reply would be: "Then give me your wife, or your child;" and there was generally sufficient power behind the demand to enforce payment in some form. If a whole clan stubbornly refused payment, it would be threatened with an attack from a more powerful hostile clan, and, in one way or another, the Malays managed to keep them in abject poverty. The arch-villain, Makota, used to assert that he liked to get even their cooking-pots from them. Not only were the Dyaks robbed, but in most instances they were compelled to carry to the boats the very plunder which had been taken from them.

If a Malay was ever injured in body or estate, and the injury, however slight, could in any way be attributed to a Dyak, the latter would be fined heavily for "a fault." To seriously injure a Malay, no matter how accidentally, was ruin to the Dyak. Matters finally came to such a pass that the wretched aborigines abstained from growing crops which only brought their oppressors upon them, and, in many instances, were able to live only by secreting food in the jungles. Hundreds of women and children were seized and kept as slaves, and scores of Dyak men became slave debtors. Seriff Sahib and his brother, Seriff Muller, two atrocious pirate chieftains, both of whom were incontinently thrashed and utterly crushed by Captain Keppel and Rajah Brooke, were formerly in the habit of sending armed parties to the Dyak settlements to bring down all the young boys and girls they could catch. It is stated, on good authority, that three hundred boys and girls have frequently been captured at one time, and kept as slaves.

The Malay rulers not only permitted indiscriminate head-hunting and sanguinary warfare among the Dyak tribes, but openly connived at it. It is hard to imagine a ruler giving a powerful clan permission to attack and exterminate a weaker one, also his own subjects, but this was often done.

As a consequence, the Dyaks could no longer live in clans, but sought refuge in the mountains or the jungle, a few together; and one of them pathetically said: "We do not live like men; we are like monkeys; we are hunted from place to place; we have no houses; and when we light a fire we fear the smoke will draw our enemies upon us."

All these miseries were inflicted upon a people naturally amiable and peaceful, honest, of cheerful disposition, and almost childlike simplicity of manner. The result can be readily imagined. In two years' time, by reason of famine, sword, slavery, forced labor, and sickness, the Dyak population of Sarawak proper was reduced from 14,360 persons to 6,792, or less than one-half! Some clans were reduced from 330 families to 50 ; one of 100 families had lost all its women and children ; another had been reduced from 120 families to 2 ; and two tribes had been utterly exterminated, or driven from the territory.

Such was the condition of the people when, on September 24, 1841, the Territory of Sarawak proper was formally ceded to James Brooke, and he became its "rajah" with the fullest powers. He was the man for the hour. His first official act was the release and restoration to their families of over a hundred married women and girls who had been confined at the capital for a whole year by the former rajah. Just previous to this formal cession of the territory, there arrived at the capital, Kuching, a hundred war-boats manned by two thousand five hundred blood-thirsty Dyaks, who came to *ask permission* of Muda Hassim to attack a weaker tribe on the Sambas ! But James Brooke was there, and the petition was urged in vain.

For once it really seems that Providence directly espoused the cause of suffering humanity in sending a philanthropic statesman to distressed Sarawak. The diplomatic difficulties he encountered would have hopelessly entangled a smaller mind or crushed a weaker character. It is surprising that he was not assassinated by Makota's followers during his first year of office. But out of rebellion and chaos he brought tranquillity and order. He ruled a superior and an inferior race, masters and slaves, to the complete satisfaction of both. With a judicial wisdom unparalleled in the history of nations, he formulated a code of laws and a system of government which actually dispensed equal justice to all, in practice as well as theory, and which was entirely satisfactory to Mohammedan Malays, and heathen Dyaks.

The present Territory of Sarawak is the fruit of Rajah Brooke's policy, as inaugurated by him and perpetuated by his successor. From a territory of at first only 3,000 square miles, Sarawak has been increased by concessions until its area is now 25,000 square miles. The population of the capital has risen from 1,500 to 21,000, while that of the whole territory is 225,000, of which there are of Hill and Sea Dyaks 125,000 ; Kyans, of all clans, 30,000 ; Malays 60,000, and Chinese 8,000. The government "is able and willing to maintain order and to offer security to life and property." The Dyaks are peaceful, prosperous and happy ; head-hunting has been entirely suppressed, and piracy, on the north coast of Borneo at least, is a thing of the past. Even-handed and speedy justice is meted out to every subject so fairly that none can complain.

Criminal cases are tried by jury, but there are no lawyers in the territory, and no elaborate system of loop-holes known as "legal precedents," whereby error is systematically perpetuated and justice perverted.

The Sarawak murderer is certain to meet his just deserts, and quickly, for the native juror has not yet acquired that degree of civilized intelligence which would enable him to find a verdict of "not guilty" for a wilful and brutal murderer. A short residence in some of our more enlightened States would be a revelation to their simple minds. In Sarawak it is the barbarous custom to hang murderers as soon as their guilt is proven, instead of keeping them in confinement and trying them again and again at great expense, or putting them in prison to be pardoned out on the Connecticut plan. Sarawak has very few laws, but "a heap of justice," which is cheap, speedy, and of prime quality; in all of which she is the opposite of every other civilized country in the world. In Sarawak no innocent man is convicted and no guilty man escapes. To most of my countrymen this statement may sound preposterous and absurd, but to any one who can imagine a country absolutely without lawyers to shield criminals and thwart justice, or "legal precedents" and "technicalities" to convict the innocent and acquit the guilty, the assertion is, perhaps, not beyond belief.

Sir James Brooke's success was very largely due to the liberality of his views on all political matters. When he framed the primary code of laws for the government of his distracted little country, he pleased the Mohammedan Malays and disarmed the suspicions of their priests by incorporating in it many of the precepts of the Koran. He was extremely tolerant of harmless native prejudice. The dignity and candor of his character, his firmness and courage, and his devotion to justice won the respect, confidence, and even affection of the better class of Malays and all the Dyaks, save those who were professional pirates. The latter soon had good cause to fear him, for, with a large force of Dyaks, aided by Captain Keppel and other officers of the British navy, the pirates all along the north coast were thrashed into peaceful agriculturists, and their depredations stopped forever.

Sarawak is a model of good government. It has already been stated that the people are peaceful and prosperous, and that life is secure in all parts of the country. With a revenue, in 1879, of $229,302, the rajah managed to maintain a civil list which included about twenty picked European officers and a host of Malays; a military force of about two hundred men; fourteen forts with their garrisons; a number of light-houses; a steam war vessel, the *Aline*, and two steam launches; to pay pensions; to build two new forts; to operate a coal mine; to pay European passages to and from England; to take $20,000 for his own use, and yet have the snug little sum of $37,673 remaining from the annual revenue to the credit of the government. What a lesson for the ex-Khedive of Egypt, and others nearer home!

CHAPTER V.

FROM SARAWAK TO THE SADONG.

Hunting near Kuching.—Crocodiles in the Sarawak.—A Dangerous Pest.—War of Extermination.—From Sarawak to the Sadong.—The Simujan Village.—A Hunt for an Orang-utan.—In the Swamp.—On the Mountain.—Valuable Information at Last.

WHILE I remained a few days at Sarawak to gather information about the orang-utan and other animals before making a start for the jungles, I purchased from a Malay a very good small boat to use as a hunting-boat, and made several excursions up and down the river.

I was surprised at finding proboscis monkeys (*Nasalis larvatus*) along the west bank of the river, not more than two miles below the town. I fired my rifle at one we found sunning himself at the edge of the jungle, knocked him off his perch in a twinkling, and the next moment we sprang ashore, or at least into two feet of soft mud, and waded landward. We reached the edge of the undergrowth and endeavored to penetrate it, but after a long struggle with the thorny tangle we gave up beaten, and the monkey got away. We found another monkey, the krah (*Macacus cynomolgus*), quite numerous along the river, but, the mud was so deep and the jungle so thick and thorny that we failed to secure more than one specimen. Had this been my only opportunity we would have secured good specimens of both species regardless of difficulties; but we knew we would have better chances elsewhere.

A few specimens were brought to me at the hotel, among which was a fine female *Manis Javanica*, here called "tingeling," with a tiny young one clinging to her. The latter was quite a prize, being of a good size to preserve entire in alcohol, while the mother furnished a fine skeleton. Squirrels are abundant along the river, and my new hunter distinguished himself by bringing in half a dozen. Turtles and beetles were brought to me by the Malay small boy, and for a few days we did a thriving business. Two professional crocodile hunters brought in a *Crocodilus porosus* eleven feet long, and delivered it to Mr. Buck, the superintendent of police, for the government reward of thirty-five cents per foot. The reptile was alive, but securely bound, and Mr. Buck kindly placed it at my disposal. Having just taken a goodly number of the same species at Selangore, I decided to take the head only, and a Malay was called to decapitate the animal as it lay. He drew his "parong latok," a very heavy sword with an edge like a razor, and with two terrific blows severed the crocodile's head from its body.

Owing to the fact that the crocodiles which infest all the rivers of Sarawak Territory are voracious man-eaters and destroy several lives annually, the government is waging a war of extermination against the species, and with telling effect. During that year (1878) 266 crocodiles were brought to Kuching for the reward, 153 of which were caught in the Sarawak River and its branches, and 113 in the Samarahan; 53 were caught by one man, a Malay named Mau, and 48 by another named Bujang, both of whom follow that business exclusively. Nearly all were taken with the "alir," on the same plan as that we pursued in Selangore, described in Chapter XXVI.* The largest crocodile taken that year measured 13 feet 10 inches, and of the whole number only two others exceeded 13 feet. Two were between twelve and thirteen feet, ten between eleven and twelve, and eighteen between ten and eleven, while the remaining two hundred and thirty-three were under ten feet, the majority measuring from seven to nine feet. The amount paid out in rewards was $738.28.

Mr. Crocker gave me a huge skull of *Crocodilus porosus*, which was 2 feet 10 inches in length, and must have come from a specimen not less than sixteen feet long. Besides the salt-water crocodile, a true gavial (*Tomistoma Schlegellii*), is found growing to a great size in the Sarawak River and the Rejang, and perhaps, in nearly all the large rivers of the territory above tidal influence. I procured of Mr. A. Hart Everett, the naturalist, a very large skull of this species from the Upper Sarawak, which measured 3 feet 3 inches in length. This species, however, is much more rare than the other, and I did not succeed in securing a fresh specimen.

The information that I received concerning the orang-utan was to the effect that they inhabit the valleys of the rivers Sadong and Batang Lupar, but not the Sarawak or Samarahan, and are usually seen in the fruit season. But the fruit season had passed months

---

*Renumbered as Chapter II in this reprint.

before my arrival, the orangs had retired to the depth of the forest, and no one could give me the least information as to where they had gone, or how I could manage to find them. Three or four were killed annually on the Sadong or its tributaries, and I decided to visit that locality in search of others. Mr. Crocker, the resident of Sarawak proper, very kindly offered me the government house on the Sadong as a residence and base of operations during my stay in that region, an offer which I was very glad to accept. In addition to this he also offered me a passage in the government schooner *Gertrude*, then about to make a trip to Sadong for a cargo of coal.

One day about sunset, we dropped down the river with the ebbing tide and, catching a light breeze at the river mouth, stood out to sea. All the next day we moved quietly along, and at sunset stood in and came to anchor at the mouth of the Sadong, to wait for the flowing tide to carry us up. Late that night I was dimly conscious of the fact that something was done about the anchor, and it seemed to me that the very next minute our vessel brought up with a loud "bump" and a violent jerk. "Run aground!" I said to myself, and went on deck to see what the trouble was. It was gray dawn of another day, a mist was slowly rising from the river, and the cocks were crowing loudly among the weather-beaten attap roofs that lined the river banks. We were at anchor in the mouth of the Simujan River, where it enters the Sadong, about twenty miles up. Along the left bank of the stream were about thirty Malay houses, nestling among the cocoanut-trees, forming the Malay kampong, while on the opposite side about half as many dwellings and shops built close up to the edge of the bank made up the Chinese kampong. As is the rule throughout Sarawak, the Chinese own nearly all the shops and do nearly all the trading. What the Malays do for a living I never could imagine.

The government house stands a hundred yards above the confluence of the two rivers, and I was surprised at finding it so well-built, roomy, and comfortable. It was built to accommodate such of the government officers as might have occasion to visit this locality in the discharge of their duties. As usual the house stands on posts six feet high, and the space underneath is quite well adapted to such work as skinning and skeletonizing animals. It contains two suites of rooms, and a latticed verandah in front of each sleeping apartment, which is a capital place for keeping pet monkeys and orang-utans.

At the front of the house the steps lead up into a spacious audience-room, from the door of which there is a fine view of several miles directly down the Sadong, here a mighty river half a mile wide. The house is used as a police station by a detachment of half a dozen men, whose duties consist mainly in striking the hours on a deep-toned gong which hangs in the verandah. Ah me! that gong! As I recall its deep mellow "boom," which was always music to my ears, there rise before me pictures of half-naked Dyaks, red-haired orang-utans, dark-green jungle, wet trousers, canned salmon, green peas, and Bass' pale ale.

The grounds in front of the house are tastefully laid out, and quite filled with flowering shrubs and curious plants from the surrounding jungle, all of which seem to thrive without care.

The virgin jungle comes up to within a hundred yards of the house at the back, and the Malay kampong nestles at its edge. Near the house stands the government rice store, where the Dyak revenue (of one dollar's worth of rice per family) is received and stored. The whole establishment was then in charge of Mr. Eng Quee, the government writer, a Chinese half-caste, to whom I brought, from Mr. Crocker, a letter which proved an open sesame to all the privileges the place afforded. No one could be more obliging than I found Mr. Eng Quee, and he was of infinite service to me.

An hour after we landed, the Malay headman of the village came to pay his respects; and a little later a party of Dyaks came to be questioned regarding the possibilities of finding orang-utans. In his own country this animal is universally called the "mias," although he is occasionally referred to by the Malays as an "orang-utan," which means, literally, jungle-man, from "orang" man, and "utan" jungle.

The English name of the mias is a corruption of the Malay, commonly written as "orang-outang."

None of the Dyaks or Malays could give any definite information as to the abundance of these animals in the Sadong valley, their present whereabouts, or the best ways and means of finding them.

They assured me there were "mias somewhere in the jungle," but they could not tell me where to seek them. They thought I might kill at least one every week, which was quite encouraging, and I thought I would be satisfied with as good luck as that would be. I gave powder and lead to such of the Dyaks and Malays as were willing to hunt orangs for me, and started them out.

Two miles from the Chinese kampong, on the eastern side of the Simujan, is the government coal mine, to which a wooden tramway leads through the swamps, the only railway in all Borneo. With a letter in my pocket to Mr. Walters, the superintendent of the mine, I started to walk up the tramway, and half way to the mine I found the gentleman himself coming to see me. We were friends in five minutes. He entered heartily into my plans, and gave me much valuable information and advice. Our acquaintance throughout was a most pleasant one, and I never wearied of his sketches of jungle life. But on the subject of orang-utan hunting he confessed himself at fault. He had seen many orangs and killed several, but for several months he had not even heard of any in that vicinity.

Two days later he hurriedly sent word to me that a mias had just been seen in the jungle about two miles above the mine. In less than an hour we were at the mine, and, accompanied by Mr. Walters and several Dyaks and Malays, we set out under considerable excitement to find the animal. We followed a rugged forest path until we reached the spot, but the mias was nowhere to be seen. We divided our party and hunted about until nightfall, but found nothing save a fresh mias' nest, and so returned in disappointment.

The next day we determined to try the experiment of hunting through the forest at random. Early in the morning there arrived a Dyak named Dundang, who has the reputation of being a very successful hunter. He was a fine specimen, though too muscular to be considered a typical Dyak. His entire costume consisted of a yard-wide strip of bark-cloth wound around his loins and passed between his thighs with the ends falling down apron-wise in front. His head-gear was a strip of faded pink calico wound around his head and partly confining his long jet-black locks. He was accompanied by another Dyak, and, with them to guide us, Perera and I set out for a tramp.

No sooner had we fairly turned our backs on the coolie quarters at the mines than we were in the jungle. We had decided to try the swamp forest first, and if that yielded us nothing we would take to the low mountain which rises out of it like an island. We plunged into the swamp and for several hours waded through its miry mazes, but saw no animals save one monkey and a few small birds and insects for which we cared nothing.

The trees were rather low, as a rule, but grew very thickly together, so that their tops formed a compact mass of green foliage which shut out every ray of sunlight from the ground below. Instead of tangled and spreading brushwood, the undergrowth consisted of saplings, with the stems of rattans, rope-like creepers and lianas hanging from the tree-tops or twining in awkward, angular fashion around their trunks. The ground beneath was little more than a net-work of gnarled roots, rising out of a thick pulp of water and decayed vegetable matter often a foot deep. It was not water, for it was too thick to be called a liquid; it was not mud, for there was scarcely any soil in it; but it was as wet as water and soft as the softest mud. It is this vegetable pulp which, when washed into the rivers of Borneo, is immediately dissolved, and imparts to the streams near the coast their murky brown color.

Almost the entire island of Borneo is quite encircled by a belt of swamp forest such as the above, extending back from the seashore a distance of fifteen to forty miles, where the land rises and asserts itself. Along the coast of Sarawak, particularly between the Sambas and Batang Lupar Rivers, isolated hills and lofty peaks rise abruptly from the level forest here and there—evergreen islands rising out of an evergreen sea. Along the seashore, the jungle is low and scrubby, but it reaches quite down to tide-mark. Where the beach is clean and sandy it is fringed with graceful casuarinas (*C. littorea*), here called the arrooree tree; but where the shore is of mud, as it is between the Sadong and Batang Lupar, the mangrove forms the boundary of the jungle. A few miles back from the sea the jungle rapidly rises in height and attains its greatest altitude on the hills.

Progress on foot through the swamp is slow and difficult at best, and even the man who prides himself on his ability to follow wherever a native can lead, will find his powers of endurance put to the test when he starts out to follow a naked Dyak through his native swamps. It seems strange that any terrestrial quadruped should voluntarily make its home in these gloomy fastnesses, where there is not even a spot of dry ground large enough for a lair, and yet the sambur deer (*Rusa equina*), the wild hog, and the tiny Java deer are abundant in this very swamp. I say abundant, because several were taken there during my stay, although on the day of which I am now speaking we saw not one. The only animal we saw was a large monkey with a short tail, called a pig-tailed macaque (*Macacus nemestrinus*), which I shot and skinned.

A day in the swamp, together with two or three shorter excursions, convinced me that my way to the orang-utan did not lie in that direction. Then we tried the mountain back of the coal mine. We traversed its entire length, hunted over its top and along its sides, over sticks and stones, and across rocky gorges, but not a sign of mias could we discover. After a week spent in such hunting at random, without any success, we gave it up. Once more I began to interview the natives as fast as I could catch them, Dyaks, Malays, and Chinese as well, as to the present whereabouts of the mias. I elicited no information which I considered valuable until one day two Dyaks arrived from the head-waters of the Simujan River to buy rice at the government store-house. They informed me that they saw two mias as they came down the river, that they often saw them near their village at Padang Lake, and they gave it as their opinion that if I would go up there and hunt for three or four days I might get two or three mias, and perhaps more. "Two or three!" I held my breath in suspense until they brought out their figures, and when they said "two or three" I could have hugged them. Had they said I would find them in "millions, sir, millions!" they would have blasted all my hopes for that river. But the Dyak statement had a ring of truth in it, and I instantly decided to put their advice to the test. I felt so certain it would "pan out" well that I made arrangements to start up the river immediately, and prepared for a prolonged absence.

CHAPTER VI.

AMONG THE ORANG-UTANS.

Start up the Simujan.—Boat-roofs.—Among the Head-hunters.—A Dyak Long house.—Monkeys.—Fire-flies.—A Night on a Tropical River.—Mias' Nests.—" Mias, Tuan."—Death of the First Mias.—Another Killed.—Screw Pines.—" Three Mias in one Day!"—Laborious Work.—Swamp Wading.—Padang Lake.—Cordial Reception at a Dyak House.

JUST twenty-four hours after our interview with the Dyaks from Padang Lake we started on an expedition up the Simujan, solely on the strength of the information given us by two semi-savages. What if they were lying to me, as so many white, black, yellow, and red men had done before, and sent me on fool's errands? The stock of provisions, ammunition, and preservatives I carried in my boat showed that I fully believed every word told me by those simple-minded children of the jungle.

Mr. Eng Quee had business up the river, and accompanied me in his own boat, with two stout Malays, Blou and Lamudin. My boat was manned by a quiet and obedient little Malay named Dobah, whom I had engaged by the month, Perara, my Portuguese half-caste, Ah Kee, my servant and best man, and myself. Both boats were amply roofed with kadjangs, which make a roof at once water-proof, very light, easily adjusted, and so flexible that, when desired, each section can be rolled up and stowed away in the bottom of the boat.

These kadjangs are made of the long, blade-like leaves of the nipa palm, on the same principle as a tile roof. The leaves are each six or seven feet long by two inches wide. They are sewn together with strips of rattan, each alternate leaf overlapping its neighbor on either side, and so on until a section of roof is formed about six and a half feet square. This section is then made to bend in the middle cross-wise, at a sharp angle, so that it can be folded once and rolled up, or partly opened and made to stand up, tent-wise, when it forms the very best kind of roof for such a climate.

We started up early in the afternoon with the flood tide, and paddled along at good speed very comfortably. For the first ten or twelve miles the Dyaks have cleared away the jungle on both sides of the river for a hundred yards back, and grow their crops of "paddi" (rice) there. At that time of the year (August) the clearings were all overgrown with rank grass four feet high. About eight miles above Simujan we came to a typical village of the Sea Dyaks, and halted to pay it a visit. It stands on the left bank of the river, quite near the stream, and, from the river, one sees only the end of a house, with its single door and a long, gray, moss-patched roof running far back, in ragged lines of perspective, toward the jungle. The lower part of this structure is almost entirely concealed by the broad-leaved banana-trees which grow closely around it.

The view from the top of the bank discloses, not a collection of houses, but one immense house, one hundred and ninety feet long and thirty feet wide. It stands on a small forest of round posts, five or six inches in diameter, set firmly in the ground, and the floor is ten feet above the ground. At either end is a door, to which there leads up a small tree-trunk, cut on the upper side into notches, which serve as steps. Four rows of posts, the two outer and two middle rows, run up through the floor to the roof, and the rest are cut off at the floor.

What is really the back wall of this long village house leans outward rapidly as it rises from the floor, and is without either door or window. The front is entirely open all the way along, and the floor extends out thirty feet farther on additional posts, forming a convenient open-air platform for drying rice and other jungle produce. The ground underneath the house—it is much more like a house than a village—is damp, wet, littered and dirty, and smells feverish.

We climbed the notched tree-trunk at the end of the house and entered. A delegation of mostly naked men, women, and children met us at the door, with here and there a "Tabet, tuan!" (Good day, sir!) in friendly greeting. Directly two or three women appeared with clean mats, which they spread upon the floor so that a considerable space was covered, and we all sat down. Mr. Eng Quee opened a conversation with the old men, our Malays talked with the young men, and the women and children flocked round to have a good look at the "orang-putei" (white man), who repaid their inspection in full, principal and interest.

From the numerous posts which ran up through the house there hung a great many deer antlers, lower jaws of wild boar, parongs, back-baskets (juahs), fish-traps, paddles and spears. Naked children scudded hither and thither over the floor, chasing the fowls, teasing the dogs and playing with the little gibbon, all of which rightfully belonged to the population of the village. As we entered, we found a young woman with a five-foot bamboo pail on her shoulder just starting to the river for water; one man was sitting on the floor making a fish-trap, and another was hewing out a new door with his "biliong," or adze-axe.

We were seated in a long hall, which extended without any division the entire length of the house, and occupied a trifle more than half the entire structure. It was on the open side of the house and faced the open-air platform. Along the other side of the house, likewise extending its entire length from one end to the other, was a row of sixteen rooms, each about twelve feet square, entered by a single door from the middle passage.

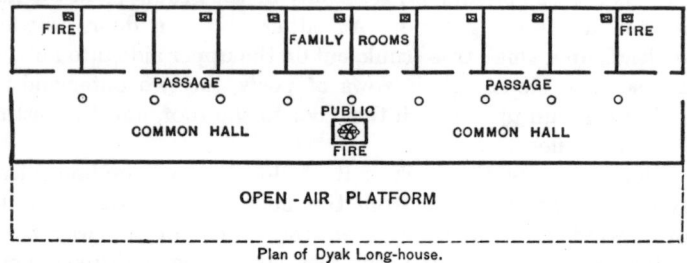

Plan of Dyak Long-house.

All the timbers of the house were lashed together with rattans, not a nail nor even a wooden pin being used anywhere. Nor were any of the timbers mortised together at any point. The Dyak idea of fastening two objects together is to lash them with green rattan; civilized man believes in nailing, pinning, mortising, or fastening with screws.

The floor was of narrow strips of the nibong palm, an inch and a half wide, lashed to the sleepers about an inch apart, thus giving a floor more open than lattice-work. The wall which divided the rooms from the open hall was of wide boards hewn out with the "biliong," placed upright, and lashed together and to a base-board with rattans. Each door was one wide board with a projecting

EXTERIOR OF SEA DYAK LONG-HOUSE.

(Sketched by the Author.)

INTERIOR OF A SEA DYAK LONG-HOUSE.

(From a sketch by H. H. Everett.)

point at the bottom for it to turn upon in lieu of a hinge. On one of the doors nearest us I noticed a figure of a crocodile rudely carved in low relief. The outline was very good but no time had been spent in working out the details.

The side of the house which was enclosed, and also the ends, were made up of wide slabs of bark lashed to the framework. The roof was of "attap," or large square sections of palm-leaves sewn together and lashed to the rafters in courses, like shingles.

Each room in a Dyak long-house represents a family, or at least a married couple, and a village is taxed according to the number of its "doors." This, then, was "a village of sixteen doors." The young unmarried men and boys slept over the hall in the loft which forms a part of every such habitation, partly for storage and partly for domiciliary purposes.

Each private room has no other door than the one opening from the passage. The floor is generally covered with mats. In a corner of the room next the outer wall is a bed of earth on which the family fire is built. At this corner the roof is so constructed that a portion of it, usually two or three rafters, can be lifted up bodily for about two feet and propped up to admit light and air, and also to allow the smoke to escape in case there should be an excess of it. There are no tables or chairs—indeed no furniture of any kind.

In the centre of the long hall a fire was burning on a bed of earth, and above it hung a bundle of about twenty human heads, or rather skulls, for not a vestige of flesh remained on any of them. Each skull was bound round securely with rattan, evidently to keep the lower jaw in place. All were black and grimy with smoke and soot, and those at the bottom of the bundle, nearest the fire, were quite charred. We were among the head-hunters, and those were trophies which our money could not buy. Thanks to the government of Sir James Brooke, those heads were all old trophies, no doubt collected prior to 1841, by the skinny and toothless old fellows who now totter about the village, and pound their betel in a joint of bamboo because they cannot chew it.

According to all accounts, the Dyaks of Southern Borneo are tame subjects in comparison with the dashing, dare-devil tribes of the north. A man may travel the whole length of the Mahakkam or the Barito and visit the villages of the most warlike tribes without being able to set eyes on more than one skull. Here in the Sadong we find a score in the first village of Sea Dyaks we set foot in, and we afterward saw a beautiful collection of forty-two skulls in the first village of Hill Dyaks we visited on the upper Sarawak.

As I had abundant opportunity later on to study the Dyaks themselves, I will not attempt here a description of the inhabitants of this village. At the termination of our call two of the women came and offered me half a dozen fresh eggs, which I accepted, and gave them in return what their souls longed for—tobacco. As we returned to the boat, all the women and children of the house trooped along after us, respectful and well-behaved to the last, to see us off—and to modestly request a little more tobacco. I duly stood treat all round with leaves from the bundles I had laid in store for this purpose, and we parted on good terms.

Just before sunset we passed the last Dyak village and clearing, and came to where the large trees and dense undergrowth clothed the banks to the water's edge and even beyond. Then we began to see monkeys by the score, and as evening approached their numbers seemed to increase as they began to perch in the branches that overhung the river, and settle themselves for the night. Sometimes as many as five or six would be seen sociably huddled together on a single bough, and often one small tree-top contained from fifteen to twenty of the little animals. They were all of one species, *Macacus cynomolgus*, the commonest in Borneo, if not of the neighboring islands as well, and by the natives it is called the krah. They are about the color of a gray squirrel, and three times as large. I think I never elsewhere saw so many monkeys in the same length of time. I counted them as we paddled along until in a few minutes I ran the number up into the eighties, and was obliged to give up the attempt. They showed not the slightest fear of us, and I could easily have killed a great many. As it was, I shot two, which was all I cared to preserve just then.

Just as darkness set in we came to a large band of proboscis monkeys (*Nasalis larvatus*), and, although we could only distinguish their moving forms for a moment now and then, their peculiar nasal cry told us what they were.

Fifteen minutes after sunset the last gleam of twilight faded out, and darkness closed over the forest. The river had narrowed rapidly, and was then not over forty yards wide. On either side a wall of green leaves rose from the surface of the stream, and the banks were quite hidden behind the leafy screen.

Just here we were treated to the most glorious exhibition of fire-flies I ever beheld. They congregated on certain trees in hundreds—if not even thousands, in some instances, and resting quietly on the leaves kept up an incessant and rapid scintillation, each insect flashing about a hundred and twenty times per minute. For three or four miles we passed in about every hundred yards a tree-top literally filled with brilliant flashes of white light, which, in the darkness, shone with novel and beautiful effect.

It gives one quite a feeling of awe to paddle along a narrow river between two dark walls of forest in thick darkness. At such times the most garrulous boatmen are quiet, the traveller's mind is filled with romantic thoughts, and the only sounds which break the sombre stillness are the measured dip of the paddles, the swish of the eddies they make, the chirp of the tree-frogs and the occasional twitter of a night-bird.

Having made several miles after sunset, we tied up to some bushes, ate a frugal dinner, and lay down in our boats to sleep. The mosquitoes were troublesome to the men who had no netting, but being provided with adequate protection I fared better. But my boat leaked from being overloaded, and I slept in water the greater part of the night.

At break of day we were off again, and soon passed the mouth of the southern branch of the Simujan. A few miles farther on we halted at a small bit of cleared ground, built a fire over the water on a pole platform which we covered with mud, and cooked breakfast. Before starting again we cleared the deck for action on Mr. Eng Quee's boat, and made ready for aggressive warfare on the monkey tribe. The kadjangs were rolled up, the supports taken down and stored away below. This "sampan" of Eng Quee's was the best shooting-boat I ever used, and, outside of Borneo, I shall never see its like again. It was a simple dug-out, about fifteen feet long by three and a half feet broad in the middle, pointed at both ends, and just deep enough to be steady. Just below the edge it was completely decked over with strips of nibong palm, and on this, amidships, I placed my ammunition-box for a seat, arranged rifle and double gun, cartridges and field-glass within easy reach. Leaving my boat to follow we again set out.

We were now some distance above tidal influence, and the river had narrowed to twenty yards, but it was still very deep and flowed swiftly. The water was much cleaner than below, and was indeed moderately clear. The banks on both sides were entirely submerged for an unknown distance back from the stream, miles perhaps, but the forest was composed almost entirely of trees. The nipa palm had been replaced by the screw pine, rasow etam of the Malays (*Pandanus candelabrum*), which formed a fringe along both sides of the river. They grew in water eight to ten feet deep and very thickly together, so that no boat could reach the shore without a great effort to get through them. The stems were from two to three inches in diameter and thickly studded with short spines. Owing to the depth at which they grew, it was sometimes possible to push them aside and drive a boat through them, when they grew rather thinly, but usually it was necessary to cut a passage in order to reach the shore. I mention them thus particularly because they afterwards caused us great trouble.

We saw no proboscis monkeys that morning, nor any others. The men had to work hard at the paddles to make headway against the rapid current. Early in the day we passed several abandoned orang-utan nests, which aroused expectations of something better, and presently we passed a green nest. From that moment four pairs of eyes sharply scrutinized every dark object or moving twig in the tree-tops as we paddled slowly and silently along. Every doubtful object was instantly pointed out and examined by the "tuan" with the field-glass.

We had just sighted another very green and fresh-looking nest, when there was an excited whisper of,

"Mias, tuan! mias! mias!" and a long arm in front of me pointed it out.

"There he is, sir! there he is!" (in Malay, of course). The light sampan fairly flew along until we came nearly opposite the tree containing our intended victim, but he had recognized the approaching danger and hidden himself in a thick clump of leafy branches. Presently we saw a big hairy arm clasping the trunk of the tree about fifty feet from the ground, but that was all. The boat was stopped directly, and as we could do no better I stood up and sent a bullet through the arm that was exposed, to stir the old fellow up. It startled him, for with an angry growl, he immediately showed himself and started to climb away. As soon as we saw his body I fired again, which caused him to stop short for a moment. Then the two Malays put forth all their strength and drove the boat as far as possible into the thick fringe of screw pines. They stood very thickly together, but their stems yielded a good deal, and by frantic pulling, pushing aside, and chopping we forced a passage through for several yards. At last we came to a dead stop; there was not a speck of land in sight, but the boat could go no farther.

WADING AFTER A WOUNDED ORANG-UTAN.
(*From Author's sketch.*)

We were near the large trees by this time, so two of the Malays seized their parongs and slid down into the water while I quickly followed with my rifle and a pocket full of cartridges. Fortunate it was for me in my wading after orangs that my rifle was a breech-loader and that Maynard cartridges are water-proof.

We went quite under water, at first, but after swimming a few yards, were able to touch bottom. We waded up to our necks in water until it got shallower, the Malays pushing ahead as fast as possible to keep the mias in sight, until presently they stood still, waist deep in the water, and pointed upward. I soon saw the mias, a fine large one, swinging himself slowly from one tree to another, evidently disabled. I immediately fired for his breast, whereupon he struggled violently for a moment, then made off in frantic haste, climbing along a straight horizontal branch by the aid of his hands alone, swinging along as a gymnast swings underneath a tight rope. He reached fully five feet at every stretch.

Presently he stopped short and let go with one hand, which dropped heavily at his side and came below his knee. For three minutes he hung there facing us, holding by one hand only. How huge and hairy he looked, outlined against the sky! Presently his hand slipped, his hold gave way entirely and, with outstretched arms and legs, he came crashing heavily down through the branches and fell into the water near us with a tremendous splash. He struggled up and turned savagely to bay, grasping the trunk of a sapling to hold himself erect. The Malays rushed at him with their parongs, and one gave him a fierce slash in the neck while I was shouting to them to desist. They were as yet wholly untrained, and would have ruined the skin in a moment. The old mias flung his long arms about, gasped and struggled violently, then quietly settled down in the water, and in another moment was dead. Then we towed him along back to the boat, lifted him in with considerable difficulty and began to examine our prize.

Truly, he was a prize. His back was as broad and his chest as deep as a prize fighter's, while his huge hands and feet seemed made with but one end in view—to grasp and hold on. His arms were remarkably long and sinewy, but his legs were disproportionately short and thick. His body was large and heavy, with a chest both broad and full; his eyes were villanously small and his canine teeth were as large as those of a small bear. His arms and legs were covered with long, coarse, brick-red hair, which grew also on his abdomen and sides, but the skin which covered his breast hung in a loose, baggy fold. The face was bare except for a thin growth of hair on the jaws and chin, which, in pictures of the orang utan is usually magnified to a luxuriant beard. His skin was of a shiny brownish-black color, darkest on the face and throat.

We transferred the body of our dead mias to the other boat and proceeded up the river as before. Nests were now quite numerous in the trees along the banks, but we saw none even fifty yards back from the shore. The Dyaks and Malays both assert that the orangs are subject to fever, and resort to the open margins of rivers and lakes for the benefit of the cooling breezes which blow there.

The nest of the orang-utan is simply a lot of small green boughs and twigs broken off by the animal, and piled loosely in the fork of a tree, or the top of a sapling. The pile is usually about three feet in diameter, and on this the orang-utan lies on his back, and sleeps.

A few miles from the scene of our first capture we came to a very fresh green nest, and Eng Quee remarked:

"Now there must be a mias very near that."

The next moment we saw the movement of a heavy body in a tree just beyond, and he added:

"There he is, sir! There's the mias!"

We paddled quickly up and directly saw the mias climbing rapidly away. I fired immediately, and the next moment the boat was driven with full force into the screw pines. We tugged frantically at the stems to force a passage, but were soon brought to a standstill. Holding my rifle above my head, I slid into the water, and this time found it only up to my shoulders. The Malays followed me closely in our wading-match, and in a few minutes we found the mias in a tree-top, disabled, as I had expected. This time my bullet went through his head, whereupon he settled back quietly across two large branches which grew close together, and remained there, dead, with forty feet of bare tree-trunk between him and us. I offered half a dollar to any one who would climb up and throw the mias down, which offer was accepted by one of the Malays. After a hard struggle up the smooth trunk, he reached the animal and sent it tumbling into the water below. Two mias in one day was far better luck than we had dared hope for.

The river narrowed rapidly as we proceeded, and at length there remained only a passage between the screw pines, which formed a barrier thirty yards wide on either side between us and the shore. In two places we found the channel choked with a wide drift of dead pine stems, completely bridging the river, and barring our progress. With great labor we cut through one drift and cut a passage around the other wide enough for our boats.

Just before reaching Little Padang Lake, we came to a spot where about forty acres of jungle had been killed—by fire, the Malays said, although I hardly see how it could have been burned. The trees stood in the water leafless, dead, and bare, save for a green epiphyte here and there on their branches. Acres of dead screw pines reared their leafless stems aloft, and the prospect was dreary enough. Winding in and out, and turning a great many times, we came to Little Padang Lake, and found it a perfect jungle of *Pandanus*. Threading our way through that, we came to forest again, and a little farther on entered Padang Lake, also a labyrinth of screw pines. As we were crossing a bit of open water, one of the Malays chanced to look back and immediately exclaimed, in an excited whisper: "Mias, tuan! mias! mias!"

Sure enough, there we espied a mias fast asleep in a little tree close to which we had passed. He lay on his back in the main fork of the tree, holding on by the large limbs.

We paddled up very quietly to within fifty yards, when he discovered us and started up. I fired at him, and, as the boat crashed into the pines, took another shot. The pines were very thick, and there was no shore anywhere. We were obliged to take to the water or lose the animal, so overboard we went, and kept our heads above water by holding to the spiny stems which pricked our hands painfully. After a while we touched a bottom of mud, and were able to wade, though the water was up to our necks. It was slow work. Our feet often got caught in vines, and roots, and sometimes we came against submerged pine-stems waist high, while up to our chins in water. Had the mias not have been hit hard, he would have escaped, for, in spite of our eagerness, our progress was slow and painful. After forty yards of wading we came up with him, and found him badly hurt, and visibly weakening. Not wishing to prolong his sufferings, I sent a bullet through his head, which smashed his skull all to pieces, and tumbled him like a log into the water. Lamudin took him in tow, and we toiled back to the boat.

Three orang-utans in one day! The men hurrahed loud and long; and I believe I must have indulged in a little shout on my own account.

When you remember, my reader, that it was for the orang-utan that I had made an expensive visit to Borneo, and up to that day had been in great doubt as to its whereabouts and abundance, you can perhaps forgive a little honest enthusiasm over the results of our first day's work.

A narrow and tortuous channel led for about a mile through a wide tract of pines, from which we finally emerged on the open lake. It was a shallow body of clear water, about five miles long by two miles at the widest part. The whole western half of the lake is filled with *Pandanus*, which also chokes it at its southern extremity. On the east they are happily absent, and the water is open quite up to the edge of the forest.

About two miles from the outlet of the lake, up the western side, is a conical mountain, called Gunong Popook, about nine hundred feet high, the end of a chain of low mountains extending westward from the lake.

It was nearly sunset when we reached the open waters of the lake and made for a Dyak house at the foot of Gunong Popook. We landed and walked fifty yards over "batangs" (saplings), passed some huge bowlders of reddish porphyry and just beyond them came to a small Dyak village, or long-house. We climbed the ladder and were greeted very cordially by a pleasant-faced young man, named Hakka, his wife Noonsong, and another woman who spread clean mats for us to sit upon. The betel box was brought out, and we all sat down for a chat. We asked if we might be allowed to stay there that night and perhaps a little longer. Of course we could stay there! Why not? Any stranger was welcome to stay; and who ever heard of a Dyak refusing shelter to a white man and the best the village afforded? They would be glad if we would honor them with a visit two months long.

Very true; a Dyak was never known to refuse hospitality to a friend, and aid when needed, in which my simple-minded savage without any religion whatever is about five thousand per cent. better than the canting, hypocritical Hindoo, who would prefer to have you sleep out in the rain rather than have your presence desecrate his mud sanctuary or even his verandah. The Dyak is the man for me.

We were informed that the whole of the open hall was at our disposal, and in a very short time we had taken formal possession. Our three dead orangs we hung high up in the trees near the house to get them beyond the reach of the lean and hungry dogs, or rather animated dog-skeletons, which roamed about. The Dyaks were really glad to see us, for to them our visit was quite an event, and had we owned the house we could scarcely have felt more at home. I gave the men and women tobacco-boxes and looking-glasses, and to the children about fifty coppers apiece, all of which were received with childish enthusiasm.

After a long confab by lantern and torch-light, I hung my hammock and musquitero, for the mosquitoes were quite troublesome, and Eng Quee rigged up his curtain in a corner close by. The other members of our party sought soft places on the floor, and being thoroughly tired with our long day's work, we were soon beyond the realms of thought or care.

CHAPTER VII.

DOINGS IN THE ORANG-UTAN COUNTRY.

Preparation of Orang Skins and Skeletons.—Return down the Simujan.—Three Orangs Killed.—A Troublesome Infant.—Accessions from Native Hunters.—Seven Orangs in One Day.—Miscellaneous Gatherings.—A Battle-scarred Hero.—The Bore in the Sadong.—Another Trip up the Simujan.—Doctoring an Injured Hunter.—The Dyak at his Worst.—Death of a Huge Orang, "the Rajah."—Dimensions.—A Rival Specimen.—Two Captives.

THE day following our arrival at the Popook village was a busy one. We had three mias to skin and also to skeletonize, for all the great apes (gorilla, chimpanzee, and orang-utan) are so rare and valuable that the entire skeleton of each specimen is carefully dissected out, and makes a complete specimen by itself, quite as valuable as the skin.

Near the house was a low platform of poles upon which the Dyaks spread their paddy to dry, and being vacant at that time, we converted it into a very serviceable work-table. We erected the kadjangs over it to protect us from both sun and rain, and, calling all the members of our party, gathered round the festive board for a picnic with the three dead mias. After each specimen had been carefully measured and one sketch made we sharpened the knives and went to work.

The forenoon was very hot and the afternoon very rainy; but we kept dry under the kadjangs and worked steadily on. It was a great bother to skin the fingers without mutilating them. Foreseeing that all my companions would very probably assist on similar occasions in the future, I took pains to teach them the *modus operandi*, and was pleased to find how intelligently and skilfully they took hold of the work in hand. It was well that I did so; for not very long after that our resources were taxed to the utmost.

My method of preserving the skins and skeletons was very simple, and I am happy to say proved entirely satisfactory. After removing and carefully cleaning the skins, we first treated them with a liberal application of arsenical soap dissolved in a little water, and then rubbed on all the powdered alum that would stick to the skin. A pole was passed through the arms, and the skins were then hung up to dry, the head and legs being distended with a little loose straw or dry grass, and the skin of the body slightly distended by short sticks placed crosswise.

In the hot, moist, bath-room air of Borneo a skin must dry immediately or it spoils. If it is hung up loosely, or in folds so that the air cannot reach both sides of the entire surface, the hair will drop off all portions that do not dry quickly. I have ventured to state the above facts for the reason that the ignorance of them, simple as they are, has entailed the loss of many a fine skin of orang, chimpanzee, and gorilla.

Orang skeletons, like all others, are prepared, in a rough state, by carefully denuding them of flesh with a knife, but leaving the bones of the various members attached to each other by their ligaments, anointing them with thin arsenical soap, then tying each skeleton in a compact bundle and allowing it to dry in the shade.

Being fully convinced that our best plan for hunting orangs lay in making trips up and down the Simujan River we decided to return forthwith to Sadong, hunting on the way down. On the following morning we loaded our boats and took leave of the hospitable Dyaks. They were loud and long in their invitations to us to come again and stop a long time, promising to do all they could to help us find animals. Having comforted them with the assurance that they would soon see us again, we embarked and set off.

Soon after entering the river, we started several troops of proboscis monkeys, but being just then in quest of grander game, we let them go, promising to call and pay our respects a little later. A little farther down we surprised an orang in the act of taking a drink. He had climbed down within reach of the water and hung at the foot of a stout sapling, dipping one hand into the water, then holding it over his mouth and sucking the water off as it dripped from the knuckles of his closed fingers. He was so busily engaged that I got a good look at him with the glass before he saw us. He was near the open water and I easily brought him down with my rifle, after which we paddled our boat in to where he fell and secured him without even getting out.

Three miles farther on I espied a baby orang up in a tree-top, hanging to the small limbs with out-stretched arms and legs, looking like a big, red spider. It gazed down at us in stupid, childish wonder, and I was just aiming for it, when Mr. Eng Quee called my attention to the mother of the infant, who was concealed in the top of the same tree. As soon as I fired at her, she climbed with all haste up to her little one, which quickly clasped her round the body, holding on by grasping her hair, and, with the little one clinging to her, the mother started to climb rapidly away.

Fortunately, we were able to get the boat in amongst the trees without much trouble, and all immediately went overboard. We had scarcely done so when a third orang, a young male about two years old, was discovered looking down from a nest overhead, which he immediately left and started to follow the old mother. As he went swinging along underneath a limb, with his body well drawn up I gave him a shot which dropped him instantly, and then we turned our attention to the female. She was resting on a couple of branches, badly wounded, with her baby still clinging to her body in great fright. Seeing that she was not likely to die for some minutes I gave her another shot to promptly end her suffering, and then she came crashing down through the top of the small trees and fell into the water, which was waist deep.

We sprang to secure the baby, but it was under water fully a minute before we found it, quite unable to swim and very nearly drowned. We managed to resuscitate it, however, then the other two were lifted into the boat and we drew out into the stream.

As soon as the baby recovered the use of all its faculties, it seemed possessed of a little devil. It was only about six months old or eight at the most, and weighed about eleven pounds, but it had the temper of a tiger. It made such persistent efforts to pull my hands up to its mouth in order to bite them that I was obliged to tie its elbows together behind its back, pinion its feet also and make it fast by a cord to the side of the boat, so that it could not reach me with its teeth. This, of course, increased its rage.

It was restless as an eel, and gave me endless trouble. Once when I was not watching, it rolled over and before I was aware of the movement seized the calf of my leg between its teeth with a perfectly fiendish expression and bit me very severely. But for my thick woollen stockings and cotton hunting trousers underneath, I think the little wretch would have bitten out a piece of my flesh. I gave him a sounding slap on the side of his head, which caused him to let me go ; but for many days after I carried a large black and blue mark in memory of him.

FEMALE ORANG-UTAN, INFANT AND NEST.
(*From the group in the U. S. National Museum mounted by the Author.*)

DOINGS IN THE ORANG-UTAN COUNTRY.

Once it tumbled overboard, and I let it get a good ducking before rescuing it.

A heavy rain came on during the afternoon but we set up our kadjangs and kept quite dry. As soon as it ceased, we took to our paddles and went down swiftly with the current, reaching Simujan at sunset, wet, tired, and hungry, but very happy in the possession of seven orangs taken in two days' hunting.

At the back of the government house, there was a wide open space, between the two bath rooms, where the roof projected over the hard ground, which made a capital open-air dissecting-room.

Mr. Eng Quee placed a table for me and there I skinned orangs and received deputations of natives who came bringing specimens, or wanting gunpowder. The ground under the house was hard, dry and clean, and my motley crew of assistants retired under the floor with their work. Mr. Eng Quee quite enjoyed the novelty of orang-skinning, and quickly became an expert hand at the business. Ah Kee, Perara and the three Malays, worked slowly and required constant supervision, but they learned rapidly.

Early the next morning after our return, came an old Chinaman to whom I had given gunpowder a week previous, escorting two other Chinamen, who carried on a pole the dead body of a good-sized orang, which he had shot the day before. I received it with open arms, paid for it, measured it, and was proceeding to remove the skin, when there arose a loud shout from those around me, and the next moment, three naked Dyaks staggered up, also bearing on a pole another dead mias. This was a fine, large "mias chappin," with the intensely black skin and the remarkable expanded cheeks, or cheek callosities, so characteristic of *Simia Wurmbii*. This was larger than any of the specimens I had taken thus far. The Dyaks said they were out the night before trying to noose a deer, and found this mias swinging himself from one tree to another, when a branch suddenly broke and let him fall to the ground. They attacked him at once with their spears and killed him. There were fifteen spear wounds in his chest, but I sewed them up carefully and entered the old fellow as No. 8. The men facetiously remarked that we had about enough mias to last through the remainder of that day.

About noon there arose another and louder shout from the men under the house, which increased to a perfect yell as a party of Malays came around the corner with another mias, the largest of all, *alive*, swinging underneath a pole which had been passed between his hands and feet after they were tied together. This was a very old male, "mias rombi" (*Simia satyrus*), without the expanded cheeks. He was much emaciated, and the Malays said he had jungle fever, which really seemed to be the case. The Malays shot him in the ankle, and, being too weak to climb fast, he fell an easy prey and was taken alive.

Had he been unhurt I would gladly have kept him alive, but I am averse to prolonging the sufferings of hopelessly wounded animals under any pretext, or keeping any animal in painful and barbarous captivity. So I quickly thrust the point of my knife into the occiput of the half-dead animal, pierced his medulla oblongata, and, with a hoarse growl, he instantly expired. This specimen measured four feet four inches in height from head to heel, and eight feet between the tips of his fingers with the arms extended.

Two hours later, the little baby orang relieved me of all anxiety on its account by dying. Blou dryly remarked that it had found dying was getting fashionable with the mias and it wanted to go with the rest. This made seven dead orangs, big and little, to skin and skeletonize in one day! I had adult specimens of both species, male and female, and two young ones; and, by a happy coincidence, the Chinese, Dyaks and Malays had almost made a dead heat in the race after specimens.

There are many good people who are at a loss to understand how a naturalist "can bear to skin and cut up dead animals," no matter how rare and interesting they are. Many wonder how he can have "an appetite to eat," and cry out in holy horror at sight of the raw flesh under his knife. Well, tastes differ, that's all. As for myself, I would not have exchanged the pleasures of that day, when we had those seven orangs to dissect, for a box at the opera the whole season through.

It is a pity that men who "don't see how you can do it" could not have been there on that memorable occasion. When we finished, there was a small mountain of orang flesh, a long row of ghastly, grinning skeletons, and big, red-haired skins enough to have carpeted a good-sized room. I forgot to eat, and did not think of sleeping till after midnight. It was the most valuable day's work I ever did, for the specimens we preserved were worth, unmounted, not less than eight hundred dollars.

It was fortunate that we had such excellent facilities for drying skins as the open space at the back of the house afforded. I applied the preservatives myself to every skin and skeleton, and watched them daily to see that they cured properly. The necessity for this constant care of them kept me at Simujan several days, during which time the natives hunted diligently, and brought me many fine specimens both dead and alive. This is the list of one day's gatherings, exclusive of insects:

>2 Spiny turtles (*Geoemyda spinosa*).
>1 Box turtle (*Emys Thurgii*).
>1 Hornbill head (*Buceros rhinoceros*).
>1 Orang-utan skull (*Simia Wurmbii*).
>3 Java deer, alive (*Tragulus*).
>3 Thread fish (*Polynemus*).
>4 Long-armed prawns (*Pæneus*).
>1 Python, seven feet long.
>1 Gibbon, "wah-wah," alive (*Hylobates concolor*).

A few days after our great orang-utan day, a Dyak brought in another specimen, which in some respects was a remarkable one. It was a male mias chappin, with cheek callosities ten inches across, and it was evidently a dwarf, though of adult age. Its height was only three feet ten and one-fourth inches, and extent of arms six feet nine inches. The hair on his arms and legs was extremely long, that on his shoulders measuring twelve to fourteen inches in length, which was the longest I have ever seen in an orang.

He bore the scars of many a hard-fought battle. A piece had been bitten out of his upper lip, and the lower lip also had been bitten through; both middle fingers were off at the second joint, leaving mere stumps; the third right toe had disappeared from the same cause; the fourth left toe and both the great toes had been bitten off at the end; one finger was quite stiff and misshapen from a bite, and, to crown all, he was actually hump-backed, caused, as I found on dissecting, by some violent injury, possibly a fall. He had evidently been a regular prize-fighter in his day, a first-class desperado. One of his canine teeth had entirely disappeared, shattered in some bloody fracas, perhaps. I warrant his enemies had good cause to remember him, for he was in prime fighting condition. But, alas! for him, his fighting days are over, and he now peacefully sits on the branch of a tree in the American Museum of Natural History, quietly eating a wax durian.

On the last day of August we made ready for another trip up the Simujan to Padang Lake. The boats were ready at two o'clock, but the tide was still at the ebb, a strong current was setting down the river, and we waited for the flow. Moreover, a great bore was expected to come up the river when the tide turned, and we were anxious to see it. Two miles down the Sadong we saw a ragged brown fringe, reaching across the broad river, and rapidly coming nearer. As it swung, like a long arm, around the point a mile below, we plainly heard it roaring like a distant waterfall. On it came, like a tidal wave, a great wall of surf, rolling and curling over at the top, backed by a rushing plain of water nine feet thick. It seemed like a thing of life and purpose, powerful, irresistible. I watched it every moment with the glass until it reached the mouth of the Simujan, where our boats lay. There were no boats on the Sadong, except two little sampans, manned by daring Malays, both of which were upset by the bore, but the occupants clung to their boats, and presently got ashore.

The height of the bore, as nearly as I could determine, was between nine and ten feet, and it travelled upward at the rate of about twelve miles an hour. At a distance of half a mile, the sound it made was like the roar of surf on a stormy beach. As the advancing wave struck the sharp point of land at the confluence of the two rivers, with a truly surf-like roar and thunder, a great volume of water came sweeping up the Simujan, filling the little ditches and catching up the boats that lay stranded high and dry on the muddy banks. In less than half a minute the little river rose eight feet, while, in the Sadong, we saw the great brown billows rolling past the mouth of our snug harbor, and chasing each other up the river in pursuit of the advancing torrent. Our light sampans swung round with the rushing current, the word was given, and we sped swiftly up the river with the advancing tide.

A short distance up we met a sampan containing two Dyaks who were bringing me two more mias, one dead and one alive. The latter was a two-year-old youngster, tied to a stout stick, with its hands above its head and its feet drawn well down and pinioned also.

It bit viciously at everything, and made strenuous efforts to seize any one who came near it. I would as soon have trusted a finger in a steel-trap as between those vicious jaws.

At last, despairing of getting a chance at any of us, the raging little wretch seized one of the fingers of its dead companion and bit it to the bone.

Both orangs were found on a tree near the Dyaks' village, and, having no fire-arms, they promptly chopped down the tree. The old one was killed with spears and parongs, and so badly cut to pieces that its skin was almost worthless. But I sent them on to Simujan, where I had left Perara to receive and take care of whatever specimens might arrive in my absence.

The Dyaks said that when the tree fell, a limb struck one of their companions and dislocated his hip, and they begged us to stop at the village and give him "obat" (medicine). An hour later we came to the village where our enterprising Dyaks lived, and, taking my box of medicines, I went ashore to see what I could do.

The house was of good size, containing about fifteen doors, and we were conducted to a room at the farther end where the injured man lay. He was not half so badly off as had been reported—a native rarely is for that matter. He lay on the floor with his injured leg lying in a swing, bared to the hip, and smeared all over with turmeric, which gave the limb an appearance of ghastly mortification.

I soon found that the hip had not been dislocated, and that the injury was only a very painful bruise. I bathed the limb with arnica and bound on a cloth saturated with the same, not so much for the effect it would have upon the injured limb as upon the mind of the sufferer.

Of course the inhabitants of the village crowded into the room and around the door to see what was going on—and such a crowd! Some had that repulsive skin disease called ichthyosis, which causes the epidermis to crack and loosen somewhat, and roll up in thousands of minute rolls, giving the otherwise dark brown body a grayish appearance, Others had large ulcerous sores on their arms and legs, which had been smeared over with turmeric and betel juice. Some had sore eyes, others had tetter and ringworm, and I think that of all the women who surrounded us in that room, about four out of every five were afflicted with visible ailments. It was the most unwholesome and afflicted crowd of Dyaks 1 ever saw, very different indeed from nearly all those I had seen elsewhere and saw subsequently.

Those who were not afflicted with cutaneous diseases were mostly old women and men, toothless and gray, with the skin hanging on their bare bodies in countless folds and wrinkles. Add to the above, tangled masses of jet-black hair, general nakedness, plenty of dirt, a little colored rattan and plenty of brass wire ornaments, and you have the most prominent features of the crowd which surrounded us. The house stood rather low on its posts, and the ground underneath was in a terribly filthy state, which, in a great measure, accounted for the ill-health of the occupants. My only wonder is that they did not die off altogether in a single year. In this village, be it remembered, we saw the Dyak at his worst, and we gladly left it behind.

Just before dark we passed the last Dyak village and kept on paddling for some time longer, until high water, in fact, when we tied up to the bushes for our evening meal, and, in spite of mosquitoes, slept soundly in the boats until morning.

About ten o'clock the next day we killed another good-sized orang, and at noon occurred the grand episode of our experience in Borneo, the death of the "Rajah," the largest orang of all.

We had just met a Malay sampan coming down the river, and, in answer to our inquiries, the occupants said they had seen no mias. Half a mile higher up we heard a deep guttural growl or roar, coming from the jungle back from the river, we thought, which put us on the alert. Presently Blou, who was steering my boat, whispered, "Mias! mias, tuan!" and struggled frantically to stop the boat. The paddlers backed water directly, although we saw nothing until the boat had backed several yards. Then we espied the knee of a large orang, who was lying on a branch about twenty feet above the water and only twenty yards from us. His body was entirely hidden by the green foliage, so I stood up in the boat and fired at his leg to rouse him.

"The Turk awoke." He started up instantly, growling hoarsely with pain and anger, and started to swing away. His reach was surprising in its length. Fortunately the water was deep, there were no screw pines to hinder our progress, and in a moment our sampan was directly under the old fellow, who then climbed high to escape us. It was a huge mias chappin, long-haired, big and burly. He growled savagely at us, and one of my men kept saying in large capitals,

"CHAPPIN! CHAPPIN! MIAS CHAPPIN! FIRE, Sir! fire! fire!—That's mias chappin, big, BIG!!!"

The men were all greatly excited, but I knew that the old fellow was ours and waited for a good shot. In a moment the opportunity came, and I fired twice in quick succession at the orang's breast. He stopped short, hung for a moment by his hands, then his hold gave way and he came tearing down, snapping off a large dead branch as he fell, and landed broadside in the water, which went flying all over us. He fell within ten feet of our boat, and we secured him without getting out.

A FIGHT IN THE TREE-TOPS.
(Drawn from the group in the U. S. National Museum mounted by the Author.)

As we seized the arms and pulled the massive head up to the surface of the water, the monster gave a great gasp, and looked reproachfully at us out of his half-closed eyes. I can never forget the strange and even awful sensation with which I regarded the face of the dying animal. There was nothing in it in the least suggestive of anything human, but I felt as if I had shot some grim and terrible gnome or river-god, a satyr indeed!

"Ahdo! Ahdo!" exclaimed Lamudin in Malay, "the Rajah of all the mias!"

We were all filled with wonder at the huge beast before us. He was a perfect giant in size, larger than any the natives had ever seen before, and the largest ever shot by a naturalist. His head, body, and limbs were simply immense, and his weight could not have been much, if any, less than one hundred and ninety pounds.

To give an idea of his size and proportions, I append his measurements, together with those taken of a man of average weight and stature.

	The Orang. (Male.)		Medium-sized Man. (Anglo-Saxon.)	
	Feet.	Inches.	Feet.	Inches.
Height, head to heel	4	$5\frac{1}{2}$	5	8
Spread of arms, between finger-tips	7	$10\frac{3}{4}$	5	$7\frac{1}{2}$
Length of arm, armpit to finger-tips	3	3	2	5
Length of hand		$10\frac{3}{4}$		$7\frac{1}{2}$
Length of foot		$12\frac{1}{4}$		10
Breadth of face		13		$5\frac{1}{2}$
Length of face		$11\frac{1}{2}$		$8\frac{1}{2}$
Circumference of head, behind ears	2	$7\frac{1}{2}$	1	$10\frac{1}{4}$
Circumference of neck	2	$3\frac{3}{4}$	1	3
Circumference of chest	3	$5\frac{1}{2}$	3	$2\frac{1}{4}$
Circumference of waist	4	2	2	$10\frac{1}{2}$
Circumference of arm		$12\frac{1}{4}$		$11\frac{1}{2}$
Circumference of forearm	1	2		$10\frac{3}{4}$
Circumference of thigh	1	7	1	9
Circumference of calf		$11\frac{3}{8}$	1	$2\frac{1}{4}$
Weight (estimated)	185 pounds.		160 pounds.	

In another chapter will be found a somewhat extended description of both species of the orang, and therefore I will not offer here any information concerning the external characteristics of the animal referred to above. He has since found a place, with several of his nearest relatives, in a huge glass case in the National Museum at Washington, where he is engaged in a sanguinary "Fight in the

Tree-Tops." In our illustration of that group, under the above title, the figure on the left is that of the "Rajah."

Late in the afternoon we arrived at the Popook village, where we stopped on our previous trip, and took up quarters as before. We remained one day to prepare our specimens, and one more in order to visit a large Dyak village, two miles above the north end of the lake, and on the day following returned again to Simujan. On the way down we took four mias, two old females and two young males, and overtook my old Chinese orang hunter in a sampan with two Dyaks and two dead mias, the latter for me, of course. One of the mias was a very large and fine one, although rather sparely built, and my mind was filled with gloomy forebodings that he was equal to the Rajah in height. When we reached Simujan I measured him forthwith, and my worst fears were realized. The animal was actually half an inch taller than the Rajah, and his height was therefore 4 feet 6 inches.

This was indeed a sad blow to us all, and cast quite a gloom over our spirits. Up to that moment the Rajah had been the tallest orang that ever fell into the hands of a naturalist, and I would fain have had him remain so. The old Chinaman had used me very badly, and I was shocked to observe that he did not feel the slightest contrition.

But, after all, the specimen I shot was considerably larger than the other, and surpassed it in every thing except height and length of arm. The Rajah outmeasured him in every other respect, had a broader face, longer and thicker hair, and a far more massive build generally. But for that disgusting half inch my specimen would have been entirely satisfactory.

During my absence Perara had received three other orangs, which made twenty-one in all. I had scarcely paid the old celestial for his specimens when a party of Dyaks arrived with two live ones. I recognized the larger as the one we met on our way up, and he was, if possible, more savage than ever. Even when I cut his bonds he tried hard to bite me, and when he was free, with the exception of a cord round his neck, the company very promptly and respectfully made way for him. I tied him by a long line in the unused bath-room, and he climbed up to the rafters, where he hung, sullenly refusing food, and even knocking the bananas out of my hand when I offered them.

The other live orang was a little fellow, a baby about six months old, of very different disposition from the other two. He was quite peaceable, not even once attempting to bite, but whined softly when I approached him, and rolled up his big brown eyes appealingly. His petition was not to be refused. I cut the bark that bound his hands and feet, and placed a pile of soft straw in the verandah for him, into the middle of which he immediately crawled and curled himself up. Thus began a great friendship between ape and man.

As a pet, the larger orang was not exactly a success. Day and night he clung to the rafters of the bath-room, as high up as he could get, sullenly refusing all food and repelling my most friendly advances. In the middle of the second night after I got him we were awakened by hearing something strike with a terrific "bang" on the bath-room floor, and, on going in, we found him lying where he had fallen, stone dead.

CHAPTER VIII.

COLLECTING AROUND SIMUJAN.

Native Hunters.—Two Orangs Killed at Simujan.—Nest-making by an Orang. —A Harvest of Mammals.—A Deputation of Dyaks from the Sibuyau.— An Inviting Invitation.—The Rise and Progress of the Baby Orang.—An Interesting Pet.—Humanlike Habits and Emotions.—A Tuba-fishing Picnic.—Third Journey up the Simujan.—Snake Curry.—A Voyage in the Dark.

I GAVE gunpowder ("obat," or gun-medicine!) quite liberally to all the natives who requested it, Dyaks, Malays, and Chinese, and in every possible way encouraged them to hunt animals for me. I found them very diligent and businesslike, and not in the least tricky or dishonest, as were the natives of India and Ceylon, whom I had occasion to employ in the same way. It was a great pleasure to deal with the Simujan people, for they were so frank and honest.

Only one of my hunters was ever guilty of a breach of trust, and that was a young Chinaman of our village, who shot a wild boar in the jungle, a mile from the kampong, and cut it up without giving me a chance to skin it. Getting word of it I went over, confiscated the head, and read the young celestial a lecture that he remembered afterward to our mutual advantage.

After getting back from my second trip up the Simujan I determined to remain some weeks at the village, and, with the aid of my native hunters, give that locality a thorough overhauling.

Early one fine morning we heard the report of firearms coming from the jungle on the right bank of the Sadong, not more than a mile below the village. It continued for about an hour, during which time about twenty-five shots were fired, when it ceased, and a Malay came with a sampan after me. I got my rifle and returned with him, and, on wading three hundred yards into the forest, we found a large party of Dyaks and Malays with a dead mias on the ground and a live one "treed" in the top of a lofty tree. They were unable to hit it with their weapons, and no wonder. They were all old flint-lock muskets, and while the Malays aspired to leaden bullets, the poor Dyaks used chunks of iron, made by cutting round iron rods or bolts into pieces an inch long. I now understood why the Dyaks had never asked me for percussion caps.

I got there just in time to see the orang build a large nest for himself. He took up a position in a fork which was well screened by the foliage, and began to break off small branches and pile them loosely in the crotch. There was no attempt at weaving, nor even regularity in anything. He reached out his long, hairy arm, snapped off the leafy branches with a practised hand, and laid them down with the broken ends sticking out. He presently got on the pile with his feet, and standing there to weight it down he turned slowly, breaking branches all the while, and laying them across the pile in front of him, until he had built quite a large nest. When he had finished, he laid down upon it, and was so effectually screened from us that I could not dislodge him, and after two or three shots I told the natives they would have to cut the tree.

Three or four Dyaks were provided with biliongs, and after hastily lashing together a few poles, to serve as a platform to enable them to get at the trunk above the spur roots, they mounted it and began chopping.

The rapidity with which those insignificant little axes ate into the tree was wonderful. In an incredibly short time—less than half an hour—the tree fell, the orang revealed himself and was promptly killed. After we got home I devoted the remainder of the day to sketching the larger of the two orangs, a fine mias chappin, in different positions. With considerable difficulty we hauled him into the top of a tree that stood near the house, put him in a lifelike attitude, with his hands and feet grasping the branches and lashed him there, after which I made a careful sketch of him from the ground.

My native hunters brought me many fine specimens of mammals, a few large birds, many reptiles and a few fishes. The most successful of all my collectors was a fine Dyak named Dundang, already spoken of, who shot four orangs, several rhinoceros hornbills, two or three proboscis monkeys, a wild hog, and quite a number of small mammals. One of the orangs he brought me had the hair on its back quite blackened and singed, as if it had been killed at close range. Upon being questioned, he said he wounded the mias, but could not bring it down, and having fired all his charges but one, he climbed into the tree containing the orang, put the muzzle of his gun so near the animal's body that he could not fail to hit, and fired.

The Malays are quite expert in catching deer. Besides noosing a fine sambur buck (*Rusa equina?*) they caught for me Java deer ("plandok"), one after another, until I cried enough. The latter (*Tragulus napu*) is the smallest of all the deer tribe, being a true pigmy only nine inches high, very trim, graceful and pretty, but, unfortunately, without antlers. The sambur was a much-dwarfed, faded-out, thin-haired representative of his species, in comparison with the noble stags of the Animallais. His antlers were also very insignificant in comparison, but as for that I have seen fully as great variation in the antlers of our Virginia deer in a far smaller area of distribution.

Two specimens of a curious viverrine animal, half cat and half otter, the *Cynogale Bennettii*, were brought in, several civet cats, a beautiful flying lemur (*Galeopithecus volans*), and a slow-paced lemur (*Nycticebus tardigradus*). The *Cynogale*, for which I believe there is no common name unless we call it the otter cat, is peculiar to Borneo, and only one species is known. Its muzzle is extremely broad at the end (2¾ inches), but narrows suddenly midway between the end of the nose and the eyes, which gives the head a very strange appearance, totally unlike that of any other quadruped I am acquainted with. The animal is 24¾ inches in length of head and body, and the tail measures 7 inches. It is covered with a rather thick coat of moderately long but fine fur, of a uniform dark-brown color. I shot in the neighborhood several specimens of the common gray monkey (*Macacus cynomolgus*), a pig-tailed macaque (*M. nemestrinus*), here called the "broque" in Malay, from which the outlandish common name of "bruh" has been evolved.

One day a party of Dyaks arrived from the head of the Sibuyau River, between the Sadong and Batang Lupar, bringing several fragmentary skins of argus pheasant, which had been taken off in native fashion for the wing and tail feathers, and also a live argus. The poor bird had had a hard time of it, and in looking at it I felt guilty of cruelty to animals. In its struggles it had lost half its body feathers, and, worst of all, when it was caught in the noose one of its legs had been dislocated. I lost no time in putting it beyond the reach of further pain.

The Sibuyau people told me that argus pheasants and animals of many kinds I had not yet found were plentiful around their vil-

HEAD OF CYNOGALE BENNETTII.
(*Sketched from life.*)

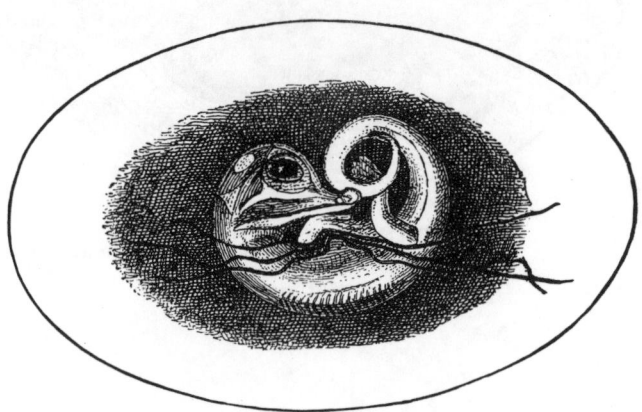

EMBRYO OF CROCODILUS POROSUS.
(*Natural size.*)

THE "OLD MAN." (YOUNG ORANG-UTAN.)
(*From an instantaneous photograph.*)

lage, and gave me a pressing invitation to make them a long visit. I determined to accept it as soon as I had worked up the Sadong region sufficiently, and told them they might expect me in a few weeks.

The baby orang mentioned at the end of the preceding chapter became a striking example of the survival of the fittest. While my first two captives were vicious to the last degree, and died promptly, without repentance, my third pet turned out to be all that heart of man could desire in an orang. He was by no means a thing of beauty, but he certainly was a joy forever.

Judged by our standard of human beauty, he was perhaps as ugly as any healthy child could be and live; but, for all that, his homeliness was interesting; it seemed to conform to a general plan of ugliness, and nothing was lacking to make it perfect. But, judged by the standard of anthropoid beauty, he was as handsome and wholesome a little orang as ever climbed. His eyes were large, bright and full of intelligence, and he had a forehead like a philosopher.

Because of his bald and shiny head, his solemn, wrinkled and melancholy visage, his air of profound gravity and senatorial wisdom, we got to calling him the Old Man, and forgot to give him any Christian name. A thin growth of brick-red hair grew straight up the back of his head and over the crown, making, in certain lights, a perfect halo around his bald, brown pate, reminding one rather forcibly of certain pictures by the old masters.

I measured him, for the first time, on October 15th, in spite of his vigorous opposition, and found that his height was $21\frac{3}{4}$ inches, extent of arms $34\frac{1}{2}$ inches, and his weight $10\frac{1}{2}$ pounds. His body was short and thick, and, like all orangs, his arms were so long and his legs so short that by stooping forward a little, his hands easily touched the ground. In walking, he invariably went on all fours, placing the back of the fingers and ball of the thumb, instead of the palm, upon the ground, and he also turned his toes under. His gait on the ground was very much like that of a man going on crutches with both feet injured alike. On the ground he moved slowly, seeming quite out of his element, but his feats in climbing and his performances on the slack-rope were highly entertaining.

He was fresh from the jungle when brought to me, but I soon convinced him that my intentions were honorable, and slowly gained his confidence. For three or four days he would not allow me to hold him in my arms unless I would let him grasp some firm object with at least one hand. The action plainly showed that he feared I would play a trick on him by letting him fall. Presently, however, I hit upon a plan which conquered his suspicion. I made him climb up to my shoulder to get the bananas of which he was very fond, and, after that, a banana held at arm's length above my head would start him to climbing my body as if it were a tree until the tempting bait was reached.

He soon became very fond of being held in my arms, and when I grew tired of holding him, he would grasp the folds of my flannel shirt and hold himself—quite an improvement upon the puny helplessness of human infants.

Next to eating seven bananas at once, his greatest delight was in sitting lazily in my lap while I sat reading, writing, or even eating, sprawling out his legs and arms, catching hold of my book, or my penholder, or pulling at the table-cloth.

Once while holding him in my lap at dinner, he suddenly made a pass at the roast duck which lay before me, and had his teeth in it before I could recover from my surprise. On one occasion when I sat eating, he leisurely climbed up the back of my chair, squatted on the topmost round, leaned lazily forward against me, and rested his chin comfortably on my shoulder. And there he sat all through the meal, watching the performance with the air of a connoisseur.

For a long time he would eat nothing but bananas and sugarcane, and I was at my wits' end to find a way to teach him to eat boiled rice. One day, however, as he was sitting in my lap while I was at dinner, I noticed that his eyes followed the journeys of my spoon with great interest, and it occurred to me that human beings always want what they cannot have. Happy thought! I began to pass each spoonful of rice close to his mouth on its way to mine. He soon began to open his mouth every time he saw the spoon coming, only to be disappointed by seeing it travel on to his next neighbor. From being merely willing to try the rice, he became very anxious when he saw it was denied him, and a little more tantalizing set him to struggling violently for the food he had previously despised. When it was finally given him he ate it with the greatest satisfaction, and thereafter, with the addition of milk, it became his daily food.

He also learned to eat with relish all kinds of cooked meat, vegetables, canned fruit and bread, and to drink tea, coffee, milk and chocolate, in all respects evincing the tastes of a human being

—except that he would not touch beer, wine nor spirits. He lived and died a teetotaler.

The Old Man soon grew fat and mischievous, and always did his best to amuse me. Many an absurd childish game we played upon the floor in highly undignified fashion. One of his favorite tricks was to seize my hand suddenly, draw it to his mouth, and make a feint of giving it a terrible bite. But he always knew that he must bite gently, which is more than can be said of any human infant I ever experimented with. Often he would entertain me for half an hour by making the most comically wry faces, for which his broad, india-rubber lips were specially adapted. He was also a great contortionist, and, having no *ligamentum teres*, the freedom with which he used his legs was at first quite surprising.

When at Simujan I slept in a tall and wide "four-poster," and the little fellow was always anxious to sleep with me. Whenever I permitted him to do so, his happiness was complete. His favorite position was to lie sprawling upon my chest, affectionately clasping my body with his outstretched arms and legs, with his head on my shoulder and his face close to my neck. Being as clean and wholesome as any human being, and without any odor of tobacco or liquor on his breath, he made a very agreeable bed-fellow until he got into the habit of snoring and sneezing so much as to disturb my slumbers, when it became necessary for him to sleep by himself. Meanwhile, I watched him closely, and did everything I could think of to arouse his mind to action, and stimulate it to act in different directions.

About this time I had another very interesting anthropoid pet, a young gibbon, which I purchased at a Dyak village. Instead of hobbling along like the little orang, which used its arms as if they were crutches, it would stand perfectly erect, partially extend its long, thin arms out sideways to balance himself, and walk across the floor with brisk confidence. When in good health it was quite friendly, and even affectionate, but in spite of my efforts to prolong its life it soon sickened and died.

On September 27th, a bore again came up the river, and on the day following the tide rose to an unusual height, about fourteen feet, covering every speck of land in the kampong, so that the Malays paddled from house to house in their sampans, and Ah Kee had to wade knee deep in water to get my dinner from the cookhouse to the table. It was like a Mississippi freshet, except that it departed as suddenly as it came.

On October 2d Mr. Eng Quee got up a grand tuba-fishing party, and invited me to make one of it, which I was very glad to do. We rose at midnight and started down the river with the ebb tide. I lay down in the boat and slept until we arrived at the mouth of the Ensengi River, a large creek which empties into the Sadong from the west, about six miles below the village. We found there a number of Malays in sampans, patiently waiting for daybreak, and, after a good deal of time-killing banter, all hands lay down and went to sleep.

At daybreak the little fleet of canoes started up the creek, and, after paddling about two miles, the stream rose above tidal influence, and the banks were thickly fringed with pandanus. The rendezvous was about four miles up.

When all had arrived there were present twenty-three sampans, manned by about sixty Malays. The first thing in order with the Malays was the usual breakfast of boiled rice, which many had brought cold, wrapped in banana leaves, and others cooked on the spot. After that, all fell to work to prepare the tuba, which is the fine, fibrous root of a climbing plant (a species of *Menispermum*), which possesses a powerful narcotic principle, and is grown for the special purpose of taking fish. It was done up in small, close bundles, the thickness of a man's wrist and six or eight inches long, and was dry and hard.

The bundles were distributed so that each boat received four or five, each man procured a stout little club of green wood, and the pounding began. The game was to reduce the tuba to a pulp, and for an hour sixty clubs beat a lively tattoo on the root bundles as they were held on the edges of the boats. A quantity of water, perhaps twenty gallons, was dipped into each boat, into which the tuba was dipped and wrung out from time to time, until it gradually softened under the pounding process and was reduced to shreds. When water was squeezed out of the tuba it had a white, frothy appearance, like soap-suds.

As fast as the bundles of tuba were reduced to fine shreds, they were chopped up with a parong, and the particles mixed with the water in the boats. When all the root had been thus pounded and chopped up, the Malays procured lumps of clay and dissolved them in the solution until it was made quite murky. Each boat contained about twenty gallons of this narcotic extract.

The stream was about forty feet wide and eight to ten feet deep, the current was swift and the water rather murky.

COLLECTING AROUND SIMUJAN

We waited until the tide was half out, and then, after selecting a good place, the boats drew close together, the word was given, and with a ringing cheer the extract was quickly dipped up and thrown into the stream. As I looked at the small quantity of tuba-water and the volume of water in the creek I must confess to entertaining doubts of the result.

Having performed the act of faith, we began at once to look for fish. The stream absorbed the tuba-water as though it had been so much dirty soap-suds, and not a trace of it was to be seen five minutes after. We drifted slowly down to where there were curves and quiet eddies in the stream, and each man looked for what he considered the most likely place for a fish to rise. Presently we saw two little fellows floating helplessly at the surface, and the man nearest them kindly took them in out of the wet.

Each man had a small dip-net and a "grains" with two or three prongs. The spear-head was set in the end of a bamboo handle so that it would come out when a fish was struck, and of course the spear-head was made fast to the handle by a stout line. Mr. Eng Quee had provided me with a spear, which I was very anxious to use.

Just as our boats reached a wide bend in the stream, a large fish showed its slimy, black back at the surface, just out of our reach. My first thought was that it was a porpoise, it was so large and black. Presently it appeared again and floated for a moment with its back out of water. It was certainly four feet long. Mr. Eng Quee and one of his Malays threw their spears at it but missed. Then I skipped to the bow of my boat, and finding myself within reach of the fish drove my spear into its side. It gave a lunge forward, almost throwing me overboard and upsetting the boat, and then—Oh! my soul! the line snapped! Down went the huge fish, and we never saw him again. I hoped that some one of the party would see him and take him in, but was disappointed.

Fifteen minutes later, another big fish of the same kind came up, was speared by two Malays, and after a gallant struggle was secured. It was a little over three feet long, scaleless, with a broad, flat head, somewhat like that of a catfish, a thin body, small dorsal fin and the anal fin very broad and long. Its color was blackish-brown, with three light bands along the middle of the side. Altogether nine large specimens of this species (*Wallago leerii*) were taken during the day.

The tide was still running out when we arrived at the mouth of the creek, and many fish were found stranded on the mud along the banks, dead and dying. The Malays waded along at the water's edge, knee deep in mud, to secure those that came ashore, and also others that rose to the surface close to the bank.

Just at the mouth of the creek we found numbers of small fish floating at the surface, of which we easily secured fifteen with our dip-net. All but three were thread fishes, a strange species of *Polynemus*, which is readily distinguished by the extremely long, white, threadlike filaments, more than twice the length of the whole fish, attached to the pectoral fins. This is, in more respects than one, a very curious fish, as may be seen by an examination of the excellent figure given herewith.

The Malays were desperately fish-hungry, and I could not induce them to sell many of their largest fish, but I consoled myself with the purchase of the smaller ones, and also a very fine large turtle which was caught in a net.

Among the most interesting species taken were *Periophthalmus schlosserii*, our old friend of the Selangore mud banks, the air-breathing *Ophiocephalus*, and the celebrated gourami (*Osphromenus gourami*), a large and fine fish of great economic value, and well known to ichthyologists, especially those engaged in fish culture, from the numerous efforts that have been made, many of them successful, to acclimatize it in various countries from the East Indies to the United States. I found it native to Selangore, where I obtained one very fine specimen. Since there is already an abundance of literature on the gourami, I will add only a reference to the accompanying illustration, which is a reproduction of a figure given by Dr. Theodore N. Gill in his paper on this species, which appeared in the Report of the U. S. Commissioner of Fish and Fisheries in 1876.

On the tuba-fishing pic-nic referred to above, I was fortunate in securing a specimen of the very rare and curious little pike-head (*Luciocephalus pulcher*),* the jaws of which are capable of being protruded far forward, thereby rendering the mouth sub-tubular. The name, *Luciocephalus*, meaning as it does, "pike-head," is a very apt one, for the head certainly much resembles that of the familiar pike or pickerel of our home waters. The fish, however, is

---

* For the identification of the fishes I collected in the Sadong River and its tributaries (35 species), I am under obligations to Dr. Tarleton H. Bean, Curator of Fishes, U. S. National Museum.

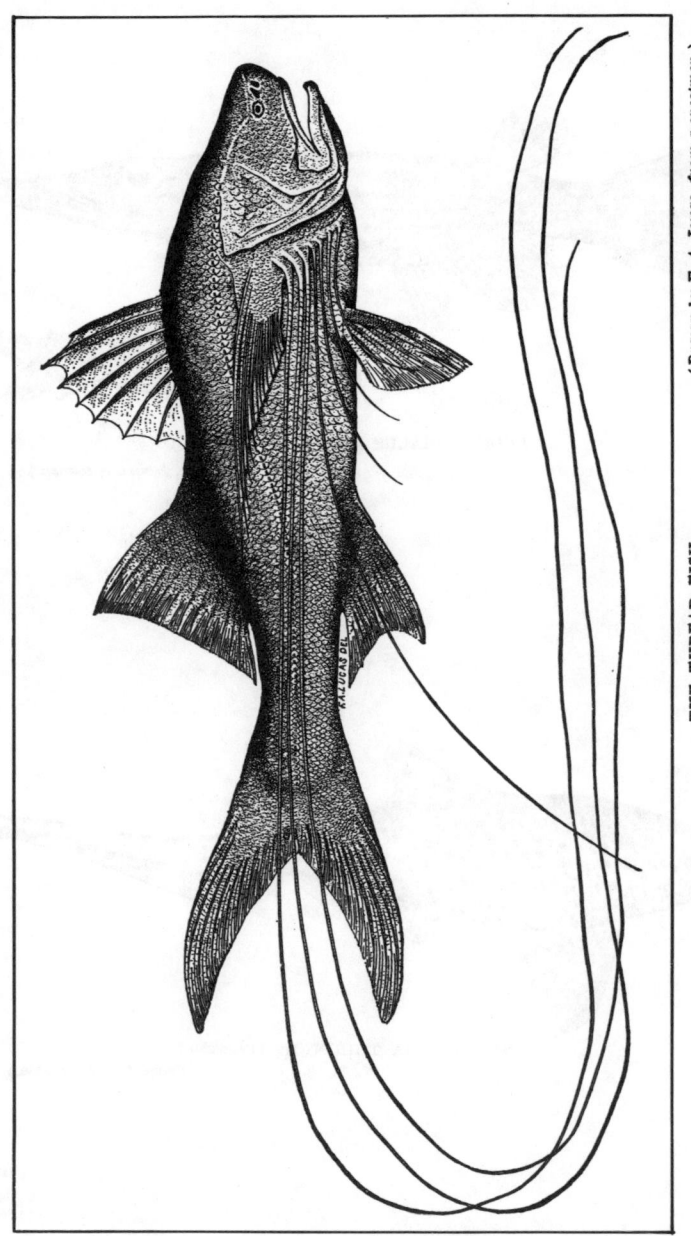

THE THREAD FISH. (*Drawn by F. A. Lucas, from a specimen.*)

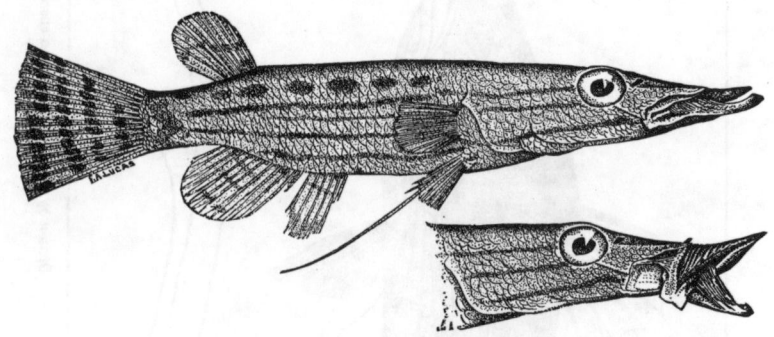

LUCIOCEPHALUS PULCHER. (Page 386.)
(*Drawn by F. A. Lucas, from a specimen.*)

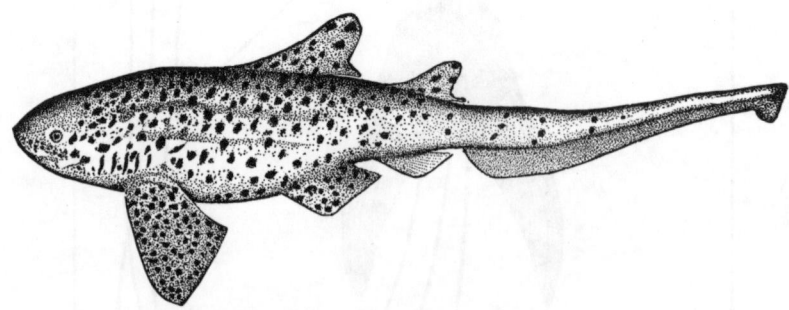

STEGOSTOMA TIGRINUM. (Page 256.)
(*From Author's sketch.*)

not at all related to the pike, but is nearest akin to the peculiar fishes with labyrinthiform pharyngeals, known as the *Anabantids*, and comprising, among others, the climbing fish and gourami. Its combination of peculiar characters renders it an object of great interest to naturalists, and by them it is considered to be the representative of a special family,—the *Luciocephalids*.

The next day my hunters brought me a rhinoceros hornbill, two proboscis monkeys, a live slow-paced lemur (*Nycticebus tardigradus*) and a brilliant emerald-green tree-snake (*Passerita*), about six feet long, which was the most beautiful serpent I ever saw. A Dyak boy brought it in his hands, and I received it in mine without any of the revulsion of feeling one ordinarily feels in handling a live snake.

It was a sociable sort of a snake, not in the least nervous on account of its captivity, and I kept it alive for some hours, and allowed it to crawl quietly over my table and around the room. I was quite charmed with its splendid color, lithe, beautiful form, and graceful movement. It was a painful matter to both of us when I was at last obliged to consign it to the alchohol can.

Late in the afternoon of October 4th, I started on my third and last trip to Padang Lake, with the intention of living at the Popook village for two or three weeks. Our starting was delayed by the arrival of a large civet cat, a wild cat, and a wild hog's head, all of which had to be attended to immediately. I took the little baby orang with me, partly because I did not like to risk leaving him, and also because I liked his company.

Darkness overtook us before we had gone far, but it was a clear moonlight night and we expected to make a long pull before tying up. Very soon, however, the sky became overcast with heavy black clouds, making the darkness very intense, and the lightning and thunder foretold an approaching storm. Just before it broke, we came to a tiny Dyak hut, about eight feet square, recently erected at the edge of the bank, and, making fast to the shore, we quickly climbed the ladder and craved shelter. "The man of the house" was at home, with his wife and two children, and we were received with true Dyak cordiality. A dammar torch was burning near the door, and in a corner a small fire was smouldering on a bed of clay. The hut which sheltered us from the pouring rain was of the kind frequently seen along the Sadong and Simujan, a mere temporary erection, built in three days, and occupied only while the owner was planting a crop of paddi and afterward while harvesting it.

Learning that we were interested in animals, our host exhibited a water-snake about four feet in length, which he had caught in the river that afternoon, and intended to eat. He said it was a clean snake, because it lived on fish. Ah Kee expressed some surprise and incredulity at his intention, whereupon the Dyak immediately proceeded to roast the serpent on the fire and strip off the skin, preparatory to making a snake curry. He said that his people eat large lizards also.

As soon as the rain ceased we proceeded, but before long it began anew, so we tied up at the first Dyak village we came to, and made ourselves comfortable until morning.

The next day was beautifully clear and balmy, of the kind which makes mere existence a delight. We paddled up stream in high spirits, shooting a monkey now and then, halting at noon for a good square meal on a fine bit of dry ground, left so by the greatly lowered waters of the stream. When it came time to eat, my stomach was empty and craved supplies; but it utterly refused Ah Kee's oft-repeated stewed duck, rice, and yams. My appetite called for a new deal, and Ah Kee responded with a tin of "biscuits" (crackers), another of American pressed beef, and a can of delicious cherries, all from San Francisco. How appetizing was that ration of home-grown beef and fruit!

The water in the river was about three feet lower than we had before found it, and dry ground was noticed in several places. Just before sunset we became involved in a chase after a big troop of proboscis monkeys, which consumed considerable time and left us wet, tired, and baffled. Then darkness fell and it began to rain. We were four miles from the Popook village and with a labyrinth of screw pines to go through in the dark, but we were in no condition to remain all night where we were. The two Malays who paddled Eng Quee's boat announced their determination to stay where they were until morning, so I got into my own boat, and told my boys we would go on. The Malays declared it was impossible to go through the screw pines in the dark, but we left them to their own devices and proceeded.

I think I never saw a blacker night. It rained steadily, though not in torrents, and the lightning aided us very effectively. My little Malay man Dobah did the steering. Ah Kee and Perara sat under the kadjangs and paddled, while I sat in the bow, paddling also, and acted as a pilot. How we ever found the entrance to that blind passage through the pines will always be a mystery to me,

THE GOURAMI.

and how we ever got through that narrow, zigzag tunnel in the dark without going astray also passes my comprehension at this time. In many places the channel was so filled with floating *Pandanus* stems as to be almost impassable, and many times our boat-roof was caught by overhanging branches and nearly dragged off. Aided by the lightning flashes, and the slight reflection on the open water, I was able to spy out the passage a few yards at a time and give directions to the steersman.

At last, to our inexpressible relief, we emerged on the open water of the lake, and headed north. By this time the clouds had lifted a little, and we were able to distinguish Gunong Popook. After several trials we found the landing, and a few moments later climbed the ladder of the village. Great was the astonishment of the Dyaks when they saw a white man enter at the door, rifle in hand, with a little red-haired orang-utan clinging to his shirt. There was a large party of visitors in the village, and when we told them from whence we came since nightfall their surprise was profound.

" And who showed you the way? " they demanded.

" The tuan " (mister).

" Ah-doe! Ah-doe! Ah-doe! "

We were wet, cold, and hungry, but all these evils were speedily corrected, and our enjoyment of them was intensified by the thought of Lamudin and his companion in their wet boat on the river, plagued by darkness, rain, mosquitoes and hunger.

CHAPTER IX

COLLECTING AT PADANG LAKE.

A Hunt on Gunong Popook.—A Lost Hunter.—A Handsome Dyak.—A Reception by Torchlight.—More Orang-utans.—How an Orang Sleeps.—Proboscis Monkeys.—Living *versus* Stuffed Specimens.—A Remarkable Nose.—Luckless Gibbon-hunting. — Luckless Wild-hog Hunting. — Mud and Thorns.—Picturesque Vegetation.—Fresh-water Turtles and Fishes.—Return to the Sadong.

I SPENT a most delightful fortnight with the Dyaks at the Popook village. The weather was continuously fine, the Dyaks were agreeable and interesting, the jungle yielded a good harvest of specimens, and every day there was something new to see and to do.

I presently sent Lamudin and his companion back to Simujan, and with my three other men settled down comfortably to live and work.

My first experience was a rather ridiculous one for me, and consisted in my getting lost, almost within sight of the village. During the afternoon of the day following our arrival, we heard some wah-wahs (gibbons) crying in the tree-tops, far up the steep side of Gunong Popook, and, hastily catching up my shot-gun, I started for them.

My boy Perara was also hunting on the mountain, and, before I had quite reached my game, he fired twice, close-by, which scared the wah-wahs into silence and out of the neighborhood. I climbed on until I reached the summit of the mountain, which is a perfect cone only a few yards across at the top. Just as I reached the summit, a female sambur deer ran along the steep slope, forty yards below me, in full view. Having only small shot in my gun, it would have been worse than useless to have fired.

Presently, I began to slowly descend. As I was quietly stooping down to examine some shells, another sambur, also a doe, trotted up, halted, and stood stock still in full view, not more than twenty yards away. I thought of Balaam and how he wished for his sword, and sympathized with him while I thought of my rifle. She impressed me as being the least handsome of all the deer tribe, excepting, perhaps, the female moose. After we had stared at each other a few seconds she trotted off, and a few moments later I saw a stag of the same species, whose antlers were in the velvet. It literally rained sambur because my dish was bottom up.

After wandering about for some time to no purpose, I set out to return to the house. Half way down I shot a black monkey or "bijit" (*Semnopithecus femoralis*), slung it over my shoulder to carry home, and made for the clearing on the mountainside. After a slow and painful struggle through several acres of thorns I heard a dog bark, saw the edge of the clearing, and knew that I was near the house. At last I reached the edge of the clearing and heaved a sigh of relief, but lo! it wasn't our clearing at all! I had never seen it before, and knew that there was no such spot within a mile of the Popook village. The explanation was not difficult. In coming down the mountain I had made altogether too many degrees of longitude at the top, which brought me out on the west side instead of on the south. It was almost sunset, there was no path leading south from the clearing, and I knew that I could not possibly make my way through that thorny jungle at that time of day without getting lost and benighted.

Seeing smoke at the farther end of the clearing, toward the north, I went toward it, resolved to bivouac in good style, and, if it became necessary, roast my black monkey and sup on it. But I found a path leading away from the clearing, and followed it up rapidly. After walking about a mile, I came to a small Dyak house of four or five doors. Calling out the inhabitants I said to them in Malay, "Give me two men go Popook Dyak house, quick!"

They asked a question or two which I did not quite understand, and therefore answered somewhat at random. They civilly invited me to come in and sit down, and chew betel with them, but with equal civility I declined and urged them to come on. Straightway two of the young men arose, took a fresh chew of the betel, girded up their loins, tied on their parongs and said they were ready. I said we had "better go lake, go boat," and we started for the lake at once.

Both my guides were as fine-looking Dyaks as any I saw in Sarawak Territory. One was a youth about seventeen years old, with an intelligent, even handsome face, a beautifully-moulded form, erect carriage, and easy, graceful movement. On the score of good looks and general physique he could discount nine-tenths of all the white boys I ever saw.

The two were dressed alike, in decidedly picturesque costumes. The head-dress was a clean turban of bright scarlet cloth, neatly wound around the head, with a loose end falling over the left ear. The crown of the head was wholly uncovered, and a profusion of jet black locks fell over the top of the turban. The "chawat," or loin-cloth, was also scarlet cloth disposed in ample folds, fringed at both ends, one of which hung down apronlike in front, and the other at the back.

Each of the Dyaks wore behind him, suspended by a cord around the waist, a shield-shaped mat of many colors, which quite covered the body from the loins half way down to the thighs, and was evidently worn to sit upon. One of these protectors was ornamented by a border of cowries sewn on close together all the way round.

Their parong sheaths were each bedecked at the end with a bunch of the most showy wing and tail feathers of the argus pheasant. The persons of my guides were further ornamented by several copper rings worn in each ear, which proclaimed them to be Seribas men, bracelets and armlets of finely-plaited rattan, and leglets of beaded rattan worn just below the knee. Taken altogether they were as handsome savages as one could wish to see.

On reaching the lake, which was about a mile from the house, the Dyaks found two paddles that had been hidden in the grass, dipped the water out of a sunken canoe, and, getting into it, we set off just as it grew dark. As we neared the Popook village we heard people calling for me far up the side of the mountain, but I was not able to make them hear my answering shout. As soon as we reached the village the gong was beaten and several shots fired to call back the four Dyaks and Dobah, who were then far beyond the clearing. I was very well pleased to find that they had turned out so promptly to look for me; going, as they did, naked and barefooted, in the dark, into thick jungle among rocks and thorns. As they were returning, one of the Dyaks was charged upon by some large animal, presumably a deer, knocked down, considerably bruised and dreadfully scratched, besides receiving a cut on his leg and another on his ear. The suddenness of the assault and its mysterious nature caused great excitement and a volume of loud talk. I served out tobacco to the crowd and dressed the wounds of the injured party with arnica and court plaster, which pleased all the Dyaks very much and placed us all on confidential terms.

The natives sat by and looked on with great curiosity while I ate my supper. Afterward they examined my shoes with great interest, and one man succeeded in putting one of them on. They also inspected my feet closely, and a comparison of theirs with mine was the cause of much merriment.

I took advantage of their good humor to ask them about the little metallic plates on some of their front teeth, which looked like gold. I found that each upper incisor and canine tooth was capped by a smooth plate of copper, held in place by a pin driven into a hole in the tooth. The Dyaks showed me how the hole is drilled (with a bow), and one imitated the agony they endure during the operation. He was a good actor, and his facial and bodily contortions and writhings excited roars of laughter.

The next day, while again climbing up the mountain after wah-wahs, my Dyak companion discovered an old female orang-utan seated quietly on a branch not more than thirty feet distant. I fired at her, and my bullet killed both her and the baby which she was holding in her arms. Although she was very small, only 3 feet 6 inches in height, she was so old her teeth were worn down to mere stumps, and several had entirely disappeared. Her hair was rather short, on account of which the Dyaks declared her to be a "mias kassar," and therefore different from the other varieties, "rombi" and "chappin."

On the morning of the third day, I took one Dyak and Dobah, and set off in my boat to visit the southern end of the lake. It was delightful weather. There was not a ripple on the surface of the lake, which lay like a polished mirror, reflecting the blue sky and its fleecy clouds, the dark-green mountain and the fringe of forest trees along the banks. Scarcely a bird's song broke the stillness. It was like a landscape in a dream—sunny, silent, balmy and clear. One day in such a spot is worth the toil of half a year to gain it.

Half way down the lake we discovered a fine old orang, lazily finishing his morning nap. His nest, which was nearly three feet across, was not more than fifteen feet above the water, and he lay sprawled out upon it, flat on his back, with the sun at the back of his head, sound asleep. His hairy arms and legs were thrust outward and upward, and his hands (an orang has hands on his legs, if you please) were firmly but mechanically grasping the largest branches while he slept. The back of his head was toward us, and, after silently paddling up to within fifteen yards of him, I stood in the boat to observe and afterward to make a rough sketch of him on the inside of an envelope.

While we were watching him, he snored almost continously, "not loud, but deep," until presently the flies bothered him and he awoke. With a slow, awkward sweep of his ponderous right arm he drove the flies from his face, and a moment later was wide awake. He was just rising to a sitting posture when my rifle-ball caught him between his shoulders. He sprang up quickly, gave a deep growl, flung himself forward into the tangled mass of green vines and branches which surrounded the nest on three sides, and was instantly lost to view. He went crashing forward for a few yards and then stopped ; there was a moment's silence, then a heavy fall and a dull splash. Lamudin and Blou went into the water and worked their way in to where the old fellow lay, and presently towed him out.

We went on down to the head of the lake, which, like the western side, is completely filled with screw pines growing in the water. A small creek called Batang Rejang empties into the lake at this point. We entered it and paddled up until it became so obstructed with overhanging branches that further progress was impossible.

On the way back we encountered a large troop of proboscis monkeys, and, by a sudden assault, I succeeded in killing two fine old male specimens. As usual, they were over water, and, being swift climbers and quite shy, were hard to kill. I saw, altogether, during my ramblings in the forests of Borneo, perhaps a hundred and fifty proboscis monkeys ; and, without a single exception, all were over water, either river, lake or submerged forest. As long as they are in sight they are very conspicuous objects, choosing the most commanding positions in open tree-tops. Once I saw thirteen in one tree, sitting lazily on the branches, as is their habit, sunning themselves and enjoying the scenery. It was the finest sight I ever saw in which monkeys played a part.

The cry of the "blanda," as the natives call it, is peculiar and unmistakable. Written phonetically it would be " honk," and occasionally "kee-honk," long drawn and deeply resonant, quite like the tone of a bass viol.

As the name would imply, the most striking feature of the proboscis monkey is its nose. In old male specimens this organ reaches its grandest proportions, and is truly enormous in length, breadth and thickness. It hangs from the face like—well, totally unlike any-

PORTRAIT OF A PROBOSCIS MONKEY.
(*From a sketch by the Author.*)

thing else in the world, coming quite below the lowest point of the chin, shaped like a pear except for a furrow down the middle and a contracted septum, which causes the organ to terminate in two points. It is broadest at the middle of the free portion instead of at the base.

Nothing could be more unnatural than the noses of all the stuffed proboscis monkeys I have yet seen in museums. They do not even suggest the natural form or size of the organ. The pictures of the animal sin against nature in the same fashion, and, in order to set *Nasalis* right before the world and vindicate his nasal character, I fixed my best specimen on a branch in a natural attitude, and drew a picture of him, to scale, a copy of which is submitted in the accompanying engraving.

The proboscis monkey, which, by the way, is found only in Borneo, is a large animal and of striking appearance both in form and color. Its face is cinnamon brown, and its body conspicuously marked with reddish brown and white, the tails of old specimens, being white as snow. Taken altogether, *Nasalis larvatus* is, to the hunter-naturalist, a very interesting object of pursuit, and were he not partially eclipsed by the orang he would be the most famous quadrumane in the East Indies.

I tried six different times, on as many days, to get a shot at the family of wah-wahs which called to us daily from the summit of Gunong Popook, but the mountain was so steep and the tree-tops so thick that I did not even get a shot. At last I gave it up as a bad job, and determined to reserve my efforts for the Sibuyau, where they were said to be plentiful. Dundang, who followed me up the Simujan in order to hunt for me, killed one fine large specimen during my stay at the lake, but where he shot it I could not quite understand. He also killed more proboscis monkeys for me, a wild pig, two small orangs, and a few other animals. Black monkeys (*S. femoralis*) were numerous within two hundred yards of the house, and Perara succeeded in killing several, which was about all he did kill.

Wild hogs were so plentiful in the jungle that the Dyaks had built a pole fence four feet high around three sides of their clearing to protect their crop of rice. Both Mr. Houghton and Eng Quee had assured me they had seen wild pigs which stood thirty-six, and even forty, inches high at the shoulders, their great height being due to the unusual length of their legs, developed in the animal's struggle for existence in low, swampy forest.

The accounts I had had of the wild pig made me very anxious to secure at least one large specimen. But, although they were so abundant in the jungle about us as to seriously threaten the rice field, I did not even get sight of one in my first week's hunting on Gunong Popook, so I determined to try for them in the swamps. The oldest Dyak in the village, who was therefore an experienced hunter, offered to guide me to the most likely spots, and, with a stout, active lad, named Munkah, to accompany us, early one bright morning we set out.

For several hours we toiled through the swamp, wading through water and thin mud of various depths from ankle to hip, and finally crossed it and came to high ground, at the edge of which we expected to find wild pigs feeding on the fallen fruit of a tree the Dyaks called ejoke. But the pigs were not there. Then we took to the high ground, and for some hours longer we tramped up and down a succession of the steepest of hills, covered with the thorniest kind of jungle. Thorns, did I say? Well, I meant fish-hooks, needles, pins, tacks, and porcupine quills.

Magnificent spreading palms (*Livistona sinensis*) grew thickly everywhere; very beautiful to the eye their long, slender stems were, but always set with rows of stout and sharp thorns, curved just the wrong way for comfort, and always ready to catch a passing victim. The branches of a worthless climbing rattan (*Calamus*) were particularly cruel. This species is very abundant, climbing over the underbrush and sending out many long, slender branches which droop like those of the weeping willow. The end of each is leafless for about two feet from the tip, and the slender, supple stem resolves itself into a long row of animated trout-hooks. The way those threadlike stems will reach out to seize a victim and then hang on, is enough to make one believe them an invention of the devil. One will catch you suddenly by the ear and hold you very still, while another flies back from the man ahead of you and rakes you across the cheek like a fine saw, cutting a neat little gash as it goes. Again, one will spring suddenly and lay hold of your neck with a score of needlelike points, while others fasten themselves in your clothes, or upon your bare hands.

If anathemas could kill, I would take bell and candle and so curse every thorn-bearing plant of the tropics, that beside my anathema the curse of the Catholic Church on Victor-Emmanuel would read like a blessing. In all the vegetable kingdom, there is nothing so useless and wholly objectionable as a thorn, especially the

COLLECTING AT PADANG LAKE.

accursed fish-hook thorn of the tropics, and if any intelligent reason can be assigned for either its deliberate creation or its evolution, it would be balm to my wounded cuticle. For my part, I consider the thorn one of nature's unmitigated blunders.

Our long tramp was wholly fruitless, for we saw not a single object worth shooting. Fortunately for my collection, my native hunters were more successful, for Dundang sent in a large broque (*Macacus nemestrinus*) and a baby of the same species; a friendly Dyak brought a large soft-shell turtle which he caught in the lake, and Perara managed to shoot a bijit.

A few days later, Hakka and I made another trial for wild pigs to Gunong Poondah, a low mountain a short distance to the north. We went by boat quite to its foot, up an arm of the lake, and along a narrow creek which led through a bit of lovely forest. The mossy tree-trunks were often covered with beautiful orchids, small ferns, and other parasitical plants, while palms of many species rose out of the water and drooped over the banks. The warm, still air, the subdued light of the forest, and the profusion of picturesque vegetation made up a bit of tropical forest scenery which quite realized my preconceived ideal.

We hunted along the foot of the mountain and stalked carefully up to the ejoke trees, but saw no pigs. Once indeed we started a troop of wah-wahs, but when I was about to fire we heard unmistakably the grunt of a wild pig. Turning reluctantly from the "bird in the hand" we tried to discover the pigs, but failed, and so lost both. The Dyaks fished diligently in the lake during my stay, and everything caught was brought to me. The largest fish taken was a very handsome goby (*Eleotris marmorata*), seventeen inches long; and the most interesting were three species of climbing perch, *Anabas scandens* and two others.

After a fortnight's sojourn at the Popook village, I felt satisfied that I had exhausted that locality, and, when Mr. Eng Quee's boat arrived, we loaded up, took leave of our friendly and hospitable hosts —not without regret, on my part, I am bound to say—and returned to Simujan without hap or mishap.

CHAPTER X.

FACTS ABOUT THE ORANG-UTAN.

Distribution of the Orang-utan.—Its Affinities.—External Appearance.—Remarkable Facial Ornament (?).— Color of Skin.—Hair.—Eyes.—Mode of Fighting.—Pugnacity.—Food.—Unsocial Habits.—Young at Birth.—Nesting Habits.—Locomotive Powers.—Inability to Walk or Stand Erect.—Height of Adults.—General Measurements.—Two Species Recognized.—Characters of *Simia Wurmbii* and *Satyrus*.—Individual Peculiarities.

BORNEO is truly the land of apes and monkeys. Among its fourteen species, five of which occur nowhere else,* are found the following very interesting forms: the orang-utan (two species), the proboscis monkey, the gibbon, the slow lemur, tarsier, and the flying lemur.

For an island, Borneo is favored with a great variety of very interesting quadrupeds, both large and small, and a far greater number of species peculiar to itself than any of its neighbors of the Archipelago can boast. So far as known at present, it has ninety-six species of mammals, thirty-three of which, or more than one-third, are not found elsewhere. The largest species are the elephant, rhinoceros, tapir, wild cattle, sambur, and wild hog, and the most interesting are the apes and monkeys, insectivores, bats, and porcupines.

The genus *Simia* occurs in northern Sumatra, but its distribution in Borneo is so much more extensive that we may well say the latter is the home of the orang-utan. It inhabits that wide belt of low, forest-covered swamp forest which lies between the sea-coast and the mountain ranges of the interior, extending entirely around the western half of the island. But even this great alluvial plain is inhabited by the orang in certain districts only; although

---

* The following are the species peculiar to Borneo: Hylobates concolor, Nasalis larvatus, Semnopithecus rubicundus, Semnopithecus chrysomelas, Semnopithecus frontatus.

all those portions which are covered by lofty virgin forests seem to present the same features. In the Territory of Sarawak the orang, or "mias," as it is called by the natives, is found along the rivers Batang Lupar and Sadong and their small tributaries, such as the Lingga and Simujan. It does not occur at all along the Sarawak or Samarahan rivers, but farther west it is found, though more rarely, from the river Sambas to the Kapooas, which latter lies directly under the equator. It is also found in Kotei near Samarinda, at the mouth of the Mahakkam, and also on the Tewah River, which flows into the Barito from the east, almost directly under the equator.

Leaving the genus homo out of the question, the orang occupies the third place from the highest in the animal kingdom. The gorilla (*Troglodites gorilla*) is given the highest place, next in order is the chimpanzee (*T. niger*), after which comes the orang-utan (*Simia Wurmbii* and *satyrus*), followed by the *Siamanga syndactyla*, the link between the orangs and the gibbons (*Hylobates*). The orang well deserves the place it occupies. It agrees with the gorilla and chimpanzee in positive size and quality of the brain, but its fore-limbs, as compared with the hind ones, are longer than theirs, while they are also proportionally shorter than those of *Siamanga* and *Hylobates*. The heel-bone (*calcaneum*) is proportionally longer in *Simia* than in *Hylobates*, and its thumb is also better developed than that of the gibbons. Among the higher apes, the orang comes nearest to man in the number of ribs (twelve pairs) and form of the cerebral hemispheres, but differs from him in other respects, especially in the limbs, more than do the gorilla and chimpanzee.

The chimpanzee approaches man most closely in the character of its cranium, its dentition, and the proportional size of its arms. The gorilla is more manlike in the proportion of the leg to the body, size of the heel, curvature of the spine, form of pelvis and absolute capacity of the cranium. In its habits the orang resembles the gorilla and chimpanzee, which are not gregarious, while the gibbons are.

The most striking feature of the orang is its great size and general resemblance to man. The chest, arms and hands are especially human in their size and general outline. Since the animal depends mainly upon these members for the means of locomotion they are necessarily of massive proportions. The natural position of the human hand at rest is with the fingers slightly bent, but that of the orang is with the fingers tightly closed, and, when measuring our dead specimens, we often found it an absolute impossibility to straighten a single finger without cutting the tendon in the palm of the hand. Thus, when an orang is asleep, the most natural position he can assume is to firmly grasp a branch with each hand.

Male individuals of *Simia Wurmbii* are distinguished by their wonderful cheek callosities, each side of the face being greatly expanded and flattened into a thick, semi-circular disk extending vertically from the top of the forehead to the angle of the jaw. This remarkable feature is a sexual characteristic, for it is never possessed by the female orangs. So far as I have been able to determine, these facial callosities are purely ornamental, since they are not controlled by voluntary muscles, and are composed merely of tough, white, semi-cartilaginous tissue. In different individuals these callosities vary in width from ten to thirteen and one-half inches.

The skin color of orangs varies according to age, as follows: In infants and all young individuals up to three or four years of age the skin is generally chocolate brown, yellowish on the abdomen and in the palms, while the skin surrounding each eye to the edge of the orbit, and the entire muzzle, or projecting lower portion of the face, is of a more decidedly yellowish or raw-sienna color. Individuals between childhood and middle age vary from dark-yellowish to blackish-brown, the latter color largely predominating. Very often the face and neck is almost or quite black, the palms light-brown and the breast and abdomen mulatto-yellow. In old specimens, especially males of *Simia Wurmbii*, or the "mias chappin" species, the skin is everywhere a deep, shiny-black, except in the palms, where, from constant wear on rough bark, the cuticle lies in several thick, calloused layers, and is of a dirty gray color.

The hair of orangs varies greatly in color, quantity, quality, and distribution, and has no bearing whatever on the question of species. Speaking generally, it may be described as brick-red, or to be exact, of the color known to painters as Indian-red. It may be said, however, that marked differences in color are found almost entirely on adult male specimens. On all others, it varies but little from pure Indian-red; but on old males it often assumes a faded yellow or raw-sienna color on the arms and legs.

It is always longest on the arms, shoulder-blades, and thighs,

FACTS ABOUT THE ORANG-UTAN.

and shortest on the breast, abdomen, and back. The face and throat are quite bare except for a scanty chin-beard of uncertain length in adult specimens, the longest hairs never exceeding four inches. On the flat cheek callosities of *Simia Wurmbii* there is a curious growth of very short and uniformly dispersed hairs not more than one-eighth of an inch in length, which lie so closely upon the skin as to escape notice except upon very close inspection.

On the back of the arms and thighs, and on the sides and shoulder-blades of old male orangs, the hair is long, coarse, straight and thick, sometimes reaching a length of from twelve to fifteen inches.

On most individuals of this class, the entire back will be found almost bare from the neck down, having been worn off in the nest. On younger specimens, the hair on the back is thick, and longer than on the abdomen. The back of the hand and the fingers are thinly covered with short stiff hairs. On the forearm the hair grows upward from the wrist to the elbow, where it meets the downward growth on the arm, and the two come together in a point.

The eyes of adults are always very small, with iris of a dark chestnut-brown, and no white visible. The teeth are invariably very much discolored by vegetable acids and juices, and the base of each tooth is always black.

On most of the *Wurmbii* there seems to be a superabundance of skin on the throat and breast, for it is often found to hang in a great baggy fold. Externally, the orang seems to have no neck at all, the head being set squarely down upon the shoulders. The chest is massive to correspond with the arms and head, but the pelvis is small, and the lower limbs are small, short, and comparatively weak. The orang never sits down as do the gibbons, and therefore has no ischial callosities like the *Hylobates*.

There is no *ligamentum teres* in the orang, and the absence of this permits great freedom of movement in the lower limbs. Indeed, the legs seem to possess almost as much freedom of movement as do the arms. I have often seen my little pet orang hang to a rope, with one arm at an angle of fully seventy degrees and, with the greatest comfort imaginable, reach up with his leg at the same angle and grasp the rope with his foot.

Some naturalists attach importance to the facial resemblances of different orangs. I have never seen living specimens of the Sumatran orang, but so far as Bornean species are concerned, I am certain that each individual differs as widely from his fellows, and has as many facial peculiarities belonging to himself, as can be found in the individuals of any unmixed race of human beings.

Male orangs are much given to fighting, and often bite off each other's fingers and toes. The upper lip, also, is often found in a mutilated condition from the same cause. I have never heard of their biting off each other's ears, as human roughs do occasionally, but a few hundred years more of evolution may bring their intelligence up to that point. Indeed, may we not confidently predict that this is the next step in intellectual development the orang will take, if he is ever to approach nearer to man.

It is the natural instinct of an orang to seize and bring the offending hand of another to its mouth, instead of moving its own heavy head and body to the object. Thus, in every imaginable way do the powerful and capable limbs and hands serve the inert body and head upon all occasions.

The battered condition of one of my male specimens has already been described (Chapter XXXI.)*; another orang, No. 34, male *Wurmbii*, had almost lost the edge of his entire upper lip. It had been bitten diagonally across, but still adhered at the left corner, and the wound had evidently healed very quickly, for that triangular piece of upper lip still hung dangling down two inches from the corner of his mouth. He had also lost an entire finger.

No. 36 had lost a piece out of his upper lip, and one of his left toes had been bitten quite off.

During the fruit season, which is from the middle of January to the first of May, the food of the orang is the durian, mangosteen, and rambutan, which are usually found upon the hills. There are also other fruits which ripen at different times, such as the raso and kapayang, but of the former the orangs eat the shoots only. Besides these, they devour the shoots of the *Pandanus*, and also the leaves of certain trees. During the months of May, June, and July, they retire far into the depths of the forest and are exceedingly difficult to find, but during the season of the heaviest rains, *i.e.*, from August to November, when the forests are quite flooded, they are found in the vicinity of the rivers.

The orang is quite solitary in his habits, the old males always being found alone; nor are two adult females ever found together. On two occasions I found three individuals together, but one was an old female with a nursing infant, and the third was her next oldest offspring, apparently about a year and a half old, who had

---

*Renumbered as Chapter VII in this reprint.

not yet left his mother's side to shift for himself. The female orang has but one young at a birth, and from the instance just cited, I infer that it does not leave its mother until nearly two years of age, by which time it is fairly supplanted by a successor.

The size of the young of the orang at birth is quite remarkable, considering the small stature of the adult female. My twenty-eighth specimen was a gravid female 3 feet 8¾ inches in height, carrying a fœtus which weighed 7 pounds 3 ounces, and was, of course, fully developed.

The nest of the orang-utan has already been described. He usually selects a small tree, a sapling in fact, and builds his nest in its top, even though his weight causes it to sway alarmingly. He always builds his nest low down, often within twenty-five feet of the ground, and seldom higher than forty feet. Sometimes it is fully four feet in diameter, but usually not more than three, and quite flat on the top. There is no weaving together of branches, for they are merely piled cross-wise as a natural consequence of their being broken off on different sides of the nest. In short, the orang builds a nest precisely as a man would build one for himself were he obliged to pass a night in a tree-top with neither axe nor knife to cut branches. I have seen in the forest one or two such nests of men where the builder had only his bare hands to work with, and they were just as rudely constructed, of just such materials, and in about the same general position, as the average orang nest.

During one day's travel along the upper Simujan River we counted thirty-six old nests and six which we set down as new or fresh. I have never been able to ascertain to a certainty, but it is my opinion that an orang, after building a nest, sleeps in it several nights in succession, unless he is called upon to leave its neighborhood altogether. Certain it is that whenever a hunter finds a perfectly fresh nest he may with confidence expect to find the builder somewhere near it. An orang never uses a nest after the leaves become withered and dry, no doubt for the reason that the bare branches afford an uncomfortable resting-place. I never saw nor heard of any house-building by orang-utans, though I am led to believe that some individuals may have a habit of covering their bodies with branches for protection against the dashing of the rain-drops during a heavy storm. My little pet orang would invariably cover his head and body with straw or loose clothing the moment it began to rain, even though he was under a roof.

Even under the most favorable circumstances, orangs are neither graceful nor active in their movements. I think we may justly consider them the most helpless of all the quadrumana. Owing to the great weight of their bodies, and the peculiar structure of their hands, they cannot run nimbly, and never dare to spring from one tree to the next. The smaller monkeys gallop madly along the larger branches, with outspread arms, legs, and tail, leap recklessly from the tree-top, go flying through the air for several yards, and fall sprawling and unhurt upon the side or in the leafy top of the next tree. Not so the orang-utan, with his huge, flabby stomach, fleshy thighs, and massive head. His weight, of one hundred and twenty to one hundred and sixty pounds, compels him to move slowly and circumspectly so that he may not find himself falling heavily to the ground. Owing to the disproportionate shortness of his legs, his progress depends mostly upon his long, sinewy arms, and very often he goes swinging through a tree-top by their aid alone. I have frequently seen them swing along beneath the large limbs as a gymnast swings along a tight rope, reaching six feet at a stretch. When passing from one tree to another, he reaches out and gathers in his grasp a number of small branches that he feels sure will sustain his weight then swings himself across.

Upon the ground the orang is a picture of abject helplessness. In his native forests he is very seldom known to descend to the earth, and so far as my experience goes, I have never seen nor heard of a single instance of the kind. True, he climbs down when thirsty until he can reach the water with his hands, but this occurs where there is no dry land to walk upon.

The orang-utan is utterly incapable of standing fully erect without touching the ground with its hands. I have seen many orangs in captivity, but not one of them ever stood erect upon its hind legs for a single instant, and for orangs to be so represented in drawings or museums is contrary to nature.

There has been considerable discussion in regard to the maximum size attained by the orang-utan, and its general measurements. Mr. A. R. Wallace, in his work on the "Malay Archipelago," pp. 72 *et seq.*, makes the following statements:

"I have myself examined the bodies of seventeen freshly-killed orangs. Of this extensive series, sixteen were fully adult, nine being males and seven females. The adult males of the large orangs only varied from 4 feet 1 inch to 4 feet 2 inches in height, measured fairly to the heel, so as to give the height of the animal if it stood perfectly erect; the extent of the outstretched arms from 7 feet 2 inches to 7 feet 8 inches; and the width of the face from 10 inches to 13½ inches. The dimensions of other naturalists closely agree with mine. The largest orang measured by Temminck was four feet high. Of twenty-five specimens collected by Schlegel and Müller, the largest old male was 4 feet 1 inch, and the largest skeleton in the Calcutta Museum was, according to Blyth, 4 feet 1½ inch; and no specimen has yet reached Europe exceeding these dimensions, although the total number must amount to over a hundred. On the whole, therefore," concludes Mr. Wallace, "I think it will be allowed that up to this time we have not the least reliable evidence of the existence of orangs in Borneo more than 4 feet 2 inches high."

The total number of specimens of the orang-utan of both species, killed by me and my hunters, was forty-three, every one of which I carefully measured while fresh, recording each measurement the moment it was made. I saved the skin of every one of these specimens, and the skeletons of all save three or four of the very youngest ones.

No fewer than seven of my specimens exceeded the maximum height for orangs as given by Mr. Wallace, viz., 4 feet 2 inches, even by the most liberal measurement. My tallest *Simia Wurmbii*, or "mias chappin," measured 4 feet 6 inches from head to heel, and the next in size 4 feet 5½ inches. Then a *satyrus*, or "mias rombi," measured 4 feet 4½ inches, two other *Wurmbii*, 4 feet 4 inches, and 4 feet 3 inches respectively, a *satyrus*, 4 feet 3 inches, and a *Wurmbii*, 4 feet 2½ inches. Only one specimen measured exactly 4 feet 2 inches, and the remaining nine fell below that height. One male specimen, with hair which grew to a length of 12 to 15 inches, in some places, measured only 3 feet 10¼ inches in height. The largest female measured 4 feet, and the smallest adult female 3 feet 6 inches.

These measurements were a great surprise to me, and, feeling that their accuracy might some time be questioned, I made and recorded them with unusual care and exactness. To obtain the height it was my practice to lay the animal upon its back with the legs held straight by an assistant, then holding the blade of a large knife flat against the top of the head, it was thrust perpendicularly into the table or the earth. Then, while an assistant held the top of the head against the first knife-blade, I pressed another blade firmly against the bottom of the heel and thrust it into the earth also. After moving the animal aside a tape line stretched between the inner surfaces of the knife-blades gave the height of the animal. Not a single figure was ever trusted to my memory alone, and my largest orangs were each measured and recorded twice.

From the subjoined table of measurements it will be seen that orangs vary in their proportions in precisely the same way as human beings. Some are short and thick-set; and others are more slenderly built and longer limbed. Specimens Nos. 6 and 9 have short legs and bodies but unusually long arms, while Nos. 43 and 38 are just the reverse. It will also be noticed that the breadth of the facial callosities of *Wurmbii* bears no relation whatever to the size of the animal. The tallest specimen of the whole series, No. 18, measured only 11¼ inches across the face, while No. 25, which stood three inches shorter, and was much smaller every way, measured 13½ inches at the same point.

Measurements of Orang-Utans, Adult Males and Females.

(Given in inches.)

	No. 18. S. Wurmbii, ♂	No. 13. S. Wurmbii. ♂	No. 9. S. satyrus. ♂	No. 43. S. Wurmbii. ♂	No. 25. S. Wurmbii. ♂	No. 38. S. satyrus, ♂	No. 8. S. Wurmbii. ♂	No. 21. S. Wurmbii. ♂	No. 26. S. Wurmbii. ♂	No. 34. S. Wurmbii, ♂	No. 6. ♀	No. 35. ♀	No. 37. ♀	No. 28. ♀
Height, from head to heel..	54	53½	52½	52	51	51	50½	50	49½	48¾	48	45½	42	44¾
Extent of outstretched arms	95½	94¾	96	88½	90	88	88¼	86	84¾	88	87¾	79	74½	74½
Length of arm and hand from armpit............	41	39½	40	38	37	36	37	35¼	35	36	33	34¾	31¾	32
Length of hand...........	11½	10½	11½	10½	10	10½	10	9¾	10½	10½	10½	9¾	9	9
" of foot...........	13½	12½	13½	12¼	12½	12½	12		12¾	12½		11½	10½	10½
Breadth of hand,..........	3¾	3¾	3½	3¼		3¼			3	3½		2¾	2¾	2½
" of foot....	3¾	3½	3½	3		3¼			2¾	3		2¾	2½	2½
Circumference of head (perpendicular).....	30¾	31¼	26¼	29½	28½	26½	27	25¼	26¼	27¼	24¼	22¾	22¾	22⅞
Breadth of face	11¼	13		12	13½		12½	13½	7	9	5½		6	5½
Circumference of neck......	26¼	27¾		25½	27½	21¼			23	22¼	21	17	16	16¾
" of chest......	42	41½	32	40¼	39½	36½	31¼	37¼	38¼	36¾	32	31¾	28½	28¼
" of loin... ..		30½		28½	26¾	25¼			26	25¾	26		21	22
" of arm.......	12½	12½		11¼	11			11¼	10¼	10½				
" of forearm...	13½	14		12¼	12¼				11½					
" of wrist......	9			8¼					7¾					
" of thigh....	18	19		17	15				13½	15¼				
" of calf......	11¾	11½							9¾					
			Sick with fever.								With young.	With young.	With young.	With fœtus.

Of the orang-utan there are two clearly defined species, and only two, viz., *Simia Wurmbii* and *S. satyrus*. While the points of difference between the males of the two species are strongly marked and unmistakable, both externally and anatomically, the females are all very much alike in their external appearance, but readily distinguishable by their skulls.

Male specimens of *Wurmbii* are distinguished by their remarkable cheek callosities, already described, *which are observed in young as well as old individuals*, and also by the joining of the two temporal ridges on the top of the skull to form an elevated sagittal crest, of varying height. In females and young males the temporal ridges subside to the level of the skull either at or before meeting in front of the parietal suture, and are continued backward in a rough line, almost to the lambdoidal crest.

In the skull of the male *satyrus* the temporal ridges pass backward and slightly converge, but still remain widely separated until they diverge again at the back of the skull and rise to form the lambdoidal crest. The skull of the female shows no continuous elevated ridges, but a rough line instead, which scarcely rises above the level of the skull. No female skull in the collection made by me possesses either the two continuous temporal ridges or the elevated sagittal crest, but the rough lines correspond to the elevated ridges of the males of their respective species in every case, and leave their identity unmistakeable.

Orangs are liable to possess individual peculiarities to a greater extent than perhaps any other of the apes or monkeys. To illustrate: No. 26, *Simia Wurmbii*, with a very prominent cranial ridge, was utterly destitute of facial callosities or any signs of them, and until dissection, was supposed to be a *satyrus*. No. 13 had a nail on the hallux of its hinder hands. No. 21 had four molars in each side of its lower jaw, while the other forty-two orangs had only three each. The distance between the temporal ridges of *satyrus*, and the elevation of the sagittal crest of *Wurmbii*, varies greatly in different specimens.

We will not say anything about the place the orang has in the long chain of evolution; but, while abstract argument leads hither and thither, according as this or that writer is most ably gifted for the same, there is still one argument or influence to which every true naturalist is amenable, and which no one will ignore who has studied, from nature, any group of typical forms. Let such an one (if, indeed, one exists to-day) who is prejudiced against the Darwinian views, go to Borneo. Let him there watch from day to day this strangely human form in all its various phases of existence. Let him see the orang climb, walk, build its nest, eat, drink, and fight like a human rough. Let him see the female suckle her young and carry it astride her hip precisely as do the coolie women of Hindostan. Let him witness their human-like emotions of affection, satisfaction, pain, and rage,—let him see all this, and then he may feel how much more potent has been this lesson than all he has read in pages of abstract ratiocination.

CHAPTER XI.

A MONTH WITH THE DYAKS.

Journey to the Sibuyau.—The River.—A Malodorous Village.—Barriers.—Proboscis Monkeys and Flying Lemurs.—Head of Canoe Navigation.—Swamp-wading.—Our Journey's End.—A Lodge in a Vast Wilderness.—Fine Hunting-grounds.—Source of the River.—Hunting Gibbons.—Lively Sport.—Gibbons' Remarkable Mode of Progress.—A Mias.—A Successful Hunt.—Affection and Courage of a Male Gibbon.—Helplessness of the Baby Orang in Water.—A Live Tarsier.—More Gibbons Shot.—Argus Pheasants.—Dyak Mode of Snaring.—A Deadly Pig-trap.—A Shiftless Village.—A Magnificent Bird.—Curious Rodent.—Visit to Lanchang.—A Village of Head-hunters.—Trophies of the Chase.—A Fine Dyak Specimen.

It was only a bunch of argus pheasant feathers that lured me from Sadong to the Sibuyau, to stay a month with the Dyaks, for better or worse. The promise of wah-wahs, also, had something to do with it, I suppose, even though they are hard to shoot. The Dyaks said their settlement had never been visited by a white man, and in spite of all I could learn from them, the nature of the country remained a profound mystery. But then, the greatest charm of travel is going to places one knows nothing at all about, and satisfying one's geographical curiosity.

Behold us, then, starting down the Sadong with the turning of the tide, early on the morning of October 28th. At home the trees have taken on their gayest autumn tints, but here the forest is still clad in the same persistent, never-changing, monotonous green it has always worn.

Under the kadjang roof of the old Malay headman's large boat, there sit the "orang putei" (white man), "orang China" (Chinaman), and the "orang utan" or jungle man, my little pet, while three stout Malays furnish the motive-power. Perara and Dobah are coming after us in my own boat. It is a delightful day, quiet, clear, and warm, such as fills a man with a sense of keen enjoyment, provided his digestion is good and his conscience clear. My little baby mias seems to enjoy his surroundings as well as the rest of us, for, with true childish instinct, he leans lazily over the edge of the boat and dabbles in the water with his hairy brown hands as it sweeps past the side.

On reaching the sea, we put up our much-mended sail and steered eastward along the coast for a few miles, until, when almost within the mouth of the Batang Lupar, we came about sharply and ran into the mouth of the Sibuyau. A conical mountain rises on the east bank, at the foot of which is a small Malay kampong, and the house of Seriff Hassan, the Port-clearance clerk. We stopped long enough to deliver our papers and hastened on up stream with the flowing tide, to get as far as possible by night-fall.

The Sibuyau is a small stream, not over a hundred yards in width at the mouth, and for a long distance up the banks are prettily fringed with nipa palms. There are a few paddy fields along the banks and the usual accompaniment of flimsy little temporary huts on stilts, reminding one of birds' nests.

About sunset we reached a Dyak village of eight doors standing close to the bank, at which we stopped for the night. It was a miserably dirty and foul-smelling place, or at least the ground underneath the house was giving off an odor like an ancient pig-sty. The Dyaks were almost as dirty as their surroundings, but they were civil, and immediately produced, for us to sit upon, two of the finest mats I ever saw of Dyak manufacture. I tried to buy the smaller one of the two, but they positively refused to sell it. Perhaps their mat-maker was dead.

We had a long confab about the prospect of getting up to the settlement at the head of the river, and were told that the way was long and difficult; that our large boat was too large to go at all; that they had no boats which could take us; and, furthermore, that they would not go with us under any circumstances. Being unable to see my way out of the difficulty which had suddenly presented itself, I slung my hammock and mosquitero and went to sleep.

In the morning three of the Dyaks agreed to go with me, for a consideration, to help with the large boat; but, when the time came to start, they and two others put their weapons and dogs—I mean dog skeletons—and cooking pots into one of their own canoes, got into it, and paddled off down stream. With a devout wish, expressed in four languages, that they might "go to the devil," we determined to paddle our own canoe, and immediately set off. I changed places with Dobah, thus leaving the four Malays and Ah Kee to manage the large boat.

After a few miles, we passed the limit of the nipa palm, and then the screw pine took its place. As the stream became more narrow the fringe on either side became wider and almost impenetrable in density. About noon, we came to where the channel was blocked by thousands of *Pandanus* stems, which had drifted together and formed a wide barrier like a "jam" of pine logs. The top of the drift was covered with rank grass, which bound the whole mass together—sometimes strongly enough to walk upon.

During the course of the afternoon we passed eight or ten such barriers; and each one cost a struggle. There was always a passage cut large enough to accommodate small sampans; but our large boat was heavily laden, and the passage had to be indefinitely enlarged. We were all of two hours in getting her through one drift, which was finally accomplished by cutting a wider passage and then hauling on her from the small boat made fast a few yards in advance, while others lifted on her at the same time. No wonder the Dyaks were chary of trusting their muscles in our keeping for that day.

During the afternoon we saw several troops of proboscis monkeys. They were not so shy as on the Simujan, but sat unconcernedly in the trees, watching us as we went by. As night approached we tied up to the bushes at the edge of a fine bit of open water, fourteen feet deep, and shifted our baggage so that we could lie down. After a most refreshing bath in which all participated, we ate our rice and turned in. Ah Kee and the little mias had a long and violent dispute as to whether they should sleep together, of which question the mias took the affirmative side and finally carried the day.

The large boat leaked badly, and, but for Ah Kee, I think we should have filled and gone down before morning. Being unable to swim he felt a lively interest in keeping the craft afloat, and baled her out five times during the night.

As we proceeded, the next morning, we entered a perfect labyrinth of screw pines, but fortunately there were no more bad drifts and we wound our way along very agreeably. During the forenoon we came upon a troop of proboscis monkeys which contained about thirty-five individuals—the greatest number of that species I ever saw together. I could not resist the temptation to "collect" one of the handsomest specimens of the lot, and the shot started two flying lemurs (*Galeopithecus variegatus*) just out of range. They spread their parachutes to their widest extent, launched boldly out of a tree-top, sailed slowly through the air at an angle of about forty-five degrees, and alighted low down on the trunk of a tree about forty feet distant from the one they had quitted. Climbing nimbly up to the top of that tree, they sailed off again, and so on until they were out of sight.

In the afternoon the growth of screw pines ceased abruptly, and we entered a narrower and more tortuous channel which wound in and out among trees and bushes, just wide enough for our boats, but with nothing to spare. After four or five miles of this, the identity of the river was completely lost; but we followed the channel persistently, and at last found ourselves in a little canal not more than eight feet wide, that came down through the forest as though cut by the hand of man. On either side were solid banks and the trunks of great forest trees beautifully decorated with ferns, orchids and dark-green moss, while the bare stems of creepers, both great and small, hung in many a curve and twist from the branches which met far above our heads. I would like to rave a little over that scenery, and would, but for a constitutional objection to emotional descriptions.

At length our little canal led out of the forest and into an open grassy swamp of considerable width, at the edge of which we arrived at the head of navigation, and a getting-out place for everybody.

There was no house nor village anywhere in sight, but one of our Malays said we could reach one by night-fall, so four of us bundled up our beds, a cooking pot and food for one meal, and set out. Our first half-mile lay across a swamp, through mud and water from one to two feet deep, from which we landed on a bit of dry ground and crossed over to another stretch of morass, worse than the first. The water was from two to five feet deep, but on the top lay a carpet of matted grass which kept us from sinking down out of sight. Once I had the luck to break through and sink down to my waist before the others could fish me out. After a mile of dreadful floundering we came to some fields of growing paddy and emerged upon terra firma once more. We followed a path through a bit of fine, dry open forest, crossed a beautifully clear running brook, our canal again, or rather the Sibuyau River—and two hundred yards further on, came to a small clearing in the middle of which (welcome sight) stood a Dyak village, or long-house of five doors.

We climbed the notched sapling which served as a ladder at the end of the house, and received the customary Dyak greeting of cheery smiles and pleasant words of welcome, while one of the girls skurried off to fetch the clean mats. We were not sorry to have reached our journey's end, and Ah Kee, never too tired to get up the best meal the larder afforded, set to work, without a moment's delay or waiting to be told, and soon had ready a fine cup of tea with buttered toast accompaniment, and a plate of rice adorned with butter and sugar. Ah Kee was the prince of good servants, and I would that every traveller who knows how to treat a servant could have one like him. He was marked with small-pox and was not what an esthete would call handsome, far from it, but in the jungle, his cheerful and efficient service condoned every physical defect.

The next morning the Dyaks turned out in force and carried up our luggage, of which there were seventeen loads, at thirteen cents per load. We took the three kadjangs which formed our boat-roof and with them made a very cosy room, about twelve feet square, at one end of the long hall.

We bought of the Dyaks enough mats to cover the floor, arranged our boxes to the best advantage to serve as furniture, and, with a very handy fireplace constructed by Ah Kee, we were comfortably fixed. One side of the room was entirely open and looked out on the jungle. As soon as we had got fairly settled, all the people of the house came in to pay us a visit. The floor of my room was quite filled with half-naked men, women, and children sitting upon their hams and enjoying the novelty of calling upon a "tuan." The men were fine, healthy-looking fellows, the women were mostly rather ill-favored in personal appearance; and the children were, without exception, very dirty, but all were good-natured and polite. One little girl had ichthyosis and was exceedingly repulsive, but, happily, she did not belong to our village, and I soon saw the last of her.

Keeping Dobah with me, I paid the other Malays and sent them back to Simujan with the large boat, to return for me at the end of a month. Being comfortably settled in a house which was really very clean and habitable, we immediately began to collect. I set Perara at work shooting and skinning birds, while I devoted my attention to mammals in particular, and everything else in general. I encouraged the Dyaks of the settlement—there were two other villages not far away—to set snares for animals of all kinds, and, being at that season without money and very nearly without rice, they bestirred themselves to earn a little money. The people of our village agreed to furnish me with from two to three guides every day for a cash consideration, and they never disappointed me.

There was a fine young man in our house who was not only willing but anxious to accompany me in my hunting trips, and we fraternized at once. With him for a guide and Dobah to carry game, I set out in the afternoon to look over the ground.

On one side of our clearing lay a vast and almost impenetrable tract of swamp-forest, choked with a dense, thorny undergrowth growing in the water. On the other side, however, there rose a succession of hills, neither too high nor too steep for comfort, covered with fine high forest, while what little undergrowth there was was not of the thorny kind. There were many charming little glens and rocky ravines with small streams of clear, cold water dashing down to where three of them came together and formed the source of the Sibuyau River. It gives one a strange sensation to stand at the very source of a river, where it is a feeble brook which one crosses at a single stride. It is a satisfaction to know all about one river, at least, even though it be a small one, from its mouth, where it loses itself in the sea, up to the very springs in the hills from whence the first cupful of water starts down.

I was rejoiced at my good fortune in being led—by blind instinct, I may say—to such a delightful wilderness. It was the finest hunting-ground I saw anywhere in Sarawak. I was sure that such high ground and fine open forest must be frequented by correspondingly fine mammals and birds in great numbers, for it seemed to me just the spot an animal would choose for a home—I would have been content to end my days there, had I been a monkey—and the Dyaks assured me my surmise was correct.

In order to place before the reader a pen picture of our daily life in the jungle with the Dyaks, what we did, saw, and thought, I venture to transcribe a portion of my much despised but faithfully kept journal.

"*November* 1st.—That fine young Dyak accompanies me regularly now as a guide, and with him and my faithful little Malay man, Dobah, I went out hunting for orang-utans and *Hylobates*. We hunted far and wide over the hills, saw a great number of mias nests, but no mias. But we at last became absorbed in trying to kill a gibbon, and it soon developed into genuine sport, about the

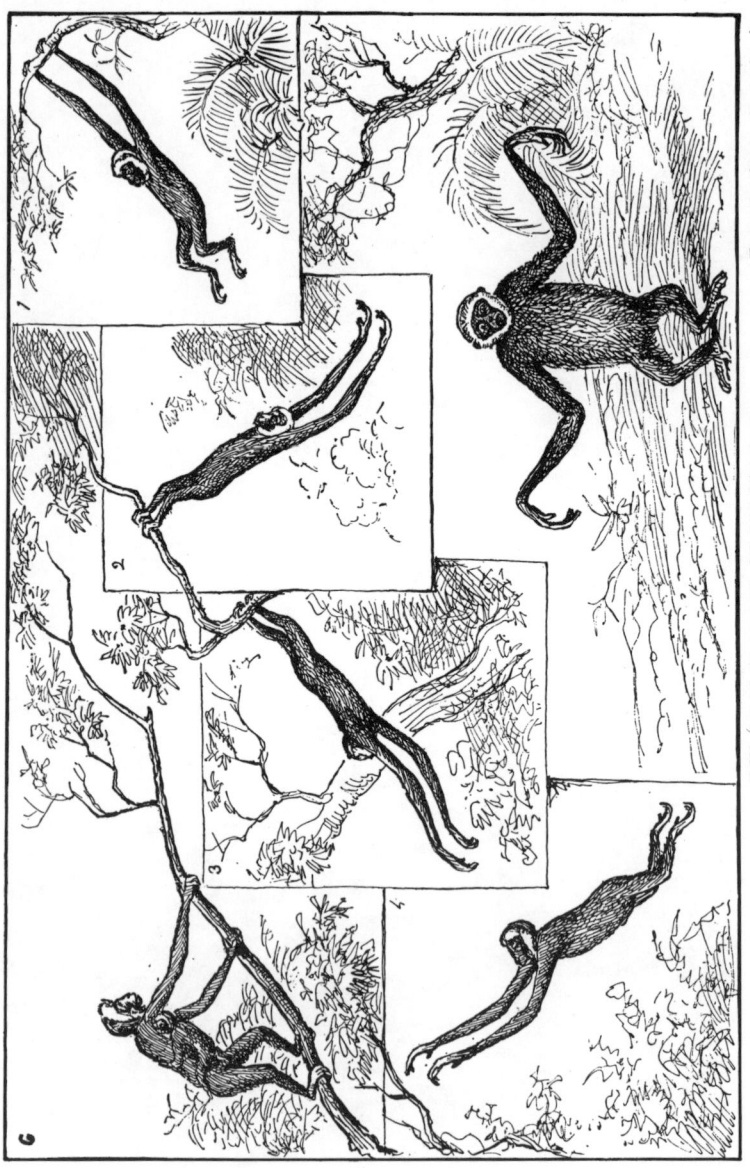

THE GIBBON'S MODES OF PROGRESSION. *(From sketches by the Author.)*
1–4. Swinging through the tree-tops.—5. Walking on level ground.—6. Climbing through the tree-tops.

only real 'sport' I have yet had in Borneo, and this is about the character of it.

"You are going along, we will say, at the heels of your Dyak guide, carrying your rifle in the hope of a shot at big game, while the guide carries your double-barrelled gun. All at once you hear a slight vocal sound and a profound rustling in the thick branches at the top of a tall tree, directly over your head.

"'Apa ini?' (What's that?), you ask in a whisper.

"'Wah-wah, tuan!' (gibbons, sir!), says the guide in the same tone.

"You take the double-barrel, loaded with No. 1 shot, and peer anxiously upward to catch sight of the animal. Ah! there he is, on the other side of the tree, and evidently making off. You cannot see his body on account of the leaves, so you steal quickly round and get directly under him to give him a surprise with a charge of shot. But by the time you get around he is apparently no longer there, for you hear a rustling in a tree-top forty yards away, and at last catch a glimpse of his lank, gray body as he swings himself out of sight, without leaving you a second for a shot. Perhaps, though, you blaze away at him, right and left, feel pretty sure you must have stopped him, and watch anxiously while you hurriedly push in fresh cartridges.

"Ha! not dead yet, for there he goes as lively as ever, this time sixty yards away. You see him quite plainly this time, and note with astonishment how rapidly he progresses by swinging himself end over end, holding by his hands while he gives his body a long swing toward another branch. His body becomes horizontal, he grasps the branch with his feet, and, letting go with his hands, swings, head downward and backward, until he comes right side again, lets go with his feet and goes flying through the air to the next branch. He grasps that with his hands, swings the other end of himself forward again, and so on. You see that by this revolutionary method he goes just as well as if he had a head on each end of his body, and that he gets along with astonishing rapidity and directness.

"This will never do. He is about to get away from you, on fair ground. You take your direction, stoop forward, and dart hurriedly along in the direction the gibbon has taken.

"You run a hundred yards at your best speed, and stop, expecting to find him directly over your head. Ha! the branches shake. There he is, fully fifty yards away! Then you get mad, drop your hat, grip your gun firmly, draw your head well down between your shoulders, and, with one eye to the front, go tearing through the underbrush like a wild bull, down the hill at full speed and at the imminent risk of breaking your neck. You dart nimbly through every little opening, and choose a practicable route with surprising quickness of eye, as a monkey does when running through tree-tops.

"After a hundred and fifty yards, good measure, you stop short, cock your gun, and glare wildly upward to catch sight of your prey as quickly as possible. In three seconds your greedy eyes have scanned every tree-top within gun-shot, and at last you see some branches shaking, a hundred yards away, on the opposite side of a deep ravine! No use! he has beaten you in a fair race, and goes on swinging gayly from tree to tree, leaving you to sit down panting like a steam-tug, bathed in perspiration, wishing for a drink of water, and puzzled to know whether you ought to laugh or get mad.

"Then you proceed to comfort yourself by calling to mind the fact that the trees are very tall, and it is almost impossible to see a gibbon on account of his gray body harmonizing so well in color with the leaves on which the sun shines; that his hair is fine and close, and his body and limbs so lean that to shoot at one is almost like shooting at a skeleton; that they never stop running until three or four legs are broken; and finally, that they fly a great deal faster than you ever had an idea they could anyway. But, all the same, you pronounce it genuine sport and acknowledge that you have met your match. And so you draw off to the nearest stream, throw yourself upon the sand, drink about two quarts of clear, cold water, and proceed to repair damages generally.

"So far, I have had five just such experiences as the above with wah-wahs, though the most notable occurred to-day. I had two such chases, felt sure of killing at least one, had three snap shots, and not a single gibbon did I get. They are valuable animals, a skin being worth at least $20, to say nothing of the rarity of good ones, and one specimen represents a good day's work—when taken! To hunt them is the most exciting work I have done for some time, violent exercise to be sure, but good to improve one's wind. The troop we started this morning had at least ten individuals in it, the most of them full grown and large.

"In the afternoon shot a goat sucker and four black monkeys (*Semnopithecus femoralis*); saw nothing else except one small gibbon, which I chased, of course,—for practice!

"Rain at night. Thermometer, 80 degrees F. at 8 P.M.

"*November 2d.*—The name of my young Dyak guide is Le Tiac. He is just about my height, build, and age, a stout young fellow, and the only difference between us is that he is a Dyak and I am an Anglo-Saxon—which makes all the difference in the world.

"We went out in the morning, far and high on the hills, and saw, at first, only some big rhinoceros horn-bills (*Buceros rhinoceros*), at which we got no shot. Too many trees for us to see through before they took flight. Heard a troop of wah-wahs crying, stalked up to them with the greatest skill—and did not see even one. Disgusting! Little Dobah was taken with an attack of chills and fever on the way home.

"When we reached the clearing at noon we noticed how hot it was out in the open, whereas in the jungle it was pleasantly cool, damp, and intensely shady. Had we been hunting in the sunshine all the morning, we would have been done up long before the time we returned. The forest is so shady one does not even think of the sun; but in the house we felt the heat. Then we took our deliciously cold bath in the stream near the house, changed clothes, and after a modest breakfast lay down with "Chesterfield's Letters" for a rest. At such times I always lie on the floor near the Old Man, and he takes great delight in teasing me in various ways. He pulls my hair, butts me with his head, sits on my stomach, climbs all over me and wrestles with my bare feet, all in the drollest and most comical way, as only a mias can.

"At 3 P.M. we went out again, without Dobah, and, in about an hour, we saw a mias rombi swinging across a deep ravine. I fired two shots and killed it directly. It fell what seemed a great distance, to the bottom of the ravine, and landed in a very picturesque spot, just beside a clear gurgling stream, that came tumbling down the rocky gorge. This mias, No. 39, female, is not a large one. Le Tiac peeled some strips of bark from a sapling, tied its elbows together behind its back, fixed a broad smooth head-strap, and prepared to carry the animal alone. I proposed to sling it over a pole and help him get away with it, but he preferred to carry it alone; so he backed it and carried it, unassisted, up the steep side of that deep ravine to the top without resting, then down the long ridge and so on home. I can kill ten mias easier than one wah-wah.

"Thermometer: morning, 80 degrees F.; noon, 90; night, 82.

"*November 3d.*—A good score to-day. Just after I had finished measuring the mias killed yesterday, and was preparing to set out for the usual morning's hunt, a troop of gibbons began whistling—their cry sounds like whistling, and is easily imitated—in the jungle close by, in fact within a hundred yards of the house. Le Tiac and I were after them in less than a minute. It so happened that several paths had been cut through the jungle just where the gibbons were, and, by their help, we were soon close to our prey. We saw one or two of them swinging off in the distance, and at last I caught sight of a fine large one, feeding quietly on leaves, within gun-shot. I fired both barrels to make sure of a kill, and, in a minute or so, as I was walking under the tree to see where my wah-wah was, down it came with a heavy "thud" within two feet of me. A little more and it would have fallen on my head.

"To my surprise it was immediately followed by another, a young one this time, which fell flat on its face on the soft earth a yard further off. We picked it up and found it was very much alive, having only a wound in the neck, and Le Tiac held it while I reloaded and looked for others. The little one set up a terrible cry and kept it up steadily, which created a great commotion amongst the other wah-wahs. They were all running away, but on hearing the cries of the little one, two came back and came as near as they dared, but kept so well concealed that I could not get a shot. Then we carried the little one about and let it cry while we ourselves kept very still. It was, perhaps, a mean thing to do; but in collecting, necessity knows no law, every wild animal must die some time, and gibbons are too valuable and hard to get for us to let one go through sympathy. Under all other circumstances these animals are exceedingly timid, and flee at the slightest alarm, but this time two of them returned in response to the cries of one of their children in distress. It was a mean thing to do, I know, but when, at last, I got a fair shot at a large wah-wah, of the rescuing party, I disabled him so that he could not get away. He climbed to the topmost branches of the tree he was in, which was about ninety feet high, and I fired at him from below. I was surprised at the shooting it took to collect him.

"Altogether I fired seven shots with my No. 10 gun, loaded with four drachms of powder and two ounces of No. 1 shot, before he fell, and, to my still greater surprise, I found on examining the body only one bone broken—a tibia. I expected to find the leg and arm-bones mostly smashed to bits. The specimen was a large male, and met its death solely on account of its paternal affection, sympathy, and genuine courage in the face of danger. It measured as follows: length of head and body, 1 foot 7 inches; entire reach of arms and legs, 5 feet 1 inch; extent of outstretched arms, 5 feet 1 inch; hand, $6\frac{1}{2}$ x 1 inches; foot, 6 x $1\frac{1}{4}$ inches; weight, $10\frac{1}{4}$ pounds.

"The young specimen was about one-third grown, but its brain being affected and its spine injured by the shock, I killed it immediately for conscience's sake. Late in the evening, when I went down to the creek to bathe, I took the little mias along to see if he could swim. I gave him a perfectly fair chance, for instead of pitching him plump into the water as we do dogs and puppies I waded with him in my arms out to where the water was waist deep, and then poising him on the surface let him go, much against his will. Did he swim? Hardly. He turned heels up in an instant and his old head went down as if it had been filled with lead instead of brains. Instead of striking out vigorously with his arms and legs as other animals do, those useful members simply stuck straight out from his body like four sticks and moved slowly and feebly, first one way and then another, as the old fellow sank to the bottom. I waited a moment to see if he would, in any measure, recover himself, or come to the surface, but he only turned horizontally in the water and remained a foot below the surface, stiff and helpless. I waited until it would have been cruelty to have left him longer, and then, like Pharaoh's daughter, I drew him out. He did not whine or scream, but you should have seen his face. Its expression of injured innocence and disgust at the whole business spoke as plainly as words. But he was soon all right and after wiping him dry I put him down upon the pebbly bank while I went in for my bath. The little rascal began slowly climbing up the bushes, in a listless, indifferent manner, to throw me off my guard. By and by I went out to make him come down, but he was already beyond my reach, and instead of obeying me he gazed down upon me with a superior, patronizing air, and went on climbing higher. Very soon he was twenty feet up, with jungle all around him, and he had evidently made up his mind to go from our gaze like a beautiful dream. It was just sunset, and if not caught within ten minutes he would be a total loss. I shouted for help and the Dyaks came running down with axes and parongs to chop down trees if necessary. But one of the men espied a slanting tree-trunk, and, by its aid, he climbed nimbly and silently into the top of the tree containing the mias while we below kept the little rascal's attention directed to ourselves. He was not aware of this adroit flank movement until he looked up and saw the naked Dyak reaching down from above to grab him. The little fellow was thoroughly terrified by the monstrous apparition, and scrambled down in wild haste, until he landed in my arms, and clung to me for protection. The Dyaks enjoyed a hearty laugh at his expense.

"*November 4th.*—Had a long, tiresome tramp in the forenoon, over the hills and through the hollows, but saw not a thing worth shooting. Myriads of leeches, however. A Dyak brought me a female argus pheasant in poor plumage. Skeletonized it and ate the flesh for dinner. It was palatable, but neither good nor bad. It had no particular flavor, but was tender, and therefore acceptable.

"Another Dyak brought a flying dragon (*Draco volans*), and a beautiful little tarsier (*Tarsius spectrum*), alive and unhurt. Although it is a monkey, it jumps like a kangaroo, which it is enabled to do by means of its very long hind legs. The peculiar structure of its cervical vertebræ permits great freedom of movement with the head, which it easily turns in a complete circle, starting with the face turned directly backward. It is a very erratic little creature and bit me as severely as it was able when I took it out of its cage. Wishing to make a drawing of it, I placed it on a pole held almost perpendicular, where it hung for half an hour with its face toward me as still as though conscious of the fact that I was taking its picture. The structure of its hands is very peculiar. Each long slender finger terminates in a flat round disk which acts like the sucker of an octopus, and enables the little animal to hold on to a limb by the side pressure of its hands and without grasping, as all the other monkeys do. The eyes are very large, and of a clear liquid brown color, proclaiming the nocturnal habits of the animal.

"Dobah still has fever, Perara is complaining, and would like to have it also in order to escape work. Ah Kee is a jewel, cheerful and companionable. He has just made me a very creditable sleeping suit, pajamas and baju.

"*November 5th.*—Three argus pheasants and a jungle cock were brought in, all of which I bought and prepared. Having become somewhat acquainted with the inmates of our house, I have commenced to lecture the women on the desirability of bringing their children in contact with clean water at least once a month. They received my lecture as a fine bit of humor on my part, but I think they were ashamed nevertheless.

"*November 6th.*—Early in the morning we heard another troop

THE TARSIER.—(TARSIUS SPECTRUM.)

(From a sketch by the author.)

of gibbons whistling in the jungle close by, and in twenty minutes we were under them. Shot a fine old couple, male and female, and a young one belonging to the latter. Allowed two other small ones to get away on account of their tender age.

"*November* 7*th.*—Out hunting all the forenoon. Came upon a troop of gibbons, had a fair chance at an old female and let her get away through sheer stupidity; didn't fire when I had a chance, hoping to get a better one. Saw a number of traps set by the Dyaks to catch argus pheasants and small quadrupeds. In this instance a low hedge of green boughs had been built from one ravine to another across a ridge in the most inviting part of the forest. The hedge is a careless affair, about two feet high, but withal so cunningly made that I actually walked into one of the traps without seeing it! At every rod or so a clean gap is left just wide enough for a bird or small mammal to walk through without suspicion, and while in mid-passage he will suddenly be yanked heavenward by a 'twitch-up,' as we boys used to call it.

"The Dyaks make this very effective little engine of destruction by bending down a stout bush close by the gap in the hedge, previously trimming off all the branches, tying a thin strip of soft bark to the end of the bush and making a noose at the other end of the thong. Then a little platform about a foot square is made with small palm-stems, a trigger is set underneath it to hold down the noose and hold up the platform, then the noose is placed upon the latter and opened as wide as the platform will allow.

"When the bird, or small beast steps upon the platform it instantly falls, the thong is freed, the bush springs up, and the noose is jerked tight around the leg of the victim. Of course the bird is jerked high in the air, sometimes dislocating the leg, and is bound to hang there until the traps are visited. The Dyak twitch-up is very effective, but the objections to it are that it punishes the victim cruelly before it dies or is found and killed, and also that the noose, in most cases, chafes off the feathers of the thigh and sometimes even the hair and skin from the legs of mammals. In that particular hedge I counted eleven traps, all very neatly constructed. We also saw a machine called a peti, to kill wild pigs, which made me shudder. Three stout, little, two-inch saplings had been selected which grew close beside a jungle path in such a position that when cut off seven feet above ground and tied together at the top they formed a perfect tripod, leaning over the path. A fourth sapling was cut, about five feet of the stem taken, and one end firmly lashed in with the other three at the upper end of the tripod. Into the free end of the fourth sapling, which was about two feet above the ground, was firmly fixed a piece of hard, well-seasoned bamboo shaped like a dagger, a foot long and pointing inward. The sapling was sprung out by main force and fastened at the lower end by a string stretched across the path with a trigger attachment. The point is, that when a pig comes tripping gayly along the path on his way to the Dyak's paddy field to see how the crop is getting on, and thinking no guile, snap goes the trigger-spring and he is instantly transfixed by a bayonet of bamboo. How it must hurt! The worst of it is that occasionally an unsuspicious Dyak comes unawares upon one of these infernal machines, gets the sharp bamboo driven through his thigh, and usually dies in consequence.* Two more pheasants were brought in. Perara shot a beautiful *Cymbirhynchus*, and, in spite of its name, he assured me he killed it with one shot.

"*November 8th.*—Out all the forenoon with Le Tiac and Dobah, who is well now, thanks to quinine, but saw nothing. On our way home, passed a Dyak house and clearing a mile distant from ours. The house was a small one, four doors, and the dirtiest, most higgledy-piggledy and utterly dejected looking habitation I have seen amongst the Dyaks. The women must read novels to excess; for the place would do for a picture of the reign of indolence. The way through the clearing to this house was over tree-trunks which sometimes took us fifteen feet from the ground. I am now becoming so accustomed to pole-walking that I look upon a batang as thick as my arm as a very good road. Give us this day our daily bath. How deliciously refreshing is a leisurely dip in the clear, cold water of the shady creek after a five-hours' tramp up hill and down dale!

"One of our Dyaks brought in a superb male argus pheasant (*Argus Grayii*), which I took supreme pleasure in skinning. What a truly splendid bird! Such delicate richness of coloring is not found in any other bird of my acquaintance. In life, the feathers have a soft, velvety nap, and at the same time a satin-like

---

* Shortly after the above was written a Kalakah Dyak named Bakir, hunting gutta on the upper Sarawak, was killed by a "peti," or pig-trap of the kind described above. The lance entered his groin and passed quite through his body. To the credit of the Sarawak Government it should be stated that these traps are now prohibited under heavy penalty, and the owner of the one which killed Bakir was promptly fined $100, or four years' imprisonment.

sheen which is not to be found on dry, preserved specimens. The longest wing feathers measured two feet seven inches in length, and the two long tail feathers, three feet two inches. One such bird as this, a creature fit for Paradise, compensates for a thousand petty annoyances. My last lamp chimney broke to-night, of its own accord, which is a calamity indeed, for the lamp is now useless. When my candles are all gone, the evenings will be very long.

"*Saturday, November 9th.*—Just as I was starting out, a curious porcupine (*Atherura fasciculata*) was brought in, which had been caught in a pheasant snare. Most unfortunately, the snare had caught three of the legs and so badly chafed and cut the skin as to greatly damage it. It was a very singular animal, twenty-six inches in total length, of which the tail was nine and a half; the body was covered with flattened, gray spines an inch and a half long. I left Perara to remove the skin, with strict injunctions to work carefully; but when we returned, three hours later, he came to me and plaintively said, '*Can't* skin that animal, sir!' Sure enough, the skin was in ruins, the tail off, and also one leg, and the body torn in many places. On examination I found the skin had no more strength than a sheet of wet writing-paper, so we reconsidered the previous motion and took the complete skeleton, but saved the skin for purposes of identification. Being pretty well tired out, I decided to rest during the afternoon, and the clerk of the weather took advantage of our remaining in-doors and sent down a rain.

"*November 11th.*—Le Tiac brought in two more atheruras, and as Perara declared it was impossible to skin them successfully I went to work and skinned both. Both were injured on the legs by the snare, and it required careful work to make skins of them. Whenever Professor Ward wishes to take the conceit out of one of his young taxidermists I will tell him to have one of these wet-paper skins mounted. If I am not mistaken there will be some bad language used by somebody before these skins are mounted 'in the highest style of the art.'

"I have not seen in this region a snake of any kind until one was brought in to-day. It was only five and a half feet long; head, underparts, and tail a beautiful vermilion; two narrow, white stripes along the back, one along the side, and the intervening space bluish black. Two more flying dragons came in at the same time.

" The women of our village have begun to make the children

wash daily, so every morning they all form a procession and march down to the creek, where they proceed to remove the dirt of the previous day. The first step toward civilization is cleanliness; creeds can come a long ways after. Sent Dobah and Le Tiac to the Sadong to bring me some more Spanish dollars and other useful things. They will return in about six days.

"*November 12th.*—Now that Le Tiac is away, Gumbong will be my guide, philosopher, and friend in the jungles. He is a good, active fellow, and knows every inch of the forest. To-day we went out northeast, and at last heard wah-wahs calling to us. Killed an old male, female, and a young one.

"In the course of our wandering we came to a small clearing, in the centre of which stood a Dyak village, of ten doors, called Lanchang. We visited it, and found the house is a very roomy one, well built and well kept, roofed with thin boards, and having an extensive platform of poles adjoining the open side for its entire length, level with the floor, evidently intended to accommodate a large crop of paddy. Our arrival was greeted by a chorus of 'ohs' and 'ah-dos' from the old men, old women, and children. All the able-bodied men and women had gone into the jungle to collect gutta, rattans, dammar gum, honey, and, in short, anything which they could find of any value. One fine young fellow who was just starting out, struck me as being the handsomest Dyak I had ever seen. His name is Ne Siak. He is about twenty-two years of age, tall for a Dyak, finely formed, with a strong and even handsome face, and erect carriage. Around his middle he wore only the customary bark-cloth chawat, but a scarf of blue cotton-cloth was flung carelessly around his neck from behind, one end of which spread over his left shoulder. A rather faded bandanna was tied turban-wise around his head, with a tuft of hair straying out at the top, while down his neck and upon his shoulders fell a mass of glossy, raven-black hair in the prettiest natural ringlets imaginable. At his side was the usual parong, in its wooden sheath, adorned with a bunch of argus feathers at the lower end, and, slung securely at his back, was a long, cylindrical basket (juah), open at the top, itself a fine specimen of Dyak handiwork. In one hand he carried a stout spear, and the other was free. I looked at him in undisguised admiration, until he stepped nimbly down the ladder at the end of the house and disappeared in the jungle.

"The children were, as usual, very dirty, and some of the women and older girls were but a shade better. Hanging upon the posts of the long hall were an unusual number of antlers from the *Rusa*, and lower jaws of the wild hog. After we had seated ourselves upon the clean mats, we saw hanging directly over our heads a bunch of fifteen human skulls, also trophies of the chase. They were fleshless and bare, often toothless and jawless as well, charred and backened with the smoke of several years. I expressed a desire to buy one, but the people of the house were unwilling to negotiate, at least at a reasonable figure. The standard value of a trophy head in the Sarawak Territory is $60, and there are none on the market even at that price."

CHAPTER XII.

A MONTH WITH THE DYAKS—*Concluded*.

Leeches.—Model Making.—Poor Shooting-Boots.—Bad Ammunition.—A Big Buttress.—Wild Honey.—Human-like Emotions of the Baby Orang.—My Guides go on a Strike.—Flying Gibbons.—Boils and Butterflies.—Bear and Muntjac.—Delicious Venison.—Le Tiac's Omen Bird.—Dyak Shiftlessness in Trade.—Gathering Gutta.—Le Tiac Climbs a Tapong Tree.—A Perilous Feat.—Ah Kee gets Lost—A Torch-light Search in the Swamp.—Another Bear.—Return to the Sadong.—The Last Orang.—The Nipa Palm.—A dangerous Squall.—Nesting Habits of the Crocodile.—Farewell to the Sadong.

"NOVEMBER 13TH.—Long before daybreak, we heard wah-wahs whistling off in the jungle in two directions. They are evidently early risers. We went for one company of them as soon as it was light, but, although we expected to find them within two hundred yards of the house, they were more than a mile away, in the swamp. Had three fair shots, failed to bring down anything, and returned crestfallen. Started a civet cat and fired at it—also without result. After coffee at the house, we went out again, but got nothing except about twenty leech-bites. Leeches swarmed where we went to-day, and we were badly bitten. There are two kinds—one being the common, short, lead-colored species; and the other twice as long, with a narrow, yellow stripe along each side of its body. The bite of the latter is most painful.

"Perara shot a yellow-necked hornbill and two other birds, one of which proved to be the celebrated Dyak omen bird (*Harpactes rutilus*, Vieill), a sub-genus of the trogons, not at all rare on the Sibuyau. The Dyaks at the house noticed it at once, and expressed a desire that we would not kill any more of them, a request to which we readily acceded.

"To-day I selected and bought a number of ethnological specimens of the Dyaks, including spears, parongs, biliongs (axes), bark cloth and sundry smaller articles. After considerable encouragement and advice I got Gumbong to work making me a model of a

Dyak long-house, to be a fac-simile of the real thing. I am to pay him a dollar for it when it is completed. His only objection to making it was a lack of confidence in his ability to make something entirely new and heretofore unseen. But he caught the idea very quickly and went to work at once. Another Dyak has undertaken to make for me a model of a prau (large boat), to be likewise complete in every particular.

"*November 14th.*—Killed a gibbon in the morning. Perdition seize all English-made foot-gear! My 'superior London-made shooting-boots' (shoes), the best in the market at Singapore, went entirely to pieces to-day, after precisely two-and-a-half months' wear. The soles came off bodily. Would they had been immortal! The hunting-shoes made for me at Rochester lasted me through fourteen months' constant wear in all sorts of wet and dry weather; through muddy swamps and over rocks as well. Now I shall be obliged to wear my Sunday (!) shoes to hunt in, and they, being also of the best English make, will probably last me through the month.

"*November 15th.*—Shot a half-grown mias. In the afternoon, Perara came running in from the jungle to tell me to come and shoot two mias chappin which he had just seen about a mile from the house. We ran all the way back to the spot, up hill and down, splashing recklessly through mud and water—and of course the mias were both gone. And of course we failed to find them. This is the third time the boys have played that little game on me, and made me nearly drown myself in perspiration.

"*November 16th.*—A disgusting day's work. Having nearly exhausted my stock of Berdan primers, I loaded all my shells yesterday with Ely's. To-day, in the course of a long jaunt, we found two troops of gibbons, and five cartridges out of nine failed to go off. One fine chance after another resulted in the ghastly metallic 'click' of the hammer, which always chills a hunter's marrow and makes him think unutterable things. In spite of my hard work and good opportunities I killed not even one gibbon, and at last, tired out and disgusted, we started home. But I was doomed to have Tantalus' cup offered me once more. On the way a fine wild hog presented himself at fifty yards and stood still. I quickly drew a bead on his head with my rifle, pulled the trigger—'click,' and away went the hog.

"*November 18th.*— On going out with Le Tiac and Dobah we found a fine, large porcupine (*Hystrix longicauda*) caught by a hind foot in a twitch-up, and held to its death by a slender bark cord, which one nip of its sharp incisors would easily have severed. Poor, stupid animal. We came upon a large tapang tree which threw out one magnificent buttress fourteen feet long, twelve feet high where it left the tree, and three feet high at the other end. This curious spur-root was a natural plank, two inches in thickness, with perfectly straight sides, covered with thin, smooth bark. I had often heard and read of these buttresses, but not until seeing one did I at all understand what they are like. As I looked at that immense natural slab, hewn out by the hand of nature, I thought of Robinson Crusoe, and how he would have leaped for joy could he have found such ready-grown shelves and tables in his forest. With considerable labor, I climbed into the top of a small tree growing farther down the hill, so as to get a good view of the buttresses, and in that uncomfortable position sketched the foundation of the tree.

"Perara distinguished himself to-day by killing a gibbon, and also a fine flying lemur (*Galeopithecus variegatus*). These two specimens, our porcupine, and a *Cynogale Bennettii*, which was brought in by one of our Dyaks, gave us work enough for the afternoon. We ate the flesh of the porcupine, which was good enough, although rather neutral in flavor. As we were obliged to work indoors all the afternoon, it rained half the time. As a general thing, the gnats, moths, mosquitoes, and other insect abominations are so bad at night that it is almost impossible to read or write with any degree of comfort.

"*November* 19*th*.—A blank day for me. Perara killed a female orang with my No. 16 gun and No. 1 shot! Of course the animal was roosting low. I am feasting now on wild honey, brought yesterday by a foreign Dyak, who sold me three quarts of nice strained honey for twenty-five cents. My boys protested against the extortion, and declared I need not pay more than fifteen cents, but I would have been ashamed to buy honey for which a Dyak climbed perhaps eighty or ninety feet, at less than eight cents a quart. Were I to climb to the top of a tapang tree for honey it would cost the buyer at least a hundred dollars a quart, if I got any.

"Hot cakes, butter and honey go well together, or at least my baby orang thinks so. Whenever Ah Kee begins to set the table —the box, I mean—for a meal, the Old Man is all animation. He rises instantly from his straw, where he has been lying lazily playing with his toes or making up faces, and gets as near the table as

BUTTRESSES OF A TAPANG TREE. (From a sketch by the Author.)

his line will let him go. By standing as nearly erect as he can, stretching his neck to the utmost, he can just see the dishes on the box, and watch for the plates of food. As the crisis approaches, he grows more and more excited, whining, coaxing, and pleading with his eyes for the food which is just beyond his anxious fingers. If I sit down and begin to eat without feeding him, he looks at me reproachfully, his nether lip drops disconsolately, and he whines in an aggrieved tone. If I still refuse to serve him, his whine rises to a shrill, child-like scream, and he throws himself flat upon the floor, kicking and shrieking like a spoiled child. This was the most human action I ever saw in ape or monkey. More than once I attempted to discipline the little brute with a small switch to see if I could make him stop screaming, but, true to the impulses of nature, he only screamed the louder.

"The Old Man evinces a decided liking for me, and also for Ah Kee; but is shy of strangers. Whenever a dog makes his appearance in our room, or it thunders hard, the little fellow makes straight for me, as fast as he can come, climbs quickly up my legs and nestles in my arms for protection. The Dyaks consider him unusually bright, even for an orang, and several have travelled miles on purpose to see him.

"*November 20th.*—Two argus pheasants and a civet cat (*Viverra tangalunga*) were brought in yesterday, and to-day we prepared their skins. Le Tiac finished making a fiddle for me, and when he delivered it I paid him sixty cents as per agreement. After looking at the money a quarter of an hour, he came to me and said he would rather keep the fiddle, so I gave it back to him, and he returned the money. Foolish fellow. He can make a fiddle any time in a day and a half, but he cannot find a market for another in ten years, I venture to say. But I shall have that fiddle yet, all the same.

"When we arrived here, Ah Kee assured me there was not a cent of money nor a measure of rice in the house. Since that, they have earned enough in various ways in my service to enable them to send off twice, to buy rice; but now they are getting stomach-proud, and are prepared to kill the goose that lays the golden eggs. For example: the old man, Gumbong, who has hunted with me during the past week, made up his mind last night that thirty cents per day is not enough wages, and he has therefore struck for fifty. Ah Kee lectured him roundly, and I told him to go to the blazes; but he declared that he would not for less than fifty cents a day. To my greater grief, Le Tiac has also struck on the same grounds and there is a coolness between us. He was somewhat surprised when I told him I should not want him any more.

"*November* 21*st.*—Leaving the Dyaks to amuse themselves indoors as they saw fit, Dobah and I went out hunting and killed a gibbon with the rifle at rather long range. The way these animals can swing along is something marvellous. To-day I saw one going down hill through the tree-tops where the forest was rather open, and, for fifty yards, he went as straight as though he had been shot out of a cannon, He flew straight along without an instant's pause or hesitation, always turning end over end. Talk about the 'poetry of motion,' this is poetry set to music. A gibbon seems to progress entirely by the sole act of his will, and without taking the least thought as to the means.

"*November* 22*d.*—Two more argus pheasants in the morning, and rain in the afternoon.

"*November* 23*d.*—A boil which has been coming on my elbow has at last arrived in full force, and I am quite demoralized. A hammock and a boil do not go well together, especially when the latter is on so salient a point as one's elbow. Spent all last night and to-day in trying to make the thing comfortable. Noticed, very disinterestedly, a great number of butterflies flitting about the wet ground underneath the house. There were at least a dozen species —all large and brilliantly colored. An entomologist would have a fine time of it among them, and the Dyaks would bring him hundreds at one cent each. To me they are no temptation. It is impossible to collect and care for small objects, like insects, except at the expense of large and important ones, like mammals. It is so far my policy to shun small things, that I do not even pretend to shoot and skin small birds.

"*November* 24*th.*—The boil and I are more comfortable. Spent the day reading Maury's 'Physical Geography of the Sea'—one of the most charming books I ever read, deep but clear, like Lake Tahoe. What a pity all writers on scientific subjects have not Maury's wonderful ability to write clearly and to the point.

"*November* 25*th.*—When I started out in the morning, with Dobah, Le Tiac repented and offered to go with me on the terms of our old agreement, so we took him. Started out to make some sketches in the jungle, but took my rifle on general principles, though not expecting to use it. After a long and skilfully conducted chase of a troop of gibbons, they finally eluded us altogether.

As we were toiling disconsolately up a steep hill we heard a sudden rustling and saw the movement of some wild animal in the bushes close to our path. I thought it was a wild pig. An instant later a dark object came shuffling rapidly toward us, growling as it came, and we saw it was a bear. The absurd little beast was actually charging us. When it was within ten paces I gave it a ball exactly between the eyes, which settled it forever. The instant my shot rang out, another and even smaller bear appeared, also above us, and came shuffling down the path, evidently intending to flank us.

"Le Tiac cried out excitedly, 'Bruong, tuan! Bruong!' whereupon the second bear wheeled about and started back up the hill as fast as he could go. Remembering my bear experience in the Animallais, I determined to stay by my first victim and make sure of that one at least. I fired two snap shots, however, at No. 2; but he was so much concealed by low bushes that I missed both times and he got away. The one we had was a full-grown female *Halarctos Malayanus*, but it weighed only 60 pounds,—too small to make our grizzly a square meal! Its total length was 36 inches exclusive of tail (1 inch), and its height at the shoulders was 18 inches. This bear is, I believe, the smallest species known. Its hair is short, very even, smooth, and glossy black everywhere except on the breast, where there is a cream-colored patch shaped like a V. Le Tiac joyfully tied the little beast into a bundle, took it on his back, supported by a strip of bark over his forehead, and we trudged on to make our sketches.

"On reaching the spot where the large argus pheasant was caught in a twitch-up, we all sat down and I began to work. We had sat there very quietly for nearly an hour, when suddenly Dobah exclaimed in a whisper, 'Kejang, tuan!' I looked in the direction he pointed, and, sure enough, down below us, a hundred yards or so, was a pretty little muntjac (*Cervulus aureus*) walking jauntily along the side of the ravine. I fired and it disappeared. My companions rushed down the hill and found the little animal lying dead behind a log, shot through the heart. It was a beautiful little buck, with perfect horns. After I finished my sketch, Le Tiac backed the bear, Dobah shouldered the muntjac, and we marched home.

"The Dyaks are rather demonstrative. As we approached the house on the open side, the inmates quickly espied us, and we were greeted by a deafening chorus of 'ohs!' and 'ah-doe, ah-does!' as men, women, and children bawled and squealed out their astonishment and delight. Ah Kee's whole face and head was covered with one vast and all-pervading Chinese smile of delight at our good luck. The secret of all this joy lay in the fact that our game was thoroughly eatable. We gave the Dyaks the flesh of the bear, which they cooked and ate immediately, and kept the muntjac meat for ourselves. Ah Kee boiled down a quantity of it and made the richest and most delicious soup I ever tasted. An epicure who would not gush over the flavor of the muntjac would be unworthy of the name. It certainly surpasses, in exquisite delicacy of 'game' flavor, all the other meats I ever tasted.

"*November 26th.*—In the jungle during the forenoon, to small purpose, and in the afternoon it rained. Le Tiac started off this morning on a six days' tramp after gutta, but about noon he heard the cry of an omen bird, of the kind called brah-guy, on the right hand, and he was therefore obliged to return and wait two or three days before starting again. He told me that if the bird cries on the right hand or behind one who is starting on a journey, it is a bad sign and he must return at once; but if it cries on the left hand or in front of him he can go on without fear. If he should go on after hearing the bad omen he would have bad luck—either be taken sick, cut his hand or foot, or perhaps the gutta-percha trees would not run any sap when cut. He declared that only once did he venture to go on after hearing the bad omen, and before he returned he accidentally cut his hand with his parong.

"The Dyaks generally attach great importance to the omens or signs which they recognize in the appearance or cry of certain birds, quadrupeds, and insects, in connection with the more important undertakings of their lives. In the Kyan country of the upper Rejang, a large head-hunting expedition of over one thousand warriors, which had just set out on a grand foray, was instantly turned back and broken up by a little kejang (muntjac) which ran across the line of march in front of the expedition. Newly-married couples are sometimes obliged to separate on account of hearing a 'deer cry' within three days after their nuptials, in order to prevent the death of one or the other within a year.* Insects often warn warriors of the presence of their enemies, and again assure them that they may rest securely for the night.

"What a glorious thing it would be for the American farmer's boy if omen birds could be introduced into the United States. He

---

* St. John.

would certainly hear one cry on the right hand when starting to the field on a 'show day,' and at least twice a week in the autumn months, when the young prairie chickens were flocking around. The lazy school-boy would listen eagerly for them as soon as the strawberries and cherries ripened; and a little later, in melon time, when the days were awfully hot, he would hear an omen bird calling to him from every fence-post on the right as soon as he started off to school. The omen bird would supply a long-felt want, and no true American farmer's boy would be without a flock of them. No other bird would be so safe from harm, or protected with such tender solicitude. Had omen birds been as plentiful as blackbirds on the Iowa prairies, I might have remained a farmer boy much longer than I did; but without them, life on the farm was unendurable.

"A Chinese trader came to the village to-day, to trade rice for gutta-percha, wax, etc. The Dyaks are either very stupid, very lazy and shiftless, or all three together. Instead of taking their gutta down to Kuehing, where they could sell it at 60 cents per cattie ($1\frac{1}{3}$ pound), and buy rice at ten to eleven gantongs for a dollar, they loaf around the village until a sharp Chinaman comes along and takes their gutta at $37\frac{1}{2}$ cents per pound, in exchange for rice at five gantongs to the dollar, and cheats them in the weight of both!

"Ah Kee took his wooden steelyards and showed me how a Chinaman can cheat in weighing an article. By the insertion of a tiny wooden peg beside the string which holds the weight at the place where the end passes through the beam, it is easy to make an article weigh too much or too little, as the weigher chooses. He assured me most solemnly that Chinese traders nearly always cheat ten per cent. in everything they weigh, when dealing with simple people like the Dyaks.

"*November 27th.*—Went with Gumbong to see how he collected gutta. A mile from the house he found a gutta tree, about ten inches in diameter, and, after cutting it down, he ringed it neatly all the way along the stem, at intervals of a yard or less. Underneath each ring he put a calabash to catch the milk-white sap which slowly exuded. From this tree and another about the same size, he got about four quarts of sap, which, on being boiled that night for my special benefit, precipitated the gutta at the bottom in a mass like dough. The longer it was boiled, the harder the mass became, and at last it was taken out, placed upon a smooth board, kneaded vigorously with the hands, and afterward trodden with the bare feet of the operator. When it got almost too stiff to work, it was flattened out carefully, then rolled up in a wedge-shaped mass, a hole was punched through the thin end to serve as a handle, and it was declared ready for the trader. I have seen the Dyaks roll up a good-sized wad of pounded bark in the centre of these wedges of crude gutta, in order to get even with the traders who cheat in weight, but I have also seen the sharp trader cut every lump of gutta in two before buying it. If he found bark, you may well believe he did not pay for it at the price of gutta. The crude gutta has a mottled, or marbled, light-brown appearance, is heavy and hard, and smooth on the outside.

"*November* 28*th.*—To-day Le Tiac announced his intention of climbing a large tapang tree we saw in the forest a few days ago, and I went along to see it done. His object in climbing was to secure some bees' nests, which we saw hanging to the under side of the largest limb. Some torch-wood was taken along with which to make a smoke to protect the climber from the bees. The tree was a grand specimen of its kind, about five feet in diameter at the base, covered with fine-grained, soft, white bark, straight as a ship's mast and without the smallest limb or knot for fully a hundred and twenty feet up. It towered grandly above its neighbors, and to any one but a Dyak its top was utterly inaccessible. Hanging from the under side of the largest and lowest limb, was a good bees' nest, simply a naked, triangular piece of white comb, but we could not see any bees flying around it.

"A Dyak 'ladder,' by courtesy so called, reached from the ground to the branches, put up the previous year, the Dyaks said, but still strong. It was a very simple contrivance, but one requiring a bold man, utterly destitute of nerves, either to put it up or ascend it. It consisted of seven twenty-foot bamboo poles held almost end to end alongside the trunk by sharp pegs driven into the soft wood about two feet apart, first on one side of the poles and then on the other, to which the bamboo poles were lashed by rattans, and held firmly about eight inches from the tree. These pegs served as the rungs of the ladder. The builder was obliged to let the ends of the poles overlap a few feet in order to build the ladder with safety to himself. Just imagine yourself a hundred feet from the ground, clinging to a shaky lightning-rod and hauling up another section twenty feet long, to put in place and peg fast at the lower end, so that you can climb it and make it fast as you proceed!

"Le Tiac had few preparations to make. He wore only his chawat, which he adjusted securely, tucking the ends in tightly so that they would not catch on the pegs and trouble him. At his back was securely fastened a juah (back-basket) to receive the comb if it contained honey. His torch was made up securely, and slung from his neck by a cord, so that it would hang down his back lower than his feet. It was then ignited and waved to and fro, until it smoked freely, and he started up. He threw his weight heavily on the first bamboo to test its strength, and also tried the second, more cautiously; but they held firmly and on he went. It was like climbing a tall factory chimney by the lightning-rod, and a very shaky one at that. It was the most daring feat I ever witnessed, and I regretted that the audience was so small. But the climber did not seem to miss the crowd which his exploit would have attracted in civilized America. He went up, hand and foot, with the most perfect ease and nonchalance, until he had scaled the dizzy height, and seated himself astride the lowest limb to rest a moment and gaze off over the top of the jungle. It actually made my head swim to look at him and imagine myself in his place. Taking his torch in one hand, he held it in readiness and crawled out along the bare limb until he was within reach of the coveted prize. He examined it first on one side and then on the other. 'No honey!' he shouted down as cheerfully as though his climb was a matter of perfect indifference. To our exclamations of disgust, he replied with lofty smiles, and leaving the comb untouched he began to descend, and soon reached the ground without accident.

"I am told that accidents do happen to honey and wax-gatherers now and then, from a fault in the construction of the ladder, but very rarely. Sometimes a number of bees' nests are found on a single branch, and the climber gets so badly stung as to cause him to fall. Where there is any danger on account of the number of bees, two or three Dyaks go up together to make the attack; and, while one gathers the comb, the others protect him from the bees with the smoke of their torches.

"*November* 28*th*.—A day of rain, which I spent in the house conversing with the Dyaks, through the interpretation of Ah Kee. They are a very remarkable people morally, and I have conceived a great admiration for them. The more I see of them, the more I see in them worthy of respect. I regret that I cannot spend several years among them and see all kinds of Dyaks under all kinds of circumstances.

"*November* 29*th*.—Last evening, after making my daily entry in this journal, an incident occurred which promised to turn out very seriously. Ah Kee is very fond of hunting, and often takes my gun and goes off hunting by himself. This afternoon, after my dinner was over, he took the big gun and went out. He did not return at the usual time, and, just at sunset, I was standing in the door expecting every moment to see him put in an appearance, when, all at once we heard two reports of his gun coming in quick succession, muffled and faint, and so distant that the sound barely reached our ears. It seemed at least three miles off, and I instantly exclaimed, 'Ah Kee is lost!' I told some of the Dyaks to go at once in the direction of the sound and find him if possible. Perara and I began firing our guns, and kept it up at intervals all the time. The Dyaks and Dobah went as far as they could before darkness came on, and I heard them calling and calling, but without an answer. I waited to see if Ah Kee would come nearer, or if the men would find him, and, at last, after it had grown pitch dark, we heard another muffled 'boom!' even fainter and farther away than before, and I saw that if we did not go and find him, he would have to stay all night in the jungle and perhaps longer.

"Now, under certain circumstances, a night in the jungle is no laughing matter. Ah Kee was in the worst swamp in the country, without a parong or knife, or any means of making a fire, perhaps with all his cartridges expended, wet of course, nothing to eat, and tormented by myriads of mosquitoes and leeches, to say nothing of the fear of poisonous snakes or pythons, or of being attacked in the darkness by a bear or a tiger-cat. We knew that even if he heard our firing, he could not possibly come to us in the pitchy darkness of that tangled, thorny jungle, and if left alone, he was just as apt to go directly away from us as any other way. If not found before to-morrow, he might wander where we could not find him, and, all his cartridges being expended, he would be unable to signal to us. Ah Kee was a faithful fellow—perhaps the best servant I have ever had—and he was devoted heart and soul to my wants and my interests regardless of himself. So I decided, in two seconds, that we must find him at once.

"I called the Dyaks and told them to prepare torches and a good supply of wood, while I put on my hunting gear. Taking my revolver and rifle, with a bag half full of cartridges for each, and a small bottle of gin, we set out. Perara seemed to think it a good joke on Ah Kee, and declared he had often told him not to go far away; but I quickly silenced him by saying that there was no possibility of his (Perara's) getting lost, for he seldom went out of hearing of the house, and that if he had had pluck to go a little farther now and then, he might have shot something. We took a torch of wood called 'suloe,' which is full of resin and burns brightly, and, with two extra bundles of it, we set out—three Dyaks, Dobah, and I. The big alarm-gong was brought out and loudly beaten, and, taking our departure by its sound, we went in the direction of Ah Kee's last shot. We were soon half-knee deep in water and ooze, but with the aid of the torch we got on reasonably well. At intervals I fired a shot as we proceeded, and the men kept calling. After going a mile or so we heard a shot far away on our left. We said that must be Ah Kee and we turned that way. After a long time we heard two shots on our right and to the rear. The men all said it was Ah Kee, but I declared it came from the house, and was Perara's gun. No, they were sure that it was Ah Kee, while I persisted that it was Perara, so we came to an undecided standstill. They did not want to go on, and so I reluctantly consented to turn back in the direction of the last reports.

"For several hours we wandered about, firing the rifle and calling, but could get no answer, and at last had no idea which way we ourselves were going. If we had only had a compass we could have gone straight from the house in the direction of Ah Kee's last shot; but alas! my only compass had been lost some weeks before. At length the torch-wood was nearly exhausted and there was simply nothing to do but go back, get more wood, and start again. For the last time we fired the rifle; then shouted: 'Ho! Ah Kee!' until the forest rang for a mile on every side, and as the echoes died away we held our breath to listen. Only the soft twitter of the night birds and the chirping of the tree frogs answered us. The brown half-naked Dyaks looked at me and at each other in hopeless perplexity, but no one had any new plan or thought to suggest. The torch-bearer knocked the ashes from his torch, waved it to and fro until it blazed up again, and then, reluctantly enough, we turned our faces homeward.

"We had gone but a short distance, and I was just planning how we would arouse all the Dyaks in the three villages and offer twenty-five dollars in silver (a fortune to a Dyak) as a reward for finding Ah Kee, when we were startled by a deep 'boom!' from behind us, which we knew at once was from Ah Kee. Luckily we caught the direction exactly. In less than a minute, two men had received hurried directions to hasten to the house for more wood and to come after us with all speed, along the track we would cut through the jungle from the spot where we stood in the direction of the shot. The two Dyaks and I then wheeled about and started through the swamp, slashing our way rapidly along, climbing over fallen logs, tearing through thickets and stumbling through mire, but keeping the direction very carefully. Every hundred yards we would stop and call: 'Ho-o-Ah Kee-ee!' At last we heard a faint, a very faint 'O-o-o-o-ho!'

"'Hurrah, boys! Now we've got him!' and with one joyous, simultaneous yell, which woke the echoes far and wide through the swamp, we settled down to the task of cutting our way to him. The water here was nearly knee-deep, and the palms so dense and thorny that we were forced to cut a passage for every step we advanced. It took us a good half hour to get to him from the time we heard his first answering call. But we kept calling and he answering, so as to keep the right direction, until we were within a few yards, when, cutting through a perfect *cheval de frise* of palms, whose leaves were twelve feet in length and set with thousands of thorns, we saw a black object wading slowly toward us through the water and the darkness—and Ah Kee was found!

"His wide trousers were rolled about his knees and hung upon him in rags. His 'pig-tail' was wound tightly around his head, his body scratched and bleeding, and, taken altogether, he was a forlorn spectacle. He said he had taken off his clothes, because they caught on all the thorns and hindered him from creeping along. He put on his clothes, took a drink of gin, and as soon as the supply of wood arrived we started home. I was very glad to find him and he was equally glad to be found. He had two cartridges remaining, which he proposed to save to defend himself with, if attacked by any wild animal.

"He had fired only four times in all, and the others were Perara's marplot shots. Ah Kee heard our firing from the house, and tried, by climbing a tree, to get the direction, but after getting it could not keep it ten minutes. Even when we were firing every five minutes, he went first in one direction then another, then back again, utterly unable to go straight. The forest is so thick that it is almost impossible to judge of direction by sound. Ah Kee got lost in trying first to shoot a wah-wah, and then in following a hornbill as it flew from tree to tree. At last we got to the house amid general rejoicing. And what do you suppose was Ah Kee's first act after getting into his dry clothes? He built a fire and made a nice cup of tea for me! That act describes his whole character.

"*November 30th.*—This morning Gumbong and another Dyak brought in the little bear which escaped us the day we killed the other. It was only about half grown, and they captured it alive. How it did bawl and struggle as it lay on the floor, bound hand and foot. It was a very pretty little specimen, a foot high and twenty-two inches long, with a coat of smooth, fine, inky-black hair. The Dyaks had the good sense to sell him to me, body and soul, for a reasonable price, and his skin was soon added to my collection. Better that, a thousand times, than a life of miserable captivity among the Dyaks.

"True to his engagement of a month previous, Blou arrived to-day with the large prau and two other Malays to take me back to the Sadong. He also brought a large packet of letters, which I received most gladly. After all, the greatest pleasure of jungle life is getting letters from home. Sent eight loads down to the boats, and Dobah slept there.

"The model Dyak house, prau, and the fiddle Le Tiac made and loved, not wisely but too well, were all delivered to-day, together with more bark-cloth, body ornaments, and musical (!) instruments. The three articles first mentioned were very well made and showed that Dyak mechanical skill is of no mean order when encouraged a little.

"*December 1st.*—At peep of day, we were up and off, bag and baggage. Of course the Dyaks assisted us in getting away with our plunder. The men went with us to the river, and the women who remained at the house, were loud in their protestations of regret at our departure. They said they would be very lonesome when we were gone. I think each of the women said good-by about fifty times, and as we left the clearing they stood on the ladder and in the door, calling Malay good-bys to 'Tuan,' 'Ah Kee,' and 'Pleira,' one after another as fast as we would answer them, and then begin again. They kept it up until their voices were lost in the jungle behind us, and then a dog at the house set up a dismal howling, as though he, too, were affected by the universal sorrow. It was awful work getting across the grass swamp, and afterward over the wretched 'batangs,' for the remainder of the distance. The batangs were small smooth sapling stems laid end to end over the mud, wet and slippery, so that we occasionally took a sudden slip into the mud and water two feet deep. There are plenty of saplings about, and, but for their lack of enterprise, the Dyaks could soon cut enough to lay two or three side by side all along and make a passable road over the mud. But the idea never occurred to them, or if it did, they were too lazy too carry it out.

"Without losing a moment's time, we loaded the boats and started, hoping, by hard paddling, to make the return journey in two days. On the way down I shot my last orang, No. 43—a splendid old male 'chappin,' 4 feet 3 inches in height. He was sitting low down in a tree, comfortably humped up with his chin resting on his hand, facing us, not over thirty yards away, and he did not evince the slightest alarm at our sudden appearance. I shot him very easily, and when he let go, he fell like a bag of meal, sprawling face downward, as mias nearly always fall.

"The nipa palm grows very thickly along the lower Sibuyau, and at low water, when they are not partly submerged, they are very pretty. From fifteen to twenty finely cut leaves grow from each root, of a dense green color, and very graceful. To the native, the nipa is a gift of the gods, apparently designed to supply them with everything in which the jungles are otherwise lacking. From the leaves, the indispensable attap house-roofing is made, cheap, durable, and easily portable, and also kadjangs for boat roofs, so perfectly adapted to the purpose that even the inventive genius of a patent-making American could not produce a better appliance ; the roots when burned yield salt, from the spadix toddy is extracted, convertible into vinegar by one process, arrack by another, and sugar and molasses by another.

"Just before reaching the kampong at the mouth of the river, we came to a house where the Malays had lately been making syrup and also sugar. I tasted the former and found it delicious, better than anything of the kind I ever ate, except that made from the sugar maple. It was thick, frothy, and clear, with a peculiar sweetness in which there is a very perceptible flavor of salt. I bought two joints of bamboo full of it, about a gallon, for twenty cents— certainly not an exorbitant price—but alas, I had no buckwheat cakes! We reached the village at sunset, and have taken up quarters for the night, in a dismal, empty, and dilapidated hut on shore. Have just finished my supper—by courtesy so-called. My rations to-day consisted solely of one can of salmon (one pound) and another of green peas (one-half pound) washed down with muddy river water. This is my birthday, my third since leaving home, and I sit here in this gloomy hut, flat on the floor, with my blanket spread on the rough poles for a mat, and my ammunition-box between my knees for a writing desk, while outside it is pitch dark, the rain is pouring down, and the tide is running swiftly up. The men prefer to sleep in the boat, and I am left alone in my glory. We have had a long, hard day of it, with precious little to eat, and I will abandon this tiresome journal and seek my swinging cradle.

"*December 2d.*—Up at daylight, and Perara and I made short work of skinning and skeletonizing the mias. With a little help from Dobah we finished it in two hours. Then we tumbled into the boats and set off. The Malays are working by the job, hence their willingness to make good time. In the afternoon, as we were about entering the mouth of the Sadong, a violent squall caught us, and we came very near being swamped. We certainly would have been had not the wind ripped off our kadjangs clean and clear so quickly that we were saved from going over. Luckily we did not have the sail up. For a time it looked as if there would be an amateur swimming match in which all who could swim would participate to see who could get to shore. But we presently found a haven in the mouth of a small creek, which we ran into thankfully enough, but with passengers and cargo thoroughly drenched, and waited until the squall was over. Dined off a pint tin of hare soup, which was short measure and very thin. Reached Simujan at 10 P.M. and found my valuable collection and all other belongings in perfect safety, just as I left them."

The day after my return Lamudin found the nest of a crocodile on the bank of a small creek about four miles below the kampong; and after shooting at the old female and wounding her, he came to let me know. On visiting the spot with him I found the crocodile lying dead beside the nest whither she had crawled, mortally wounded, to watch her charge to the last. Her length was nine and a half feet.

The nest was situated on a clear strip of marshy ground, about fifty yards from the bank of the creek. It was simply a mound of dead grass, grass-roots, and earth, about nine feet in diameter on the ground and three feet high. The ground around the nest was covered with water at high tide, and the mound was thrown up to afford the eggs a resting-place above high water mark. We went to work with our hands to dig open the nest, and after removing about eight inches of warm sodden grass and earth in a high state of fermentation we came to the eggs. They had evidently all been deposited at the same time, over the top of the half-built mould, for they were disposed in a single layer. There were fifty-five of them—an unusually large number for a crocodile—and incubation had been in progress about ten days.

I took thirty-two of the eggs, at three cents each, and the remainder were eagerly purchased at the same price by the Malays of the kampong, who ate them, notwithstanding the fact that each egg contained a little embryo crocodile. I was very anxious to hatch a number of the eggs in order to watch the development of the embryo, and vainly offered five dollars for a setting hen or duck to cover the eggs. I tried to hatch the eggs in warm sand, but my going to Sarawak caused the failure of that plan also. I am therefore only able to present a drawing of the embryo as we first found it.

By this time (December 5th), I had eaten up all my provisions, spent all my money and allotted time, and having made a rich and valuable collection of what I most desired, I was ready to move on. After dining for the last time with genial Mr. Walters, I engaged passage for my two men and two mias, my collection and myself in a Chinese trader's boat bound for Kuching. Mr. Eng Quee gave me at parting a number of valuable ethnological specimens which he had surreptitiously gotten together for my benefit.

I left the little kampong with keen regret, and have ever since looked back upon it longingly. The days I spent on the Sadong, the Simujan, at Padang Lake and the Sibuyau seem like a strange, delightful dream of a sojourn in another world, where every face and form and every object, animate and inanimate, was strange and strangely interesting, and with the sweet there mingles no bitter. It was a lotus-eater's life that I led for four delightful months, free from the aggravations which beset all but jungle life.

The deep, mellow boom of the big gong in the veranda of the government house, on which the policemen struck the hours with measured stroke, and its echo, rolling through the surrounding forest like a wave, will always sound in my ears. I love to think that the hours are struck there now just the same.

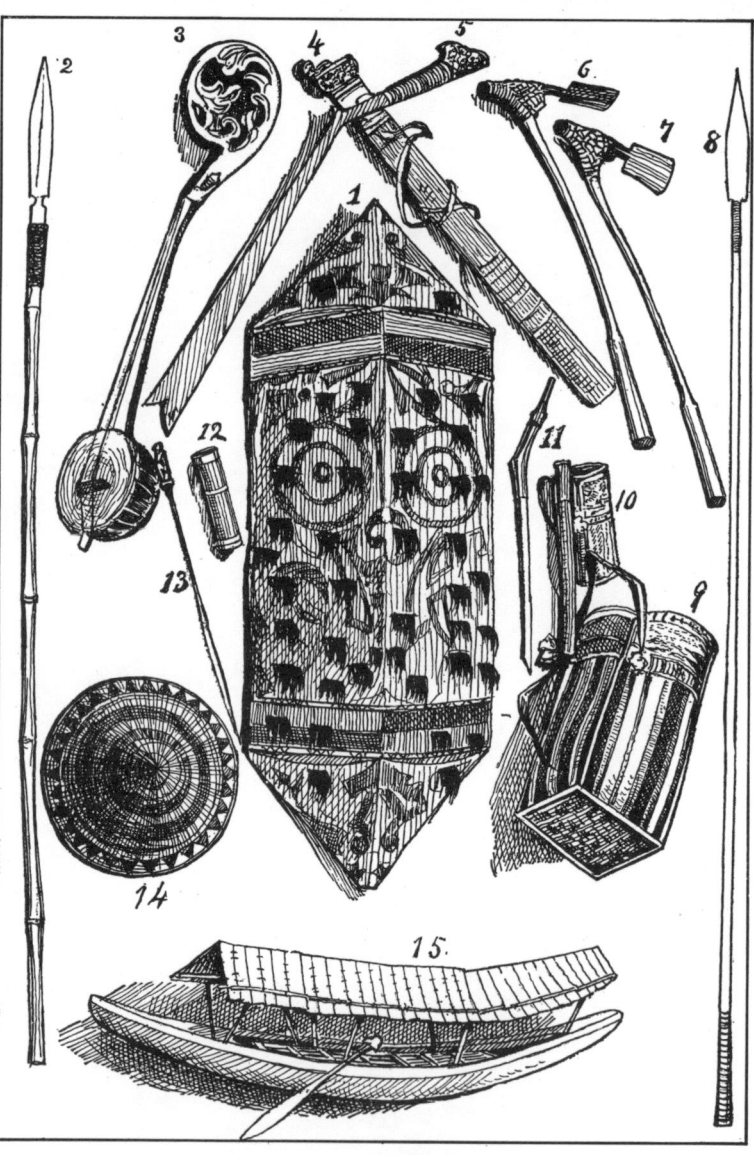

DYAK WEAPONS, UTENSILS, ETC.
(*Drawn from specimens collected by the Author.*)

1. Kyan war shield.
2. Sea Dyak spear.
3. Sea Dyak fiddle.
4. Sheath of Parong latok.
5. Parong latok. (Hill Dyaks.)
6. Biliong, to use as an adze.
7. Biliong, to use as an axe.
8. Sumpitan, used by Poonans.
9. Juah, or back-basket.
10. Sirih basket.
11. Betel knife, to accompany No. 10.
12. Chunam box, " "
13. Sibuyau Dyak measuring-stick.
    (Used in setting pig traps.)
14. Sibuyau Dyak hat.
15. Model of Sea Dyak boat, with kadjang roof.

CHAPTER XIII.

THE ABORIGINES OF BORNEO.

Civilization an Exterminator of Savage Races.—Stability of the Dyaks.—The Survival of the Fittest.—The Typical Dyak.—Four Great Tribes.—*The Kyans.*—Their Strength and Distribution.—Tribe Misnamed Milanau.—General Characteristics.—Mechanical Skill.—Modes of Warfare.—Aggressiveness.—Cannibalism of certain Sub-tribes.—Tattooing.—Ideas of a Future State.—Human Sacrifices.—Houses.—*The Hill Dyaks.*—Distribution.—Takers of Head Trophies.—Fighting Qualities.—Physique.—Dress and Ornaments.—A Curious Corset.—Weapons—Houses.—The Pangah.—Social Life.—Strict Morality without Religion.—Prohibition of Consanguineous Marriages.—Marriage Ceremony.—Honesty.—Disposal of the Dead.—A Relic of Hindooism.—Ideas of a Supreme Being and Future State.—*The Mongol Dyaks.*—Remains of Former Chinese Influence.—An Advanced Tribe.—Position.—Physique.—Dress.—Houses.—Skill in Agriculture.—Implements of Husbandry.—Independent but Peaceful.—The Muruts.—Dress and Ornaments.—Houses.—The Kadyans.—Comparative Estimate of the Four Great Dyak Tribes.

SAVAGE tribes deteriorate morally, physically, and numerically, according to the degree in which they are influenced by civilization. Those which yield most readily to the mild blandishments of the missionary, the school-teacher, and the merchant are the first to disappear from the face of the earth. Behind the philanthropical pioneer of Christian civilization, even though he bears in his hands only the Bible and spelling-book, there lurks a host of modern vices and diseases more deadly than the spears and poisoned arrows of the savage. To improve a savage race is to weaken it ; to wholly civilize and convert it is to exterminate it altogether. Like the wild beasts of the forest, the children of nature disappear before the grinding progress of civilization.*

---

* This has proven true in perhaps more than ninety per cent. of all cases in point. Occasionally, however, a savage tribe is found possessed of sufficient moral strength and tenacity of purpose to withstand the first great shock of contact with the powerful forces of civilization, and to survive indefinitely thereafter. Such tribes as are thus fitted by nature to absorb the

To the ethnologist, aboriginal races lose interest in proportion to the extent in which they have adopted modern customs and ideas. If we except the changes in customs necessarily brought about by the suppression of the head-hunting and piracy, it is safe to say that the Dyaks of Borneo are to-day precisely what they were when Europeans first landed on the island. They have mildly but effectually resisted the best efforts of the missionaries—Protestant, Catholic, and Mohammedan alike—and, being unalterably devoted to jungle life, there exists between them and the white race a gulf which the latter cannot bridge and the former will not. Wise Dyaks! Neither commerce, education, nor religion can in the least add to their happiness, and so long as they hold their present attitude all those influences combined cannot exterminate them.

By reason of their adherence to all their former traditions, customs, and surroundings, except those mentioned above, and on other accounts as well, the Dyak (by the natives pronounced Dyah) tribes of Borneo are especially interesting. In some respects they are the most remarkable people living, and their condition is well worth study.

As may be inferred from the geographical position of Borneo, the Dyaks are descendants of the Malay race, which has peopled nearly all the islands of the Malay Archipelago with the exception of New Guinea. At present it is impossible for any one to offer more than vague speculations respecting the advent of the aboriginal tribes in Borneo, and than such speculation nothing could be more unprofitable. No one can say whence this vast island was originally peopled, although there are some facts which seem to indicate that the progress of the great Kyan tribe has been from Kotei northwestward. There are well-defined traces of Hindoo influence among the Hill Dyaks in the west, and of Chinese influence in the extreme north; but not a single representative of either race exists in Borneo at the present day, except a few late arrivals. Both the Hindoos and Chinese of past centuries have either been completely exterminated by various influences, or swallowed up by affiliation with the aborigines. The traces of Hindooism are particularly insignificant, consisting mainly of the idea amongst the Hill Dyaks of a Supreme Being of some kind named

---

virtues of civilization without being weakened by its vices are not exterminated, but are substantially benefited, and go from strength to strength. It is not charged that the evils of civilization go *with* the missionary and the teacher —far from it—but it is a sad fact that they follow closely after.

Jowata; the prejudice against killing cattle and deer, and also of eating their flesh; and a few rude stone images and utensils. It is curious and worthy of note that both these great Oriental races invaded Borneo in the spirit of conquest, but both succumbed to savages of mould superior to their own—a clear case of the survival of the fittest.

Although the aboriginal inhabitants of Borneo are divided into several tribes and scores of sub-tribes or clans, they may, with reasonable exceptions, be described as one body, or sub-race, viz., Dyaks. In general terms, a Dyak may be described as a Bornean semi-savage of Malay extraction, of a yellowish brown complexion, straight, glossy-black hair, smooth face, medium stature, and active, warlike disposition. He is usually clad in a bark-loin cloth; but sometimes in a war-jacket of skin or padded cloth. He is armed with sword and spear, and possibly the sampitan also; and lives in the jungle in a long-house set high up on posts. He has no definite religious convictions, but respects his wife, and treats both her and his children well. His sustenance is rice, fowls, pigs and fruit grown by himself, and wild animals slain in the forest, supplemented sometimes by the sale of wax, gum, rattans, and gutta collected in the jungle; though these articles are generally exchanged for brass wire, beads, cloth, and other ornaments. He has no written language, makes no pottery, builds no monuments, carves but little and only in wood, works but little in iron, yet builds fine war-boats. His bearing is independent, dignified, respectful and frank, and he is honest at all times, save in war.

While it is perfectly proper to call every aboriginal inhabitant of Borneo a Dyak (for otherwise it would be necessary to coin a name applicable to all), there are, as has been already intimated, several well-marked tribal divisions, and many sub-tribes or clans, between whom there exist marked ethnological differences, and diversity in language and custom. Before proceeding to a more detailed description of the tribe with which I am best acquainted, it is necessary to a proper understanding of the subject that we take a brief survey of the entire Dyak race, or, to be exact, sub-race.

In my opinion the aboriginal inhabitants of Borneo may best be divided into four great tribes, which should be designated as follows: the Sea Dyaks, Kyans, Hill Dyaks, and Mongol Dyaks.

The Sea Dyaks are distinguished by their brave and warlike

disposition and love of conquest, their skill in building war-boats and conducting naval operations, which has given to them their name of Orang Laut, or men of the sea ; and also the fact that they never tattoo their bodies or limbs. Inasmuch as the people of this tribe may properly be regarded as the true type of the Dyak race they will be described at some length in the next chapter. Something will first be said, however, respecting the other great tribes.

The Kyan Tribe.

The Kyan tribe is numerically the greatest of the four, and it also covers a much greater extent of territory than any other, embracing fully one-half of the whole island. Its position is central, extending from the mouth of the Segah River and the lower corner of Kotei across the island to the very sea-coast of Sarawak. The accompanying map shows the extent and outline of the territory occupied by this great tribe, and the positions of its various sub-tribes, or clans, so far as known. We have information of at least eighteen sub-tribes—quite definite information respecting some, though extremely meagre concerning the majority at present, but no one can say how many more sub-tribes that have never even been heard of inhabit the unknown interior. The numerical strength of the Kyan tribe is consequently not known ; and, while it is quite futile to blindly conjecture the number of its people, we may safely believe from the facts we already have that it exceeds two hundred and fifty thousand.

On the north coast of Borneo the name Kyan is applied only to the people who inhabit the head-waters of the Rejang and the Baram rivers (about fifty villages in all) ; while the tribe as a whole is named after the Milanaus, an insignificant sub-tribe inhabiting a few miles of sea-coast, a half-civilized offshoot of the true Kyans, who do not practice head-hunting, but according to Rajah Brooke are "exceedingly treacherous." The Milanaus proper are in no sense typical representatives of the sub-tribes usually classed under that name (and even by Rajah Brooke in his "Ten Years in Sarawak," vol. i., p. 72) ; therefore, I have adopted the term Kyan as the name of the whole tribe, for the reason that the sub-tribe commonly known by that name is the largest, the most warlike and enterprising, and in every way most fit to be regarded as the type of the whole people.

Generally speaking, therefore, the Kyan tribe is distinguished

A KYAN WARRIOR.
(*From a sketch by H. H. Everett.*)

by being the farthest removed from civilization and by the practice of sundry barbarous and sometimes cruel customs; by tattooing; by the use of the sampitan, or blow-pipe, and poisoned arrows; by wearing sleeveless jackets made of padded cloth or skins of bear, leopard, monkey, or orang-utan; by the burial of their dead, especially of their chiefs, in coffins or vaults raised high on posts; and lastly (and most strangely of all), by their ability to smelt iron ore, and to use both forge and bellows in the manufacture of their weapons, which are of good quality and strangely ornamented. In addition to the above distinguishing characteristics, mention may be made of their war-shields, of hard wood, ornamented on the front with tufts of hair, sometimes dyed in various colors, taken from the heads of slain enemies.

For making forays in great force and suddenly attacking defenceless villages of real or fancied enemies for the purpose of obtaining heads, slaves, and plunder, the Kyans proper and various other sub-tribes have always been famous. They have thus acquired a great reputation for bravery and enterprise in war, but very few facts have been recorded which really justify it. In their head-hunting forays, the Kyans always went in numbers sufficient either to completely overwhelm the attacked or else to insure a retreat, in good order, from the enemy's stockade. Rajah Brooke declares with the disgust natural to the leader of an expedition against an enemy who would not stop to fight, "The Kyan warriors never fought when they could flee."

With the exception of the check which the Kyans proper experienced when they encountered the finest warriors in Borneo, the Sea Dyaks of Sakarran and Seribas, they have steadily driven all other tribes before them in their progress northward from the interior. The Sibuyau Dyaks were forced to migrate bodily from the head-waters of the Batang Lupar and settle nearer the coast, while the poor Bisayas and Muruts have been driven from one settlement to another on the Limbang River, in Borneo proper, until they are greatly weakened and impoverished. The Kyans often destroyed a whole settlement of Muruts at a single blow.

One of the Kyan sub-tribes of Kotei, the Trings, some members of which were interviewed by Mr. Carl Bock, has the reputation of being not only head-hunters, but cannibals, nor did either their chief or priestess deny the charge.* The Bugis kapitan who vis-

---

* Head-Hunters of Borneo, p. 135.

ited the Trings at home stated to Mr. Bock that they live "in large houses several hundred feet long, but extremely dirty inside, of a wretched appearance outside," and literally full of skulls taken in head-hunting expeditions.

The Kyans proper have on two occasions been publicly accused of cannibalism, once by some Sibaru Dyaks, of the Kapooas, who declared that the Kyans (their allies) on one occasion ate a Malay who was slain in battle; and once by a Malay noble, named Usup, who declared that in 1855 a few Kyan warriors took portions of the bodies of some executed criminals, which they had helped to capture when alive, roasted, and ate them. Both these instances are given by Mr. St. John.* One or two other tribes in the Dutch Territory have also been accused of exhibiting the same bad taste.

The people of the Kyan tribe are the only ones in Borneo with whom the practice of tattooing seems to be universal. Of those who live in the north, the Kyans proper, the Kenowits and Pakatans are known to practise this custom; while of those in the south, Mr. Bock states that all the Dyak sub-tribes in Kotei tattoo, except those in the Long Bleh district. The Tring women and those of the Baram Kyans tattoo their thighs very elaborately, and the women of Long Wai do the same with their feet and hands.

The Kyans come the nearest to having a religious belief, or, rather, system of formulated superstitions, of all the Dyaks. The Baram Kyans believe in a future existence, and their heaven and hell are divided into various compartments for the proper accommodation of all according to the circumstances under which they die. They pay much attention to the carving of wooden images and charms, to all of which more or less meaning is attached; still their ideas of a Supreme Being and a future state are very vague, and they have no religious rites or outward observances.†

The Trings have a well-defined belief in a tribal heaven, and a purgatory of toiling and enduring which must be passed through before the heaven can be reached. Yet the Trings practise cannibalism in war, and offer human sacrifices at the *tiwahs* (death feasts) which are made upon the return of an expedition. Mr. Perelaer describes such an event, held on the Upper Kahajan River by a Kyan clan (of which the Trings are a branch), at which forty slave debtors were put to death by torture, or by flesh wounds inflicted by the men and boys of the tribe.

---

* Life in the Forests of the Far East.
† St. John, vol. i., p. 110.

The houses of the Kyans are, in general, very similar to the long-houses of the Sea Dyaks, each of which accommodates a number of families, but very often a number of these long-houses are grouped together in regular village style.

Those of the Baram Kyans are roofed with shingles, and floored with rough boards instead of poles or slats of the nibong palm, such as are usually employed for this purpose.

The Kenowits and Milanaus in the Rejang District formerly built their long-houses on posts, from twenty to twenty-five feet high, or even more, in order that they might better resist the attacks of the hostile Sea Dyaks of the Sakarran and Seribas. Being unable to climb into the houses, their assailants directed their attack against the hard-wood posts, and worked under their shields while trying to chop them in two. Although the inhabitants above rained down stones, beams, spears, and hot water upon the besiegers, Low states that the latter were generally successful.*

The Pakatans and Poonans, wandering tribes who inhabit the unknown interior, build no houses whatever, and are, to that extent, the least advanced of all the East Indian tribes we are acquainted with. Even the open pole platforms of the Jacoons of the Malay Peninsula show a far greater advancement than the simple mat spread upon the damp earth, but one step removed from the wild beasts' lair.

THE HILL DYAKS.

The Hill Dyaks inhabit the extreme western side of Borneo, their eastern boundary being the Sadong River. As their name implies, they live away from the sea, usually upon the hills and mountains, and are essentially hill-people. Being indisposed to making piratical forays by water in great force, as did the Sea Dyaks in former times, they were usually the victims of their more powerful and rapacious neighbors. Although possessing, perhaps, fully as much courage, man for man, as the Sea Dyaks, they were never so warlike as to make fighting and plundering the chief business of their lives. The Sarawak officers say that they are far more tractable and easily managed than the Sea Dyaks.

Although they formerly took the heads of enemies slain in battle and preserved the cleaned skulls in their head-houses, they deny that they ever had that mania for head-collecting which at one time

---

* Sarawak, p. 340.

affected the Sea Dyaks. While it is true that the customs of some of the clans required that, in order to be eligible for marriage, a young warrior should be the possessor of a head taken by himself, in most of the clans of this tribe the taking of a head was not a preliminary necessary to marriage. The Hill Dyaks also claim that it has always been contrary to their customs to take the heads of white men or Malays unless slain in battle, or even of strangers from other tribes who were visiting their country.

But notwithstanding their natural ability and present peaceful habits, the Hill Dyaks have been, in their day, warriors of no mean kind. In 1840 Sir James Brooke states* that the Sentah clan embraced about one thousand warriors, and their head-house contained about one thousand heads. In the pangah, or head-house, of the village of Peninjau, on Serambo mountain, I counted forty-two skulls, or very nearly one for every two fighting men in the village, and Mr. O. H. St. John informed me that there were quite as many in the other two villages of that mountain, Serambo and Bombok.

I did not see many Hill Dyaks, and altogether, representatives of but three clans—the Serambo, Sentah, and Sow. They were so similar in both physique and physiognomy as to render it quite impossible for a stranger to detect any other than purely individual differences between them. They were, I should say, more strongly built than the Sea Dyaks, and a little shorter in stature also, all being decidedly below medium height—five feet, six inches. As a rule both the men and women were well made and muscular, their forms denoting activity and strength in an equal degree. All have that independent and dignified bearing so characteristic of both the Hill and Sea Dyaks, which, resting on a clear conscience and a foundation of good principles, goes far to make the Dyak the equal of the European.

Most of the men wore cloth jackets in addition to the bark-cloth chawat, and a head-dress of either one or the other of the materials just mentioned. The women wore only the bedang, or half-petticoat, reaching from hip to knee, but their waists were encircled by hoops of No. 6 brass wire, which lay, one upon another, from the hips upward, in an unbroken coil half way up their plump breasts, which were conspicuous above the upper coil. In the village of Peninjau, on Serambo mountain, I saw a really good-looking girl,

---

* Mundy's Narrative.

who wore a remarkable waist ornament, totally unlike anything I had before seen or heard of. It was neither more nor less than a tightly-fitting cylinder, or corset, composed entirely of brass wire of large size. One wire hoop was fitted around her waist at the hips, and another half way up her breast, between which were fastened, *perpendicularly*, brass wires of the same size and equal length, set as closely together as possible without overlaying. This curious girdle of brass was ten inches in width, and, unlike the corset of modern civilization, had no provision for the breasts, which strayed out in a most lawless manner over the top. The girdle fitted so tightly and with such rigidity that I was impelled to ask my companion, Mr. O. H. St. John, how it was removed at the approach of that interesting period in womanhood to which every Dyak woman looks forward with eager interest. He stated that when pregnancy rendered the removal of the corset imperative the old women of the village would tie the girl's hands together, pull them above her head to the utmost stretch of her arms, make them fast to a beam, and then work the girdle off over her head.

In addition to this brass-wire corset, this same young woman wore on each arm about fifteen nicely polished brass rings, or bracelets, which, altogether, reached from her wrist nearly to her elbow, like a long, close-fittting cuff of brass wire. Her entire outfit of wire was quite clean and highly polished, and in sharp contrast with her dark skin, the general effect was quite pleasing.

The Hill Dyak women sometimes wear a loosely-fitting jacket of bright cloth, but are usually seen without it. The ornaments of the men are armlets of plaited rattan, necklaces of beads, and sometimes, as I was told, of leopard's teeth, although I saw none of the latter. Neither men nor women ever tattoo in the least, and their skin is of a yellowish-brown color.

The weapons of the men consist solely of the spear and parong latok, the latter being a heavy sword of the toughest steel, very thick at the back, and with an edge like a razor, gotten up for the express purpose of splitting a head open, or cutting it off altogether, at a single blow. For a European, it is an awkward weapon to use, the hilt being very small and set on the blade at an obtuse angle, in order to give greater force to the swing of the weapon. The parong latok in my possession measures as follows : length of blade, 21 inches ; breadth at widest part, 2 inches ; thickness at back, $\frac{1}{8}$ inch at the point to $\frac{3}{8}$ at the hilt ; length of hilt, $8\frac{1}{2}$ inches ; weight, $2\frac{1}{4}$ lbs. The sheath is of wood, stained dark red, and is fastened to the body by a cord made of blue cotton cloth. This weapon and its sheath are figured in the group of weapons and utensils given elsewhere, Nos. 5 and 4 respectively.

The villages of the Hill Dyaks are composed of a number of houses of good size, elevated on posts of course, and each inhabited by several families, instead of the one continuous structure, or longhouse, peculiar to the Sea Dyaks. The departure from the typical long-house is rendered necessary by the fact that their villages are usually on mountains or hills where the surface is too rugged and broken to accommodate one continuous structure several hundred feet long by forty or fifty wide. Each Hill Dyak village contains a pangah, or head-house, a circular structure with a steep and high conical roof. That at Peninjau was about fifty feet in diameter, with a fireplace in the centre, and a broad bench running all the way around the room next to the wall, directly above which the skulls which had been taken by the community had been suspended in a row. Here and there a square section was cut in the roof and fixed so as to be pushed out at the bottom and propped open to admit light and air. The pangah is the purgatory to which the boys of the village are sent to lodge from the time they arrive at puberty until they marry. All strangers are lodged in it, and councils are held there also.

I do not know much of the social life of the Hill Dyaks except what was told me by Mr. St. John and the late A. R. Haughton, Esq.; but I consider their testimony of higher value than even the personal observations of a stranger and brief sojourner, and therefore I give it unhesitatingly.

The people of this tribe are morally the most highly developed of any in the island of Borneo, if not in the whole archipelago, which, in view of the extent of the influence Hindooism formerly exerted over them, is all the more surprising. Although they are, as a tribe, wholly without religion or any of its restraining influences, their moral principles would put to the blush the children of Israel in their best days. It is claimed that adultery is an uncommon crime (except in the case of the people of Peninjau and Serambo) among them, and there are several large villages in which the oldest men do not remember a single offence of the kind. Under no circumstances does a Dyak woman attempt to produce an abortion, the common and unpreventable crime of civilization in its highest state. But one wife is allowed, except in rare instances, where a chief is permitted two.

The customs of the Dyaks absolutely prohibit consanguineous marriages, even the marriage of cousins constituting a rank offence, for which the offenders are heavily fined, and socially disgraced as well. Marriages could be contracted in this country or in Europe with honor and *éclat* which would not be permitted for a moment among the aborigines of Borneo in their native jungle. I have already alluded to the custom of banishing the unmarried men and boys of the village to the pangah for the protection of the families.

And yet the marriage ceremony is devoid of any solemn vows and protestations, certainly destitute of even a spark of religious sentiment, and so simple and absurd as to seem little more than child's play. Indeed, it is so little thought of that it might almost be said a couple may go through with almost any ceremony they please so long as their intention is made public. In some villages a fowl is shaken a certain number of times over the heads of the pair to be wed; in others the bride and groom each take a fowl, pass it in front of them seven times, then cut the throats of both, cook them and eat them. Sometimes a marriage is celebrated by an exchange of bracelets in public; and again by the contracting parties eating a meal of rice, honey and salt together. Like honest people, it is the intention of the other that each participant in a marriage relies upon; and the ceremony merely serves to mark publicly the beginning of their marital relation.

Marriage usually takes place when a girl reaches the age of sixteen, and she is always allowed to engineer her own matrimonial schemes, and choose her partner without let or hindrance. Divorce is not uncommon, but scandal, lying, and wholesale vituperation are not resorted to to accomplish it. If a pair does not live happily together, by reason of laziness on the part of one, or bad temper on the part of the other, the dissatisfied party leaves the other, and, after a fine is paid over by the dissatisfied party to the original offender, both are free and at liberty to marry again. Separations to which both are opposed sometimes take place soon after the marriage, in obedience to certain recognized signs, such as the barking of a deer, which foretells the death of one of the parties if they do not separate. In all his social relations the Dyak is a philosopher, free from gnawing jealousy and yearning for seclusive and perpetual possession. If one wife leaves him he girds up his loins literally and coolly seeks another and a better one. Although he greatly enjoys his wife's society and co-operation in his pursuits on the farm, if she leaves him he does not allow her absence to disturb his serenity. The loss of his children affects him much more, for they are his hope and trust.

To the other virtues of the Dyak must be added that of strict honesty and profound respect for the rights of property. Whether they steal from each other I cannot say ; I suppose they do sometimes, although it must be very seldom. It is positively asserted, however, that they never pilfer from Europeans, nor even Malays and Chinese, from whom they would have a right to take something in remembrance of past oppression and extortion in the one case, and sharp practice with false weights and measures in the other.

Strangely enough, some of the Hill Dyaks burn their dead, a custom which they have clearly adopted from the Hindoos who flourished in Western Borneo several centuries ago. I believe all the people of this tribe in Sarawak Territory practise cremation excepting those who live on the Sadong. The Sadong River Dyaks bury their dead, and bury with them various articles belonging to the deceased, especially his betel box with fresh sirih leaves (black pepper), some old clothes of no value, and perhaps his spear. His land is then divided equally among his children, without discrimination for or against either sex.

The Hill Dyaks have no written language, and no social laws save the customs and traditions which have been handed down from their ancestors ; and it must be admitted that these are surprisingly well adapted to their condition and necessities. Chieftainships are hereditary, but their chiefs rule only by the consent of the governed and without the power to oppress.

The Hill Dyaks have dim ideas regarding a future state and a Supreme Spirit named Tupa or Jowata, both Hindoo names. They believe the good Dyaks go to a place under the earth, called Sabyan, where they are happy, and that the bad go to another place, also called Sabyan, where they are not happy. A few believe that sometimes their ancestors take the form of deer after death, for which reason, like the Hindoos from whom the idea was probably derived, they will neither kill deer nor eat of their flesh.

Some believe that certain of their warriors become "woodspirits," or wood-devils (antus), after death, and remain on earth to plague such of their survivors as have offended or injured them. They have no religious ceremonies or observances whatever, nor any conception of a God who controls the destinies of men for good or ill. In these people we see morality divorced from any form of religion, a state of things which we are often told is impossible. In this condition they are happy and prosperous, which, after all, is the great end of human existence.

The Mongol Dyaks.

The Mongol Dyaks, whom I regard as the fourth division of the Dyak tribes, are composed of the Ida'ans, or Dusuns, who inhabit the northeastern portion of the island; the Kadyans, who inhabit the hills in the vicinity of Brunei, the capital of Borneo proper; and the Muruts and Bisayas, who are the sole inhabitants of a long strip of territory lying between the country of the Baram Kyans on the south and the Ida'ans on the north, and stretching from near the coast of Borneo proper perhaps three-fourths of the distance across the island. While it is certain that future explorations of the interior of Sabah will add to the above several clans now wholly unknown to us, it will be noticed that the Bajus and Lanuns of the north coast are excluded from the Mongol Dyak tribe. The former are Sea Gipsies, of mixed breed, and no particular nationality, while the Lanuns, formerly the most famous pirates in the East Indies, came to the north coast of Borneo from Mindanau, one of the most southern islands of the Philippine group.

For the most definite and reliable information attainable concerning these sub-tribes we are indebted to Mr. Spencer St. John's admirable work, "Life in the Forests of the Far East," from which the following facts are drawn.

The Ida'ans are the farthest advanced toward civilization of all the aboriginal sub-tribes in Borneo, and from the fact that the language of the other three sub-tribes is nearly identical with theirs, and that they have all been greatly influenced by contact with the Chinese in former years, which influence still affects them, I consider it both convenient and desirable to group them together under the title of Mongol Dyaks. The Ida'ans, who number about forty thousand souls, and constitute perhaps more than four-fifths of the proposed tribal group, certainly differ very strikingly in many respects from the other Dyak tribes; while the three sub-tribes which we associate with the Ida'ans, certainly resemble them more than they do any others.

The Muruts and Bisayas are, in many respects, similar to the Sea Dyaks, and it is highly probable that they once belonged to that tribe; but, by the onward march of the warlike and aggressive Kyans, they became separated from the main body, ever since which time, even down to the present day, their implacable enemies have steadily driven them northward step by step, until finally, perhaps even as early as the end of the present century, their northern boundary will reach the country of the Ida'ans, and the three sub-tribes will become more closely related than now.

The Ida'ans (or Dusuns), according to St. John,* are essentially the same in appearance as the Dyak of Sarawak, the Kyan, the Murut and Bisaya. Some of the men tattoo slightly, but in an entirely different fashion from the Kyans. They are clear-skinned and have good-tempered countenances. The women, although not good-looking, are not ugly. All the girls and young women wear a piece of cloth to conceal their bosoms : their petticoats also are longer than usual, and the young girls (of Ginambur) had the front of the head shaved like Chinese girls. Near the sea-coast, the men wear jackets and trousers, but as the traveller advances into the interior, the amount of clothing gradually lessens ; cloth garments being seen on a few only at the foot of Kina Balu, beyond which the people are said to wear nothing but bark-cloth.

The houses of the Ida'ans on the Tampasuk River, Mr. St. John declares to be the best he ever saw among the Bornean aborigines. Some were " boarded with finely-worked planks ; " the doors were strong and excellently made ; and the flooring of bamboos beaten out, which in one house at least was very neat and free from all dirt. While some have adopted the Chinese custom of a separate house for each family, others occupy the usual long-house so common among the Sea Dyaks, with the open hall and a separate room for each family.

The Ida'ans are essentially agriculturists, in which pursuit they are so far advanced as to use the plough, which is very simple and made entirely of wood, and also an equally rude harrow. They raise rice, sweet potatoes, yams, maize, sugar-cane, tobacco, and cotton. " Simple as this agriculture is," says St. John, " it is superior to anything that exists to the southward of Brunei, and it would be curious if we could investigate the causes that have rendered this small portion of Borneo, between the capital and Malludu Bay, so superior in agriculture to the rest. I think it is obviously a remnant of Chinese civilization." . . . " The Ida'ans also use a species of sledge made of bamboos and drawn by buffaloes to

---

* Vol. i., p. 379 *et seq.*

take their heavy goods to market. The gardens on the Tarawan are well kept and neatly fenced in."

"None of the Ida'ans pay any tribute to any one, and no one dares to oppress them. Each village is a separate government, and almost each house independent. They have no established chiefs, but follow the counsels of the old men to whom they are related. They have no regular wars . . . and their feuds are but petty quarrels. Although every man goes armed, perfect security exists, as was proven by the troops of girls working in the fields without protection."

The only case of pilfering from a white man by a Dyak occurred to Mr. St. John, when among the Ida'ans, which may also be set down as due to the results of Chinese influence and example in former times.

The Muruts and Bisayas are numerically weakened and greatly impoverished by reason of the oft-repeated and usually successful attacks made upon them by the Kyans of Baram. They are steadily driven from one locality to another, and live in constant fear of further raids, for, be it remembered, they are far beyond the beneficent influence of Rajah Brooke's government.

"Orang Murut" means literally "mountain man," and those visited by St. John, who live in the mountain above the source of the Limbang River, he thus describes :

The men wear bear-skin jackets, and head-dresses of bark ornamented with cowries. Heavy necklaces of beads are worn by the men as well as the women, with many rings of lead worn in the rim of the ear. Some young girls have petticoats composed entirely of beads on a ground work of cloth or bark. The girls of this tribe also twist a couple of fathoms of brass wire in circles around their necks, which rise from the shoulders to the chin like a small hoop-skirt.

The Limbang Muruts live in long houses, one of which contained fifty doors, and the long hall was closed in and filled with fireplaces.

The Kadyans, who are few in number and live only about Brunei, are the only clan of the aborigines who have taken kindly to the haunts of civilization and choose to dwell near the city, and many even within it. Although like the Ida'ans, they learned their agriculture from the Chinese during the present century, the influence of the Malays has been sufficient to convert them nearly all to Mohammedanism.

Before turning our attention to the Sea Dyaks, the various tribes may be placed before the reader in a summarized form in the following manner, to show their comparative rank as viewed from different standpoints:

	Morally.	*Mentally.*	*Physically.*
1st.	Hill Dyaks	Sea Dyaks	Sea Dyaks
2d.	Sea Dyaks	Hill Dyaks	Kyans
3d.	Mongol Dyaks	Kyans	Hill Dyaks
4th.	Kyans	Mongol Dyaks	Mongol Dyaks

A GROUP OF DYAKS.

(From a sketch by H. H. Everett.)

CHAPTER XIV.

THE SEA DYAKS.

Habitat.—Number.—Sub-tribes.—Their Physique.—Sea Dyak Women.—Their Dress and Ornaments.—The Men.—Their Weapons.—War Boats.—Fighting Qualities.—Head-taking and Head-hunting.—A Mania for Murder. —Houses and House-life of the Sea Dyaks.—Communal Harmony.— Daily Occupations. — Amusements. — Music-making. — Feasts.—Gentlemanly Drunkenness.—High Social Position of Women.—The Doctrine of Fair Play.—Strict Observance of the Rights of Property.—A Race of Debt-Payers.—Morality without Religion.—Infrequency of Crime.—Dyak Diseases.—Mode of Burial.—The Future of the Race.—Can Christianity Benefit the Dyaks?

THE tribe of Sea Dyaks has always been celebrated for the bravery and enterprise of its warriors, their independence and resistance of oppression in all forms, and their success in maintaining both offensive and defensive sub-tribal alliances. In Sarawak they occupy all the territory between the Sadong and Rejang Rivers and all the tributaries of the latter up to the Kanowit River which is the boundary of the Kyan country. The largest and most powerful clans reside on the Batang Lupar and its tributaries, and the Seribas. The main body of one large clan, the Sibuyau, inhabits the Lundu River and its tributaries in the western extremity of Sarawak, where they emigrated from the Sibuyau River to escape the aggressions of the people of Sakarran and Seribas. Southward, the clans of this tribe extend to the Kapooas River in the Dutch Territory and beyond it to limits not yet clearly defined.

In Sarawak there are seven sub-tribes of Sea Dyaks, viz.: the Seribas, Sakarran, Ballow, Sibuyau, Undup, Batang Ayer, and Lamanak. The Sarawak Government estimates the total population at ninety thousand (1879).

The Sakarran and Seribas clans are the largest, and also the richest in gold and silver ornaments, jars, gongs, brass guns, and such other goods as help to constitute Dyak wealth.

In physique, the Sea Dyaks, like the Hill Dyaks, are below

medium stature, the tallest Sibuyau man that I saw being barely five feet four and a half inches while the majority were under five feet three. The men are well proportioned but sparely built, and not, as a rule, what would be called muscular. Their form denotes activity, speed, and endurance, rather than great strength ; precisely the qualities most required by a denizen of the jungle. While this is true of the men in general, it is by no means uncommon to meet thick-set and muscular individuals ; almost the first Dyak I saw, Dundang, was a fleshy native Hercules. Their movements are easy and graceful, their carriage always erect ; and in manner they are independent and dignified, though naturally polite and respectful. They have neither the insolence of the African, the fawning obsequiousness of the Hindoo nor the hypocritical formality of the Anglo-Saxon. The Dyak, in spite of his occasional dirt, is my beau ideal of a man in more respects than one, but nothing commends him to me more strongly than his simple honesty and manly independence.

The color of a typical Sea Dyak is dark-brown with a strong tinge of yellow ; his hair is jet-black and falls in graceful, flowing locks upon his shoulders instead of being perfectly straight and characterless like that of the Malays. His costume consists of the chawat, a piece of cotton or bark-cloth about five feet long wound tightly around the waist and drawn between the legs with one end hanging down apron-wise in front and the other behind. He also wears a sort of turban of red cotton cloth, or perhaps a bandanna or bark-cloth, or he may wear nothing at all on his head. As has already been mentioned, some of the Sibuyaus wear a small coffin-shaped mat depending behind from the chawat, and reaching from the small of the back half way down the thigh, evidently to be used as a seat. I have been told that many of the Sea Dyak men wear sleeveless jackets of red cotton cloth padded with cotton, when going to war, but the few I saw worn in the piping times of peace were very common-looking garments of dingy white, or coarse brown cloth, the latter of native manufacture.

The Sea Dyak women, or at least those of the Sibuyau tribe, are much lighter in color than the men, the yellow tint predominating. As a rule they are not handsome, but I saw among them a few who were decidedly good-looking, if not even pretty. I particularly remember two girls that I saw in Dundang's village, near Simujan, one of whom was his sister. Both were exceedingly comely girls, whose good features, and plump, well-moulded figures would do

A SEA DYAK (SERIBAS CLAN).
(From a portrait sketch by H. H. Everett.)

A SEA DYAK BELLE.

(From a photograph.)

no discredit to a Venus de Medici. As a rule I fear I do not appreciate the beauties of dark-skinned women, and I never yet saw one who would justify even a mild form of emotional description, to say nothing of the stereotyped raving in which the English language is often pumped dry of adjectives with which to convey a faint idea of a beautiful creature. For once, however, I was glad that the Dyak women are partial to "full dress," and I looked at those two forest belles with undisguised but respectful admiration. I remember another young woman, in a foul-smelling village near Padang Lake, whose face was precisely like that of Raphael's Sistine Madonna, except that it was brownish yellow. Her extremely pensive and half sad expression fastened my attention instantly. She had a pretty oval face of a very different outline from the typical Dyak woman, and her whole expression was strangely peculiar for a native. I imagine it was caused by love-sickness.

But the Sea Dyak women in general are by no means bad-looking. Their faces are bright, intelligent, and interesting, and I dare say others would call many of them pretty. As a rule they are handsomer than the men. Some that I saw were so clear-skinned and light as to be really a dark yellow, but sufficiently warmed with brown to make it healthy-looking, and far from disagreeable. Their eyes are always jet-black and sparkling, and their hair, which is abundant, well-kept, and drawn straight back without parting, is likewise glossy and black as a raven's wing. Their teeth, alas! are also black from chewing betel, which likewise reddens their lips for the time being. Their busts, which are always exposed, are generally plump and well-formed until old age mars all such beauty and leaves the skin hanging from the shrunken sides in hundreds of wrinkles and folds. The girls marry at sixteen and are old women at thirty.

Ordinarily a Dyak woman's sole article of wearing apparel is the bedang, or petticoat fastened at the waist by being tucked over and under a belt of rattans dyed black, and falls within about three inches of the knee. This garment is usually of native cotton cloth, and sometimes very prettily figured. The women living around Padang Lake, and a few on the Simujan, have jackets of red or brown cotton cloth with sleeves, which they always wear when at work in the fields; also wide conical hats, of Malay pattern, made very pretty with fine rattan splints dyed in various colors. Both hat and jacket are always worn when they go visiting, or trading down the river to Simujan. The picture which I remember most vividly in connection with my last trip down the Simujan, was Noonsong sitting in the stern of Hakka's prau, paddling and steering for him, clad in a jacket of turkey red, and a gorgeous Malay hat, similar to the one she made for me, her long black hair streaming down her back, the water flying from her paddle and the rain pouring down upon us all.

The ornaments of the Sea Dyak women consist of many coils of thick brass wire, sometimes loose and sometimes fitting tightly, occasionally brass spiral, worn round the waist when they are rich enough to afford it, and coils of split rattan, dyed dark red or black when the brass is beyond their purchase. Loose rings and coils of the same material are sometimes hung around the neck also, and half cover the breast. Beads I never saw worn on the neck. They also wear coils of brass wire, or else large hollow bracelets of silver, on their arms from the wrist upward, when they can afford it. Mr. Haughton informed me that ornaments of gold and silver were quite common among the people of Sakarran and Seribas, the result of their piratical habits in former times. The only ornaments I saw worn on the lower limbs, were leglets of rattan and sometimes brass wire, worn immediately below the knee, varying in number from one to five. Some of the women wore a large ornament like a silver rosette on the lobe of each ear, beaten hollow on the inside and held by being riveted through the flesh. I was told that these are made of gold when the wearer's husband is rich enough to afford it.

The men of Sibuyau wore very neatly-made armlets and leglets of braided rattan, some extremely narrow and others half an inch wide. The men of Sakarran and Seribas wear a number of brass or copper rings of different sizes in the rim of each ear one above another, the largest below, the smallest at the top, and often three or four together, two or three inches in diameter, in the lobe of the ear. With the men of these two clans, this custom is so universal that they are everywhere recognized by it. In former times the Hill Dyaks used to say, "Beware of the men with many rings in their ears; they are always bad men." I have never seen a specimen of the head-dress worn by the Sea Dyaks when on the war-path, but Mr. Haughton described it to me as a three-inch-wide band of cloth or bark-cloth with cowries sewn upon it, worn tightly around the head from which there stand up from six to a dozen of the wide, black-banded tail feathers of the rhinoceros hornbill.

The weapons of the Sea Dyaks are really insignificant in comparison with the warlike, and once piratical propensities of the people. Their arms are neither numerous in kind nor elaborate in design, and it is surprising that such redoubtable warriors have not developed weapons of better fashion, more elaborate ornamentation, and greater variety. In the matter of both weapons and shields of all kinds, the Kyans far surpass both the Hill and the Sea Dyaks. The arms of the latter consist ordinarily of a common parong or chopper, in shape, size, and weight closely resembling a farmer's corn-knife. It is not so heavy as the parong latok, nor so long; but in good hands it is enough. Like the latter weapon it is carried in a wooden sheath on the left side. Those to be seen now among the Sea Dyaks are very rough, common-looking instruments, not worth keeping as curiosities, and their sole use now is in the never-ending, but wholly bloodless, conflict which the Dyak wages with the jungle.

As before stated, the Sea Dyaks never use the sampitan and poisoned arrows. Their spears are as cheap-looking and destitute of all ornament as their parongs, being simply a piece of steel hammered into a rough-looking blade, $8\frac{1}{2}$ inches long by $1\frac{1}{2}$ wide; set into a stout handle of rattan five feet long.

I did not see any genuine war boats, and for a full description of them I must refer the reader to Low's "Sarawak," p. 216. It is there stated that "their war-boats, which are called 'bankongs,' are generally of great length, frequently as much as seventy feet. They are built very high abaft, and high forward, . . . from a flat keel, without timbers of any sort, the planks being merely sewn one to the other, or rather tied by rattans, through holes about eighteen inches apart, calked with the soft bark of a tree of the tribe *Myrtaceæ*, and payed with a preparation of dammar and oils. . . . . They are sometimes steered with a rudder, but more frequently by paddles, and from the assistance the men paddling them are able to give, they turn as on a pivot." The planks from which these boats are made are all hewn out, Crusoe fashion, with "biliongs," two only being obtained from a large tree and that only with infinite labor, it being very necessary that all the planks should be of the same length as the "bankong." "These boats, according to their size, carry crews of from thirty to ninety men, . . and I should think it probable that no boats in the world could equal them in speed."*

---

* Written in 1847.

Every Sea Dyak prau or large boat above the size of a small sampan, or dug-out canoe, is provided with a tight roof of kadjangs supported upon and lashed to a skeleton frame-work of poles. The hull is decked over from stem to stern with an open frame-work of slats of the nibong palm, or of poles, except that an opening is left amidships, whereby to bale out the craft when it leaks. All the praus, or nearly all, are made on the same plan as the bankongs, of planks sewn together with rattans.

Thanks to the benign influence of Rajah Brooke's government, my knowledge of the Dyaks as warriors was obtained wholly at second hand, chiefly from the writings of Sir James and his successor. From the first, it has been the leading principle of both to maintain peace in Sarawak, peaceably, if possible, but if not, to fight for it. The Sibuyau clan has always been the staunch ally of the government in its efforts to subdue, first the hostile and piratical sea tribes, and lastly the Kyans. The powerful and warlike clans of Sakarran and Seribas maintained a close offensive and defensive alliance, and were openly hostile toward all their neighbors. For many years their power remained unbroken and they successfully made one piratical foray after another against the Sibuyaus, Ballows, Undups, and the Hill Dyaks in general. The latter people, being badly scattered and apparently incapable of forming strong defensive alliances, suffered terribly and thousands of them were killed and beheaded, while thousands more (women and children) were made the life-long slaves of their fierce captors.

But the advent of Sir James Brooke and the forces he was able to enlist in the cause he had espoused, ushered in the dawn of a new era. The pirates of Sakarran and Seribas were attacked again and again by Captain Keppel and the forces of the *Dido* and *Phlegethon*, aided by Sir James and his fleet of Dyak warriors, and, after repeated and well merited thrashings, finally submitted.

This left but one hostile tribe in the territory, the Kyans, which submitted in 1863, since which time Sarawak has been quiet, save now and then when some act of insolence or crime rendered it necessary to discipline some particular chief by means of a small expedition. At present, life and property are as secure in Sarawak as in any country in the world.

The Dyak modes of warfare most preferred are precisely the same as those of the best trained warriors of Europe and America, viz., either to attack in overwhelming force and crush with numbers, or to take the enemy by surprise and therefore at a great disadvantage. Dyak fighting was usually done at close quarters; and the courage and dash of the combatants has often excited the admiration of trained European fighting men. In former times the villages were mostly fortified by stockades of thick planks or posts set up high all around them, while some were built on bilian posts from twenty to thirty feet high, to be more safe from attack.

From time immemorial, it has been the custom of Sea Dyaks, Hill Dyaks, and Kyans to cut off the heads of slain enemies and keep the cleaned skulls as trophies. Formerly each warrior kept his own trophies, and, in many clans, a Dyak girl would scorn a suitor who had not taken a head. A warrior's grief at the death of his wife or child could only be assuaged with a fresh head, taken by himself, of course, and the death of a chief often involved a regular head-hunting expedition. When a renowned warrior died it was supposed that he could not rest quietly in his grave until a head had been taken in his name.

After a time, however, the custom of head-hunting incidental to war degenerated into a murderous craze for making collections of human skulls, regardless of the circumstances attending their acquisition. It is charged that the Malays are mainly responsible for this result, on the ground that they encouraged the powerful tribes to attack the weaker ones, for the sake of getting as many heads as possible, while the Malays, who aided and abetted the pirates, took the plunder and slaves as their share of the spoil. The heads were no longer regarded as trophies of individual valor in the field, but all became the property of the clan as a whole, and the end sought by each was to have its collection of heads surpass those of its neighbors in point of number. Often all the adults of a village, both women and men were swept into the vortex, the children only being spared to keep as slaves.

I think Sir James Brooke showed a greater depth of wisdom in his treatment of the Sarawak natives than any one else who has ever occupied a similar position. For example, instead of preaching and making laws from the very first against all head-taking, and thereby incurring the hostility of the Dyaks, he taught them that a head trophy was an emblem of cowardice unless taken in fair fight; that to cut off the head of a defenceless and inoffensive person was a wicked murder, such as no true warrior could be guilty of without disgrace. This principle once admitted, it was an easy task to teach them the folly and crime of warring for heads alone, and to put a stop to the petty wars altogether. With due consistency however, when the wild warriors of the jungle gathered by thousands to support the Rajah during the Chinese insurrection in 1857, he gave them permission to cut off the head of every man found wearing a queue. Since that time the heads taken in Sarawak have been few and far between, and the takers have, in nearly every case, been treated as ordinary murderers.

The dwellings of the Sea Dyaks are all constructed on precisely the same plan as the one described in a previous chapter (page 355), except that, where a village is very large, a number of smaller long houses are built instead of a single continuous structure of enormous length. I have never seen a house longer than that already described, which was one hundred and ninety feet, but one of the Sibuyau long-houses on the Lundu River is six hundred feet in length and contains rooms for as many as fifty families.

Another house of the same tribe situated on a little creek below Simujan was described by Sir James Brooke as being 257 yards, or 771 feet in length!

Most of the Sibuyau village-houses are raised about eight feet above the ground; but some are twelve; and others again only four or five. Externally, they are all weather-beaten, gray, and wholly unpicturesque-looking structures, but sometimes are very prettily surrounded by banana and cocoanut trees.

Within, they are clean enough, because all the dirt and litter falls of itself through the slatted floor; but the ground underneath is usually covered with litter, perpetually wet and mouldy from the water thrown down through the floor above and, being the favorite resort of the pigs of the village, often smells horribly. Sometimes the pigs are kept in a sty underneath the long-house. As a matter of course, the old villages are the most foul smelling, and the European traveller should quarter in a new house whenever possible.

The house in which I spent a fortnight at Padang Lake contained four rooms, and was built in about four weeks by Hakka and another Dyak. All the materials came from the adjoining jungle, except the three hundred and fifty attaps composing the roof, which were made on the Sebangan River, below Simujan, and cost 72 cts. per hundred. The entire house was valued at $40.

I believe the Sea Dyaks are the only people in the world whose villages consist of a single structure under one immense roof, the greater portion of which is owned in common. No greater proof of their peaceful domestic and social habits could be desired than the fact that from five to fifty families, according to the size of the long-house, can live under one roof without coming to blows.

Fancy twenty Anglo-Saxon women living with their husbands and children in twenty rooms, along one side of a vast open hall which serves as work-room and play-room for all. The amount of quarrelling, slandering, back-biting, child-slapping, and child-fighting which would take place would be fearful to contemplate. And yet among the Dyaks I never saw or heard anything like high words, much less a regular quarrel, between either children or adults. The people with whom I lived at Padang Lake and on the Sibuyau were always light-hearted, and generally even merry. It was truly refreshing to see people so universally happy and contented.

They always rise early in the morning, or at about six o'clock; each family kindles a fire in its own private room, and boils the morning meal of rice or vegetables in an earthen pot or joint of bamboo. If they are lucky enough to have on hand the flesh of any animal, that also is boiled or roasted and forms a portion of the meal. When eating, they squat upon a mat in the centre of the room around the vessels containing the food, and all eat with their fingers. The drinking-water is contained in a five-foot section of bamboo which stands in a corner of the room. After eating, the Dyak takes a drink, rinses his mouth, takes down his parong, juah, and tambuk and prepares to set out. If he intends to go into the jungle to search for gutta, honey, dammar gum, or rattans, or to hunt or snare game, he takes with him also his spear, biliong (axe), and his dogs, if he has any. If his day's work lies in his field he takes with him his wife and older children to help plant or reap the paddi, or clear the ground, as the case may be.

Late in the afternoon he returns, his basket laden either with rice, bananas or other fruit, or such jungle products as he has been able to secure. By the time supper is eaten it is night, and time to light the smoky dammar torches, by the flickering light of which both men and women make mats and baskets, boil gutta, make new paddles or biliong handles, and work busily until bedtime. If there are visitors, work is partly suspended in order that the evening may be spent in giving and receiving the news.

About nine o'clock, the young and unmarried men and strangers climb up the ladder into the loft over the long hall, and, after stretching their limbs upon their mats, lie there singing and chattering until they fall asleep.

The married couples and their small children and girls retire to their rooms, and spread their mats upon the floor, being usually provided with dingy cotton-cloth curtains as a protection against the mosquitoes. The walls are thin and slight, but I never heard issuing from within them any sounds of curtain-lecturing, bickering, or worse still, wife-beating, such as came to my ears in the hotels at Calcutta, Colombo, and Demerara. I have often wondered what would happen if a Dyak should go to beating his wife and she to screaming. I am sure his neighbors would interfere vigorously.

It is not surprising that the Dyaks generally are fond of amusements, although they have no games of chance or mental skill. The people of Muka have great sport swinging with a long rattan attached to a high derrick and guyed to keep it from swaying to and fro. A ladder is planted a short distance off from which to start, and ten or a dozen men often swing together, the outsiders clinging to the arms and legs of the others.* The children of the Hill Dyaks at S'Impio play with peg-tops precisely as do those of England, spinning them, and throwing one spinning top at another to knock it out of place.† The Ballow Dyaks play prisoner's base and international "tug-of-war" in the most approved style, and the Sakarrans are much given to such athletic sports as wrestling, sham-fighting, jumping, running, and swinging.‡ The Kennowits are good at dancing in time to music, and entertain the visitor with a "mias dance," "deer dance," regular war dance, all in costume, and, most interesting of all, a well-acted pantomimic representation of the various events in a head-hunting expedition, the start, the journey, the surprise, the fight, head-taking, defeat, retreat, etc. §

Mr. A. R. Wallace describes his attempt to initiate some Dyak children into the mysteries of cat's cradle, but he succeeded so poorly that, out of compassion, the children took the string and showed him the proper way to do it.

The only amusements I saw among the Sibuyaus were of a musical character. The people of Gumbong's village, with whom I lived at the head of the Sibuyau, were decidedly musical, and scarcely an evening passed without a performance of some kind.

---

* Rajah Brooke, "Ten Years in Sarawak." † Hugh Low, "Sarawak."
‡ Spenser St. John, "Life in the Forests of the Far East."
§ Frederick Boyle, "Adventures Among the Dyaks."

Le Tiac was the fiddler of the crowd, but, while his instrument was by long odds the most elaborate and pretentious, the sounds it produced were by no means so pleasing as the clarionet-like notes of the numerous reeds, made like a shepherd's pipe, which the men, women, and children were so fond of playing upon in concert. The women had still another instrument, made of a piece of bamboo like a large organ-reed, the tongue of which was made to vibrate sharply by jerking a string attached to one end. The instrument was held all the while firmly against the teeth and the operator breathed forcibly upon the vibrating tongue of the instrument, thereby producing a few harp-like notes. It was a difficult instrument to play upon, but one evening, during the course of a very merry concert given by several of the women in my apartment, I wrestled with ye Dyak harp until I threw it, and succeeded in playing upon it as well as the others, to their great satisfaction and amusement. After that the greatest difficulty was to keep from laughing while we all played together.

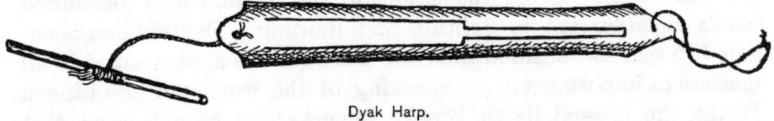

Dyak Harp.

Upon great occasions, such as the gathering of the harvest, the marriage of a person of note in the tribe, or the visit of some European of distinction, the Rajah for instance, the Dyaks gather for a grand feast. Pigs are killed and cooked, rice, fruits, and vegetables are provided and also a liberal supply of tuak, or palm toddy, upon which all the men are expected to get drunk. The company feeds to the fullest possible extent and then the dancing and drinking begin. It is upon these occasions only that the Dyaks drink liquor and get drunk, and after the women take from the men all their weapons to prevent accidents they go to work deliberately to make their husbands, lovers, and friends of the male sex roaring drunk. A Dyak girl considers it the grandest fun in the world to coax a redoubtable warrior into drinking until he is unable to stand.

I never saw a Dyak feast, nor an intoxicated Dyak, nor even a drop of the tuak which lays the warriors low at their feasts. In this connection, I feel in duty bound to quote Mr. Frederick Boyle's observations and reflections upon a feast in which he participated among the Seribas Dyaks.

"In England such a scene of drunkenness and uncouth merriment would necessarily be coarse and disgusting to the last degree, but among these savages it is not so. We did not see a single act of impropriety even among the most reckless of the revellers, and the brutality inseparable from a 'heavy wine' at Oxford or Cambridge was utterly absent. We were assured that during the whole festivity decorum would be maintained as strictly as it was in our presence, nor would any Dyak dream of violating the laws of decency and good temper. Whether this be owing to the national character, or the quality of the liquor I cannot judge, inasmuch as it was impossible for us to swallow enough of the latter to decide; but I am inclined to think that barbarous manhood and savage modesty were the principal causes of public decency. Thus it happened that a scene which, according to all precedent, should have been disgusting, turned out to be pleasantly amusing."*

So it seems the Dyak is a gentleman, even when drunk.

This reminds me to speak of woman's social position among the Sea Dyaks. From the cradle to the grave, she is considered man's equal, except in fighting and hunting. Her opinion is entitled to serious consideration, and her advice is always asked in all matters of importance. In speaking of the women of the Lingga Dyaks, the present Rajah Brooke remarks: "I soon learned that great power and influence is attached to their opinions on matters in general, and that to stand well with them was more than half of any Dyak battle."†

One great secret of the pleasant domestic and social life of the Dyaks lies in the fact that parents think too much of their children to make them marry against their will, or from mercenary motives.

The Sibuyaus believe in strict chastity, both before and after marriage, and lapses from virtue are considered highly shameful. Strangely enough, these simple-minded savages, without written law and wholly without religion, hold that in cases of unchastity, or infidelity to the marriage relation, the man in the case is equally guilty with the woman. Both stand on precisely the same footing toward the remainder of the community, and the disgrace and punishment are *shared equally by both participants* in the crime.

How very different is this from the improved customs of Christian lands. We say that what is folly in a man becomes crime in

---

* Adventures among the Dyaks, p. 248.
† Ten Years in Sarawak, I., 129.

a woman. A man may be as "fast" as he pleases, or, as his means will let him, so long as he preserves the veneering on his character. He may be guilty of open harlotry, or ruin an innocent girl every year or two, and he will still be smilingly welcomed in polite society. He goes his way securely, proudly, is highly spoken of by both men and women, and if he is only rich, is fawned upon as much as ever. How is it with the woman in the case? One single step aside from the path of virtue, one little stumble, and no matter what the temptation or the palliating circumstances, no matter how atrocious the betrayal, she goes down. Into the mire she goes, howled at and spat upon by her sisters, forsaken instantly by the whole world, and literally sent to hell. What is there on earth to-day more deplorably and hopelessly faulty than the social laws of the "highest civilization the world has ever seen?" Even the unlettered savages of the jungle have a better state of society than we.

I have already mentioned the sacredness of the rights of property amongst the Dyaks, but the actual and universal observance of these rights by any class of people in this thievish world is so phenomenal I feel that I have a right to allude to the subject again. In civilized countries, and almost all others except Borneo, every man is not treated precisely as a thief, yet at the same time he who has stealable property is careful not to put temptation in the way of a stranger. Generally speaking, I believe that out of every twenty persons there will always be found one who would steal if he had a chance to get something he very much wanted and could take without detection.

Making debts beyond one's power to pay, is a very popular form of stealing by wholesale, for the encouragement of which we have several thousand laws which furnish ample protection to the perpetrators. Half our bankrupt merchants are ruined by "bad debts," made by people who prefer that method of getting a man's goods to simple burglary.

Once more I assert, with the certainty of being disbelieved, that the Dyaks actually do not steal. I have an account of one who did once steal some gutta from a companion, but he is dead now—hanged, "in the usual manner."

Where else but among the Dyaks will a traveller dare to trust a cart-load of boxes and packages, none of them securely fastened, all filled with scores of trifles, any one of which would be dear to a native's heart, in the centre of a village of fifty strange natives with no one to watch for thieves? You can do this among the Dyaks, and lose not one cent's worth. Even the empty tin cans and boxes I threw out of the house were brought to me and shown before they were appropriated. And yet, had the Dyaks been West Indian negroes, or even like some white men I have known, they would have stolen half my goods in perfect safety to themselves.

I have never heard of a single instance of theft from any European, Malay, or Chinaman, committed by a Sea or Hill Dyak.

Their most wonderful trait, however, is their faithfulness in paying their debts. If the people of the village want goods, a trader will give them his whole cargo, if he can get them to accept it, in exchange for jungle produce *to be collected*. The day for full settlement is named by the head man, and by that day the debts are all paid. What a glorious country for an honest merchant to start business in!

Like their neighbors of the hills, the Sea Dyaks are without priests and creeds or even the faintest notion of religious observances. Their moral laws are the product of their own evolution, for we see in them no reflection of the religious customs of any of the people who have thus far come in contact with them, either Hindoos, Javanese, Chinese, Malays or Europeans.* Savage nations usually acquire all the vices, and but very few of the virtues, of the civilization which touches them, but so far the Dyaks of Northern Borneo have gone through the fire unscathed. They are yet free from the grovelling idolatry and abominable religious fanaticism of the Hindoos, the sordid avarice of the Chinese, the deceit, treachery, and licentiousness of the Malays, and the brandy-and-sodaism of the Europeans.

The Sea Dyaks believe there is a Supreme Spirit whom they call Battara, and sometimes Jawata (both of which are Hindoo names), and that the dead go to Sabyan, which is below the earth. They revere the memory of a party named Biadum, who was formerly a great chief among them, and at harvest time they make offerings in his memory, quite after our custom of firing off

---

* In asserting that the Dyaks have no religion I attach to that word the meaning which is most generally recognized, viz., a system of faith and worship, and obedience to the laws of a Supreme Being. Although modern anthropologists have agreed to consider that belief in a Supreme Being of any kind is sufficient to constitute a "religion," it seems to me highly improper to dignify with that name a vague, inconsequent notion which bears no fruit whatever, either in worship, obedience, or even love.

gunpowder on Washington's birthday. Like most ignorant people, they believe in evil spirits who haunt and annoy certain ones among the living, and are superstitious in regard to various omens of good and bad fortune.

Their crimes can be counted on the fingers of one hand; and instances of their commission are few and far between. It must be remembered that the frenzy for head collecting, which led to such wholesale murder before the advent of Rajah Brooke, was mainly due to the instigation and encouragement of the reprobate Malays who so nearly ruined the country.

As might be expected, the Dyaks are subject to but few diseases, and those of a simple nature. The most common ailment is called "corrip" (*ichthyosis*), in which the epidermis of the subject cracks all over the body and the edges roll up into little whitish rolls. The body of a Dyak so affected has a gray appearance, and, although the disease is painless, it is disagreeable to look at and very difficult to cure. Fever and dysentery are both common diseases, and also ophthalmia, which is most prevalent during the time of weeding the paddy fields in September and October, at which season whole tribes are sometimes attacked. If taken in time, it yields to very simple remedies; but many lose their sight from neglecting treatment.

Insanity is very rare, and also natural deformity of person. So far as I could learn, the Dyaks are entirely free from the long list of unmentionable male and female diseases which appear to have been developed by the human race only at its highest stage of civilization and refinement. It is a singular, though melancholy, fact that savages know nothing of venereal diseases, abortion, infanticide, and drunkenness, until they are introduced by the civilized nations of the earth.

Dyak women in confinement are attended only by the old women of the tribe, and, as might be expected from the absence of the health-destroying clothes, food, drink, medicines, and social customs, which make American women weak, they are usually seen going about their regular occupations on the third or fourth day after child-birth.

A favorite Dyak remedy for a cut, bruise, or sprain, is to expectorate a quantity of betel juice upon the part afflicted, which quickly imparts to it a disgusting yellow-jaundice appearance.

Unlike the Hill Dyaks, the people of the Sea tribe always bury their dead. I did not have an opportunity to witness an interment or even to see a burial ground, but Mr. Eng Quee told me that the Sibuyaus bury their dead in coffins when they can make them, otherwise without. They put vessels of food beside the grave, and also such of the ornaments of the deceased as are not valuable enough to be carried off by strangers. They formerly buried with their dead many valuable ornaments of gold and silver, but these tempted the low-class Malays to rob the graves, and of late years the custom has been discontinued altogether. The Dyaks select retired spots for burial grounds, never visit them except when really necessary, are averse to taking strangers to see them, and also to talking about their burial customs. They erect no monuments whatever to mark the resting place of their dead, and make their interments very quietly.

Thus ends our brief survey of the Hill and Sea Dyaks, and what does it teach us? In these strange children of nature we see all the cardinal virtues without a ray of religion, morality without ministers, the Christian graces without Christ or gospel. They keep no sabbaths, pray no prayers, build no temples, worship nothing and nobody, and acknowledge no higher tribunal than the bar of public opinion on one hand, and the Sarawak government court on the other.

The Dyak is perhaps the most happy and contented human being under the sun. His wants are few, and his native jungle supplies nearly all of them. Thanks to his state of savagery, he has not developed one-tenth of the diseases which so often make the lives of civilized people a burden. His children do not have scarlet fever, diphtheria, croup, or whooping-cough, nor does he or his wife have consumption, pneumonia, dyspepsia, rheumatism, or gout. But for the rascally Chinaman, who years ago taught him to make toddy from the palm tree, and who even now supplies him with arrack, he might to-day be without the means of getting drunk. As is the case with nearly all savages who drink intoxicating liquors, this vice is the gift of civilization.

In hospitality, human sympathy, and charity, the Dyaks are not outranked by any people living, so far as I know, and their morals are as much superior to ours as our intelligence is beyond theirs. If happiness is the goal of human existence, they are much nearer it than we. In this instance, at least, the highest civilization has not evolved the most perfect state of society, and to this extent the fundamental theories of theology, of sociology, and human evolution are utterly at fault. Borneo is no field for the missionary, for no religion can give the Dyak aught that will benefit him, or increase the balance of his happiness in the least.

We have seen that there can be, and there is, morality of a high order without any creed, religion, or education whatever. Is it possible that man reaches his highest *moral* development in a state of savagery? Is it, then, really true that as we increase in civilized intelligence, refinement, and capacity for enjoyment, our capacities and *propensities* for wickedness and harmful pleasures increase likewise? If this is the case now with mankind, will it *always* be so? These are serious questions, and I leave them with the reader.

CHAPTER XV.

A PLEASURE TRIP UP THE SARAWAK.

The *Firefly*.—Mr. A. H. Everett.—The Chinese Gold-washings at Bau.—Caves and Crevices near Paku.—Walk to Tegora.—The Cinnabar Mines of the Borneo Company.—Romantic Boat Ride down the Staat.—Trip to Serambo Mountain.—Dyak Bridges.—Village of Peninjau.—The Rajah's Cottage.—Magnificent View.—Return to Kuching.—Farewell to Borneo.—Singapore once more.—End of the Expedition.—Retrospect.—Conclusion.

I RETURNED to Sarawak (Kuching) on the sixth of December, and during the fortnight I spent in packing up my collection and waiting for the steamer, my good friend, Mr. Oliver St. John, Inspector of Public Works, treated me to a glorious trip up the Sarawak River. I say " treated me," for without him as a guide, philosopher, and friend, I should not have gone, and, when I reflect now upon the trouble he took and the miles he walked solely on my account, I feel quite as if I had wronged him.

I had collected until I was tired and sick of specimens, and that trip was made solely for pleasure. Mr. Crocker placed the government steam launch *Firefly* at our disposal for the trip, and one bright afternoon at two o'clock we started up the river with the turning of the tide. A bend of the stream soon hid the town from our view, and after getting clear of the straggling Malay kampong, we were ready to drink in the successive scenes of the new panorama which began to unroll before us.

Scene first, five miles long—banks low, uncultivated, covered with monotonous mangroves.

Scene second—the banks have risen and asserted themselves; they are clear of old jungle and covered with green paddy fields for a quarter of a mile back from the river, where they meet the forest primeval. Here and there are neat-looking houses, nestling in clumps of banana and cocoanut trees, surrounded by neatly-kept vegetable gardens. From the general look of care and thrift, we are led to hazard the opinion that fields, houses, and gardens belong to the Chinese, which proves to be the case. Two or three Chinese shops are passed; Gunong Matang, the mountain so conspicuous from Kuching, also went by us on the right, with a few other peaks of humbler elevation.

Eight miles above Kuching, the mountains of the interior rise prominently into view in long ridges with fleecy white clouds clinging to their densely wooded sides. Though not so very distant, they were of a deep blue color, and, taken altogether, were to the eye a grateful relief from the everlasting green of the level jungle.

We took in the scenery until dark and then reluctantly turned from it to the dinner table. The *Firefly* is a very comfortable little craft, but her passengers must provide their own bill of fare and table furniture. We had plenty of soup, but there was not a spoon on board, so we drank it out of our plates and proceeded to dispose of the remainder of the menu with equal facility.

The night was exceedingly dark, and how the steersman managed to keep clear of the banks was more than I could see. About twelve miles up, we came to the confluence of the two branches of the Sarawak River, and took the smaller or western stream, which soon became very narrow, but still remained deep, swift, and murky. About 8 P.M. we reached Busau, twenty-six miles from Kuching, and landed. Here we were at the terminus of the Borneo Company's tram-way system, from which the antimony mined in the vicinity and the quicksilver from Tegora is shipped down the river. Leaving our luggage to be pushed after us on a tram-car, we set out in the black darkness and walked on the tram-way four miles to Paku. At the police station we turned off and climbed a steep conical hill until we were out of breath, which brought us to the top, upon which was perched a house, to the comforts of which we were hospitably welcomed by Mr. A. Hart Everett, the naturalist.

It was a great treat to meet an accomplished Malasian naturalist on his native heath, a man who knew Borneo by heart, and was, like myself, almost wholly given over to collecting. I plied the poor man with questions until we were both fairly exhausted and obliged to open some bottles of ale. Mr. Everett was on a mission of much more importance to science than the mere collecting of specimens.

Under the patronage and support of the British Museum and the Marquis of Tweeddale, then President of the Zoölogical Society, he had entered upon a thorough and systematic examination of the caves of Borneo, in the hope of finding in the deposits upon their floors fossil remains of the forerunner of the anthropoid apes. It was faintly hoped that, even if the cavern deposits did not reveal the missing link, their fossils would at least throw some light upon the point at which the human race diverged from the catarrhine stock. Here was an evolutionist with his war-paint all on, and his weapons in his hand—pick, shovel, and sieve. Imagine the sensations of a Darwinian actually searching for and finding the link between man and the great apes! Another Kohinoor would be a mere glass marble in comparison.

Mr. Everett's methods of search were so thorough and truly searching that not even a bat's tooth escaped the sieves through which the floor deposits of the caves were put. He found the bones of bats in great abundance, all of living species, however, and one skull of *Simia Wurmbii* in a fossil state, but, I grieve to say, no traces of extinct animals nor even a prehistoric race of men. I should have stated above that another and equally important object with Mr. Everett was to obtain evidence, if any existed, of the occupation of Borneo by any primitive race anterior to its being peopled by the descendants of the Malays.

Unfortunately for science, Mr. Everett's investigations were soon after brought to an untimely end by the death of the Marquis of Tweedale. In order to reach a new field, Mr. Everett accepted a position with the North Borneo Company and went to the Kina Balu district. It is to be hoped that he may soon find the time and means for a thorough scientific exploration of the *terra incognita* lying to the south of Kina Balu—a work which no one is better fitted to accomplish than he.

When we started from Kuching I solemnly promised myself not to think "specimen" even once, much less try to collect one, but when Mr. Everett showed me his beautiful specimens of *Tupaia, Gymnura, Galeopithecus, Atherura*, and ten superb specimens of the most wonderful bat I ever saw (*Cheiromelas torquatus*), I weakened. When he brought out a huge and quite perfect skull of the Bornean gavial, a species which I had not before encountered (*Tomistoma schlegellii*), I surrendered unconditionally, and my last dollar was swallowed up in the fearful vortex of "specimens." Crocodiles always were great pets with me.

The dawn of the following day disclosed in every direction a fine view of mountain, hill, and dale—so charming a prospect, that I heartily envied Everett his quarters. The little house was perched exactly upon the summit of the steep cone, open on all sides to the breeze, with not a tree to break the view.

After coffee, with Mr. Everett accompanying us, we set out and walked four miles northwest to see the Chinese gold-washings at Bau. There was a good path all the way, through the second growth of jungle, and the scenery was highly interesting.

Bau takes its name from a peak close to the washings, from the northern base of which a remarkable pinnacle rises like a gigantic pillar with the top broken off and its precipitous face smooth and bare.

There are two Chinese companies working gold at Bau, and we visited the works of both. Both pursue the same wasteful plan. The gold occurs in very fine particles in a low hill of decomposed porphyry, mixed with a small proportion of blue limestone, manganese, etc. In appearance it resembles yellow clay. A large reservoir affords a good head of water, and, as fast as the hill is dug down, the earth is thrown into the sluices, some of which are nearly a mile long, and washed away. Three or four times a year they turn off the water and wash up the residuum by hand. It is a very wasteful process, and the Chinawomen do a very fair business in washing out the dirt at the lower end of the sluices.

The two gold companies have separate villages and two sets of shops, both well built and neatly kept. It was here that the Chinese insurrection was hatched in 1857, which taught the celestials a fearful lesson, one which it will never be necessary to teach them again. I do not suppose any combination of circumstances could now induce the Chinese to get up another row with the government of Sarawak. Like the people of our Southern States, they now declare that "rebellion must be put down."

As we passed through the village of the Sap Long Moon Kunsi, on our way back, we found a table of refreshments had been prepared for us in a cool veranda. First, last, and all the time, we were helped to tea of the very best quality (so St. John said), strong, bitter, and wholly innocent of either milk or sugar. To me it was about as palatable as soapsuds, but it was nevertheless refreshing to the inner man, and, without consulting my palate in the least, I emptied my tiny cup several times. Besides the tea, we had sugared peanuts, candied pumpkin, a preserved fig-like fruit from China, and big Chinese gooseberries to eat at the finish in lieu of pickles. Strangely enough, none of our hosts could speak Malay, but a very respectful crowd gathered to see the animals feed. At the next village, the above performance was repeated, except that we sat down to tea and fruit instead of tea and sweetmeats. We ate heartily, both by choice and as a matter of courtesy due the company. When hot and thirsty, I can eat a good many mandarin oranges out of politeness to my host.

We reached Everett's quarters about noon, and in the afternoon St. John and I went to see some caves not far away. Half a mile east of Paku is a rocky gorge between two hills, in one of which Ensunah cave is situated. The cavern extends, like a great irregular tunnel, quite through the hill, and is at least four hundred feet from end to end. In some places it is wide and high, like the interior of a cathedral, and in others contracted to a mere passage, so narrow that a man weighing two hundred pounds would not be able to get through. The sides of the cave revealed the fact that the whole hill is full of cracks and fissures. I was surprised at seeing long, slender, rope-like roots of a dark red color coming down from the trees far above, and winding about through the crevices in a most persistent way. In some parts of the cave, water was dripping down in a copious shower, and the soft limestone floor underneath was quite honeycombed with small round holes which the "little drops of water" had drilled. The earth on the bottom of the cave had all been dug up and examined by the indefatigable Chinese in their never-ending search for new deposits of gold.

After leaving the cave, we went on higher up the gorge to some of the remarkable well-like crevices which exist in the hills. They are simply holes running down through the limestone, with ragged, uneven sides, very often of no greater diameter than a common well, three or four feet, and sometimes sixty to seventy feet deep. Sometimes gold is found in the loose dirt at the bottom, and when this is the case they are worked by the Malays. In order to get down one of these holes and up again, the prospector puts sticks across the opening, jamming the ends firmly into the cracks in the sides, thus forming a ladder reaching to the bottom. There is usually a cavern at the bottom of each crevice, and it would seem that the whole hill is a mass of huge rocks, cracked and seamed throughout.

The antimony mine at Bidi was full of water and we did not visit it. With the exception of that one mine, all the rest of the antimony produced is found in surface pockets, many of which have been found, and quickly emptied, along the line of the tramway. The Honorable Borneo Company has a monopoly of all the useful minerals of Sarawak except gold, coal, silver, and diamonds; and all the antimony found by the natives is purchased by the company at forty to sixty cents per picul, according to its quality.

A PLEASURE TRIP UP THE SARAWAK. 191

On the following morning we rose early and after a good substantial "coffee," Mr. St. John and I set out to walk to Tegora, eleven miles from Paku. There is a good bridle-road and good bridges all the way, and with good company it is a delightful walk. The road is merely a narrow lane through beautiful virgin forest of stately trees and trailing lianas, mossy rocks and acres of pretty ferns.

Presently we came to the Staat River, a small, shady stream, along the south bank of which the road winds for several miles. Far below us, over its bed of clean white pebbles, flowed the river, clear and cool; at last, when we came to where the road crosses the stream on a high bridge, a deep shady pool in the bend below looked so inviting to our perspiring bodies that I begged St. John to take a swim with me. Boy-like, we "raced" in undressing to see who should take the water first, and in less than five minutes we plunged into the cool, sweet water, where not a ray of the hot sun could reach us, where the water was deep, and, thank heaven! free from crocodiles. How delicious it was, and how loth we were to leave that bath "fit for the gods." It was the first really secure and comfortable swim I had enjoyed since Jackson and I went swimming in the Orinoco, when I stepped upon a small sting-ray with the usual result, and he got nipped by a cariba fish. Verily there is little comfort in swimming in tropical rivers, especially within tidal influence, for they are nearly always dirty, and infested by sharks, sting-rays, crocodiles, and other aquatic vermin.

The last four miles of the road led over a succession of low hills, and the forest scenery grew even more picturesque and charming. At last we reached the village of Pankalan about a mile from Tegora, at which there is a police station and court-room, and also a shop kept by a wealthy Chinaman. We halted at the shop and emptied a quart bottle of champagne, a drink by no means to be despised in the jungle. After we had disposed of a "scratch" breakfast evolved for us by the Chinese shopkeeper's domestics, St. John tarried to hold court, over which he presided as magistrate. Had I but understood the Malay language I would gladly have stayed to watch the proceedings, but having no special interpreter, my presence would have been only a hindrance to the court, so I left, and walked on to Tegora.

On the way to Tegora, where we had been invited to dine and put up for the night, I met Mr. Harvey, a handsome, manly-looking young Englishman, one of the officers in charge of the mines, who introduced himself directly and greeted me very cordially. We met again in the evening at the dinner-table, and he proved to be a very jolly and hospitable host.

On reaching the mines, I found Mr. H. H. Everett, brother of our Paku naturalist, at the furnaces, weighing out bags of cinnabar dust, and close beside him on the ground stood about sixty flasks of mercury ready for shipment to London. A "flask" is a malleable iron bottle with a screw top, which holds seventy-five pounds of mercury.

The cinnabar ore comes out of a very steep, double-peaked hill composed of semi-metamorphic rock, rising to an elevation of about one thousand feet above the sea, and six hundred and fifty feet above the level of the adjacent swamp. Mr. Everett, with the most cheerful resignation and truly guide-like patience, took me into each of the four "levels" that have been mined into the hill, one above another, and gave me all the facts in the case as we proceeded. The lowest level was a new one, and the tunnel had not yet reached the ore. The other three had penetrated quite to the heart of the hill, and on reaching the paying ore it had been mined in every direction, forming a great cavern at the end of each tunnel. The miners are all Chinamen who work out the ore and sell it to the Company according to the assay. The ore was then very poor, and although the rock containad only four per cent. of mercury it was worked as a matter of necessity and at a loss, while all concerned hoped constantly for something better. In one of the levels Mr. Everett showed me a very rich pocket, which had yielded ore almost as heavy as mercury, being ninety per cent. pure metal.

The Tegora mines were opened in 1868. The first ore taken out was stamped, by which process about one-fourth of the metal was lost in the washing. Now it is smelted, and the vapor containing the metal is passed through a flue or shaft about one thousand feet long, which leads off up the steep side of the hill. The mercury is gradually condensed upon the sides of the flue, which after a time is cleaned out by men sent into it. The cleaners often get badly salivated, so much so that they are sometimes utterly helpless from the sores which break out upon different parts of their bodies. We saw two poor fellows who were helpless from salivation; and Mr. Everett himself was also badly off from an overdose of mercury.

The officers of the Borneo Company are very comfortably housed close to the mines, and in the evening at dinner we were most hospitably entertained by four of them, Messrs. Everett, Harvey, Gray and, Beecher. Every one was in good spirits, and we had a very merry time until a late hour. An Englishman may be rather rigid and formal on his native isle, but take him in the East Indies, especially in the jungles, and he is certainly the jolliest and best of companions.

On the following day, St. John and I returned to Paku. At Pankalan we took a boat and had a very romantic ride down the Staat, which saved us several miles walking. The river was low and we had to shoot a number of rapids in consequence. The boat was a small one, and at each end stood a Malay with a bamboo pole to guide the frail craft. It was certainly a charming ride. The bed of the stream was sand, pebbles and bowlders, and the banks were shales and limestone. The branches of the trees met far above our heads, giving us a continuous cool shade instead of the glare and heat of the sun, and in a quiet ecstacy of delight we glided smoothly along with the swift current, feasting our eyes upon the beauties of rock and tree, flower, fern, orchid, and mossy bank.

Often when shooting down the rapids at a great rate, with great bowlders lining our narrow way thickly on either hand, or with a wall of rock rising directly before us at the foot of the incline, it seemed as if the next instant our boat would certainly strike and be smashed into kindling wood. But no; just at the right moment, the man in the bow would quickly jam the end of his pole into a crevice or against the rocky wall, give a quick, strong shove, and send us swinging off at a sharp angle down the middle of the channel. The Malays handled the boat as only skilful and practised hands could; and it did not touch a rock even once.

After several miles of this delightful voyaging we came to the getting-out place, and, with a sigh to think the ride was over, reluctantly took to the road and walked the remainder of the way to Paku, which we reached shortly before noon. In the afternoon, while St. John held court, Everett and I strolled out to get some specimens of calc spar, antimony, and limestone, and to talk over all Borneo.

Our last day was to be devoted to an excursion to Serambo Mountain, whither my good friend St. John had invited me, for I should never have dreamed of asking him to do so much hard climbing on my account. We said good-by to Mr. Everett and set out early for the mountain, which rises about two miles east of Paku. There is a good Dyak road, or path, all the way, leading over hills, through hollows and across several very interesting Dyak bridges, built across mountain streams, above high water mark, to insure the traveller a crossing in times of flood. Evidently the Hill Dyaks are more averse to floundering through mud and water than their brethren of the Sea tribe.

The low foot-bridges are almost precisely like the hay-racks at which the cattle feed in an Illinois farm-yard. They are very ingenious contrivances, and the idea of their construction might often be copied to good advantage by the settlers of our Western States. They are built by planting two rows of long stakes in the ground slanting in opposite directions, so that a small sapling laid in the fork thus formed will be horizontal, and of the proper height for the footway. Each pair of stakes is lashed together at their point of intersection, and the bridge is further strengthened by perpendicular posts set under the footway. A pole is lashed along the top of each row of stakes to serve as a hand-rail. One of the bridges between Paku and Serambo was about a hundred feet long and nine feet high at the middle.

Sometimes the Dyaks construct very high suspension bridges across streams with high and precipitous banks, by hanging a couple of long bamboo stems with rattans or creepers from the branches of the trees which overhang the chasm. A hand-rail is also constructed, either on one side or both, but even with that, it takes a very steady-headed European to cross without breaking out all over in a cold perspiration. The Dyaks, however, trot across them, carrying heavy loads with the most perfect nonchalance, and the only accidents that occur are by the bamboos becoming rotten and suddenly giving way with a grand crash.

About an hour from Paku we reached the foot of the mountain and began to climb up the path which leads to the Rajah's cottage and the three villages of Serambo, Bombok, and Peninjau. It was a hard climb. The whole side of the mountain was strewn, or covered, rather, with boulders and angular masses of rock from the size of a Saratoga trunk to a street car, smooth, mossy, and slippery as ice. I think they must have been covered with soft soap that morning for our especial benefit. We were obliged to proceed with the greatest care and circumspection to avoid coming down with a wreck of muscle and crush of bones. In some places the rocks are so large and piled together in such rugged confusion that the Dyaks have regular ladders and foot-bridges over them, of notched saplings placed end to end with a hand-rail

DYAKS USING THE BILIONG, OR AXE-ADZE. (Page 379.)
(*From a sketch by H. H. Everett.*)

along one side. My journal for that day pantingly declares, "It was hot work to climb such a steep mountain over such a terrible jumble of slippery stones."

Near the top we came to Peninjau, a typical village of the Hill Dyaks. Besides the pangah, or head-house, there were fifteen other houses, each of which contained from three to six rooms and accommodated a total population of about five hundred persons, when the returns were all in. The houses stand just wherever they can find standing-room, with no order or regularity whatever, not a sign of anything like a street nor even a good path anywhere. They were of course built along the side of the mountain, usually with the open side up hill, and all were elevated on posts which were from six to eight feet high on the upper side, where they were the shortest. The rank grass growing all through the village and the uncommon stillness which prevailed, gave the village quite a deserted air, and, sure enough, we found only a few girls and old women in the place, all the rest being away at work on their farms.

As we passed through the village, two young women came out to look at us, who were in their turn inspected with equal curiosity. Their brass waist ornaments were of an entirely different style from any I had before seen, the thick wire being worn up and down from hips to armpits instead of in rings around the waist.

These curious corsets were models of rigidity, and closeness of fit, and being brightly polished, gave the young ladies quite a substantial air. What a magnificent protection they must be against the embraces of a too-powerful lover!

We entered the head-house, which I have already described in a previous chapter.

The heads, or rather skulls, hung in a semi-circle around one side of the room, and there were forty-two of them in all, not counting the skull of a young orang-utan, which probably some enterprising young Dyak, in haste to marry, had, in times past, palmed off upon his unsuspecting lady-love and his brethren, as the head of a fierce young Seribas Dyak.

The collection as a whole was in very good condition, the specimens being moderately clean and not at all smoked. Some had been very carelessly taken, I regret to say, as was shown by the way they had been split open or slashed across with parongs; and from some, large pieces had been hacked out. One I noticed had a deep slash diagonally across the bridge of the nose, which evi-

dently ended the earthly troubles of the owner in short order
None of the skulls were labelled with locality, date, sex, and species
as crania always should be, to be valuable.

After leaving the pangah we climbed two hundred feet higher,
and at last reached the Rajah's cottage, which has been visited by
nearly every European who has thus far set foot in Sarawak. The
cottage itself is a sort of summer-house, a veritable "lodge in a
vast wilderness," a little house on posts, with three rooms, a veranda extending around three sides, and at that time no furniture
except a table and two or three chairs.

But if the cottage is nothing of itself, the location is everything.
Back of it is the forest-clad top of Serambo, all about it are flowering shrubs, cocoanut trees, and the tops of the trees which have
their roots far below in the steep side of the mountain. Through
the cocoanut-grove in front we catch a glimpse of sea and sky, and
hasten forward to get beyond the trees. Come with me, quickly,
if you would feast your eyes on a most charming view. Fifty
yards below the cottage we stand upon a bare rock, the very
northernmost point of the summit, nine hundred and fifty feet
above the sea, with a clear view to the north, east, and west. It is
enchanting. The sun shines brightly, the air is clear, and every
object in the vast landscape is defined with unusual clearness of
detail.

Almost beneath our feet is a wide semi-circle of ferns, then the
feathery tops of the bamboos that grow lower down the steep
slope, and beyond that a sloping bank of green tree-tops which
finally mingle with the foliage of the plain far below. To the left
hand (west), and seemingly very near, rises the Semadjoe mountain
range, which forms the boundary between Sarawak and the Dutch
Territory, with Bau and Matang still nearer at hand toward the
northwest. Everett's house at Paku, far below, looks like a little
white martin-box on a tiny mound. Toward the north, seemingly
at the foot of Serambo, we can trace the winding course of the
western branch of the Sarawak River, brown and murky with the
mud of recent rains. Beyond the river stretches a wide level plain
covered with green jungle, broken only by a few light patches here
and there, either farms or second growth jungle, and a few hills
that rise high enough to be recognized as such. Far away in front,
at the edge of the sea, rises the fine peak of Santubong, with its
head thrust up into a fleecy white cloud. The coast line is clearly
defined from the mouth of the Lundu to the Batang Lupar, and

beyond it the sea stretches out toward the horizon like a sheet of frosted silver.

We can very easily make out the position of Kuching, and trace the windings of the Sarawak for a long distance, but the stream itself is visible in but one or two places. Truly, an enchanting picture in contrast with the monotonous closeness of jungle and river scenery.

Reluctantly enough, we quitted Peninjau, the "look-out," and started straight down the mountain, in the direction of Siniwan, at which point the *Firefly* was to meet us. The descent over those abominably slippery stones was, if anything, more tiresome and difficult than going up. Half way down we met a party of Dyaks coming up. As soon as they heard our voices they quickly dropped their juahs beside the path and bolted into the bushes; but after we had passed out of sight they returned, chattering and laughing, resumed their loads and went on.

Shortly before noon, after a very hot walk to the river, we reached the *Firefly*, and went down to Kuching in about three hours. For my part, I felt thoroughly tired and foot-sore, and Mr. St. John was also quite willing to rest. Our feet were badly blistered, and a large, angry boil on my left arm, which had kept me company all the way, was a companion with whom I would willingly have parted.

Thus ended my jungle life in the East Indies. On December 18th I embarked in the *Rajah Brooke* for Singapore, serenely happy with the results of my visit to Sarawak. Never has a country used me better or sent me away fuller handed. I have been treated excellently well by both natives and Europeans, have had very few annoyances, I ought to say none at all, and more joys crowded into four months than are counted in many a lifetime. My only regret is that I have not had a score of friends to enjoy it with me. The coast line sinks into the sea behind us, and the hazy blue mountains fade out against the clouds like a dissolving view. Farewell to Borneo!

"Welcome the gleaming sea."

. . . .

I remained six weeks in Singapore, making up a large collection of corals and shells, for the variety and abundance of which the place is famous. Previous to that time the season had been unfavorable for the successful gathering of marine invertebrates, but now the Malays brought me beautiful shells by the hundred and corals by the boat-load. Major Studer, our worthy consul, gave me a large room in the lower part of his house, and the use of a cool, shady court, where I bought, assorted, and packed several hundred specimens of coral of twenty-six species, and more shells than I could spare time to catalogue.

My friend Syers sent me a very nice collection of Selangore mammals, skins and skeletons, and snakes in alcohol, all of which he had gathered since my visit there. It is a pity that such an ardent hunter and dead shot with a rifle could not have his lines of duty cast in such a country as Southern India, which, in places, actually teems with noble game. Mr. Syers and I planned an expedition to the Animallais for some future year, with Theobald for a companion in the chase, and when we do actually start on the war-path in that direction some of the big game animals had better get their lives insured against accidents.

My jolly friend Hood, of the Rainbow, put in an appearance during my last days in Singapore, but I felt so down-in-the-mouth at not having sufficient funds left to get me to and through Australia, that I was but sorry company, I know. It was fated that I should not see Australia; for a hunting and collecting trip cannot, like the brook, "go on forever."

Foreseeing that I should have to cross the Pacific in winter, I determined to spare my two baby orangs the miseries of such a voyage, and, after having the Old Man sit for his photograph, I sent them both, under the guardianship of Mr. Vandevorst, to Madras, as a present to my kind friend Theobald. I could not have given him anything that pleased him better. He made a journey of three hundred and fifty miles to meet them; and they received him with open arms. Both were presented at court before they left Madras, and I hear were very much complimented on their deportment and good looks.

Early in February I turned my face homeward, by way of China and Japan, and reached Rochester safe and well, just two years and nine months from the time of my departure. From first to last I had been remarkably prospered, quite as if the prayers and good wishes of my friends had enlisted the services of a special guardian angel to accompany me at every step, in addition to the one I left behind me, whose charming missives of news, hopeful encouragement and unfaltering affection followed me everywhere—one by every mail, without a single break—without which I would have been lonesome indeed. No journey could have been more free from accidents, for from first to last I did not meet with so much bodily harm as a cut finger, and returned home with health wholly unimpaired.

Enriched by experiences in foreign lands, wealth which cannot be estimated in dollars and cents, nothing but a desire to have others share with me, through the medium of these pages, the delights of forest and field, river and sea, could have impelled me to the laborious task of writing this narrative in hours which should have been devoted to rest and recreation. But if a single reader (always excepting the proof-reader) has followed me thus far, and experienced in sympathy a hundredth part of the delight which quickens my blood as I think of the scenes which I have feebly attempted to describe for him, I can say that my labor has not been in vain.

The rifle and knife hang peacefully upon the wall, their labors done. Let me rest my weary pen also. Farewell.

Other Oxford Paperbacks for readers interested in South-East Asia, past and present

Borneo

Among Primitive Peoples in Borneo
IVOR H. N. EVANS

The Best of Borneo Travel
VICTOR T. KING

Borneo Jungles
TOM HARRISSON

The Field-Book of a Jungle-Wallah
CHARLES HOSE

Fifty Years of Romance and Research
CHARLES HOSE

The Gardens of the Sun
F. W. BURBIDGE

The Head-Hunters of Borneo
CARL BOCK

In Borneo Jungles
WILLIAM O. KROHN

My Life in Sarawak
MARGARET BROOKE, THE RANEE OF SARAWAK

Natural Man
CHARLES HOSE

Nine Dayak Nights
W. R. GEDDES

Orang-Utan
BARBARA HARRISSON

Queen of the Head-Hunters
SYLVIA, LADY BROOKE, THE RANEE OF SARAWAK

Through Central Borneo
CARL LUMHOLTZ

Wanderings in the Great Forests of Borneo
ODOARDO BECCARI

The White Rajahs of Sarawak
ROBERT PAYNE

World Within: A Borneo Story
TOM HARRISSON

Cambodia

Angkor: An Introduction
GEORGE COEDÈS

Angkor and the Khmers
MALCOLM MacDONALD

Indonesia

An Artist in Java and Other Islands of Indonesia
JAN POORTENAAR

Bali and Angkor
GEOFFREY GORER

Coolie
MADELON H. LULOFS

Flowering Lotus: A View of Java in the 1950s
HAROLD FORSTER

Forgotten Kingdoms in Sumatra
F. M. SCHNITGER

The Hidden Force*
LOUIS COUPERUS

A House in Bali
COLIN McPHEE

Indonesia: Land under the Rainbow
MOCHTAR LUBIS

Island of Bali*
MIGUEL COVARRUBIAS

Islands of Indonesia
VIOLET CLIFTON

Java: Facts and Fancies
AUGUSTA DE WIT

Java: The Garden of the East
E. R. SCIDMORE

Java Pageant
H. W. PONDER

Javanese Panorama
H. W. PONDER

The Last Paradise
HICKMAN POWELL

Let It Be
PAULA GOMES

Makassar Sailing
G. E. P. COLLINS

The Malay Archipelago
ALFRED RUSSEL WALLACE

The Outlaw and Other Stories
MOCHTAR LUBIS

The Poison Tree*
E. M. BEEKMAN

Rambles in Java and the Straits in 1852
'BENGAL CIVILIAN'
(CHARLES WALTER KINLOCH)

Rubber
MADELON H. LULOFS

Soul of the Tiger*
JEFFREY A. McNEELY and PAUL SPENCER WACHTEL

Sumatra: Its History and People
EDWIN M. LOEB

A Tale From Bali*
VICKI BAUM

The Temples of Java
JACQUES DUMARÇAY

Tropic Fever
LADISLAO SZÉKELY

Twilight in Djakarta
MOCHTAR LUBIS

Twin Flower: A Story of Bali
G. E. P. COLLINS

Unbeaten Tracks in Islands of the Far East
ANNA FORBES

Yogyakarta: Cultural Heart of Indonesia
MICHAEL SMITHIES

Malaysia

Ah King and Other Stories*
W. SOMERSET MAUGHAM

An Analysis of Malay Magic
K. M. ENDICOTT

At the Court of Pelesu and Other Malayan Stories
HUGH CLIFFORD

The Chersonese with the Gilding Off
EMILY INNES

The Experiences of a Hunter and Naturalist in the Malay Peninsula and Borneo
WILLIAM T. HORNADAY

Glimpses into Life in Malayan Lands
JOHN TURNBULL THOMSON

The Golden Chersonese
ISABELLA BIRD

Illustrated Guide to the Federated Malay States (1923)
C. W. HARRISON

The Malay Magician
RICHARD WINSTEDT

Malay Poisons and Charm Cures
JOHN D. GIMLETTE

A Nocturne and Other Malayan Stories and Sketches
FRANK SWETTENHAM

The Pirate Wind
OWEN RUTTER

Saleh: A Prince of Malaya
SIR HUGH CLIFFORD

Six Years in the Malay Jungle
CARVETH WELLS

The Soul of Malaya
HENRI FAUCONNIER

They Came to Malaya: A Travellers' Anthology
J. M. GULLICK

Philippines

Little Brown Brother
LEON WOLFF

Singapore

Main Fleet to Singapore
RUSSELL GRENFELL

The Manners and Customs of the Chinese
J. D. VAUGHAN

Raffles of the Eastern Isles
C. E. WURTZBURG

Singapore 1941–1942
MASANOBU TSUJI

Thailand

Behind the Painting and Other Stories
SIBURAPHA

The English Governess at the Siamese Court
ANNA LEONOWENS

A Physician at the Court of Siam
MALCOLM SMITH

The Politician and Other Stories
KHAMSING SRINAWK

Temples and Elephants
CARL BOCK

To Siam and Malaya in the Duke of Sutherland's Yacht *Sans Peur*
FLORENCE CADDY

Travels in Siam, Cambodia and Laos 1858–1860
HENRI MOUHOT

Vietnam

The General Retires and Other Stories
NGUYEN HUY THIEP

Titles marked with an asterisk have restricted rights.